Emotions, Ethics and Mass Atrocities

Perspectives from Scholars, Teachers and Practitioners

Edited by

Maartje Weerdesteijn
Alette Smeulers

BRILL | NIJHOFF

This publication is part of the project *Emotions In and Around the Classroom* with file number 40.5.23865.026 of the Comenius Teaching Fellows 2023 programme which is financed by the NKO (formerly NRO). The Dutch Research Council (NWO) has, furthermore, financed the open access publication of the book (file number 36.201.158).

ISSN 2666-903X
ISBN 978-90-04-75064-7
ISBN 978-90-04-75472-0 (PDF)
DOI https://doi.org/10.1163/9789004754720

Library of Congress Control Number: 2026933649

Brill Nijhoff and Koninklijke Brill BV are part of De Gruyter Brill.
www.degruyterbrill.com

Questions about General Product Safety Regulation: productsafety@degruyterbrill.com.

Cover illustration: Adam Jones, Ph.D. / Global Photo Archive / Flickr.

Dedicated to our students, past and present

Contents

PART 3
Reflections from Practitioners

Acknowledgements

We would like to start by thanking our students and colleagues across different universities, whose honesty and openness about their struggles with this topic have been inspirational and foundational. Without those students and colleagues who were strong enough to share their vulnerabilities, this book would not have existed.

We would also like to thank our contributors, without whom this book would not have been possible. We really appreciate your dedication and hard work, the willingness to unveil the personal side of your professional identity and for sharing the lessons you have learned to help others.

A special thanks also goes out to Dafne 'Nico' Mall, who helped with the English language edits of the book. It was a pleasure working with you, and you impressed us with your eye for detail. We also thank the team at Brill, Bea Timmer and Akiko Hakuno, who helped send the book out for peer review and ensured the publication process ran smoothly.

While many have contributed to this book by being there for us throughout our journey in bringing it to fruition, we are not going to mention all of you by name. You know who you are, and you know how we feel about you.

Maartje Weerdesteijn and Alette Smeulers

Abbreviations

AI	Amnesty International
BASIC Ph	Belief, Affect, Social, Imagination, Cognitive, Physical
CRSV	Conflict Related Sexual Violence
CSPC	Community Stress Prevention Centre (Israel)
DNR	Donetsk People's Republic
DPKO	Department of Peace Keeping Operations
DRC	Democratic Republic of Congo
EU	European Union
FC	Force Commander
HGS	Holocaust and Genocide Studies
HQ	Headquarters
IACHR	Inter-American Court of Human Rights
ICC	International Criminal Court
ICTR	International Criminal Tribunal for Rwanda
ICTY	International Criminal Tribunal for the former Yugoslavia
IDF	Israeli Defense Forces
IDP	Internally Displaced Persons
ISIS	Islamic State of Iraq and Syria
LNR	Luhansk People's Republic
LRA	Lord Resistance Army
MONUC	Organization Mission in the Democratic Republic of the Congo (UN)
NATO	North Atlantic Treaty Organization
NGO	Non-Governmental Organization
NIOD	Institute for War, Holocaust and Genocide Studies (the Netherlands)
OSCE	Organization for Security and Cooperation in Europe
OTP	Office of the Prosecutor (ICC)
PSVI	Preventing Sexual Violence in Conflict Initiative
PTG	Post Traumatic Growth
PTSD	Post Traumatic Stress Disorder
R&R	Rest and Recuperation
ROE	Rules of Engagement
RUF	Revolutionary United Front (Sierra Leone)
SC	Security Council (UN)
SCSL	Special Court of Sierra Leone
SG	Secretary General (UN)
SGBC	Sexual and Gender Based Crimes
SMM	Special Monitoring Mission

SRSG	Special Representative of the Secretary General
STL	Special Tribunal of Lebanon
STS	Secondary Traumatic Stress
TCG	Trilateral Contact Group (Ukraine)
TRC	Truth and Reconciliation Commission
UK	United Kingdom
UN	United Nations
UNMEE	United Nations Mission in Ethiopia and Eritrea
UNMHA	United Nations Mission to support the Hudaydah Agreement
UNMISS	United Nations Mission in South Sudan
UNPROFOR	United Nations Protection Force
UNTAC	United Nations Transitional Authority in Cambodia
VT	Vicarious Traumatization
VPTG	Vicarious Posttraumatic Growth
WFP	World Food Program
WWII	World War II

Notes on Contributors

Andy Aydın-Aitchison
is Senior Lecturer in Criminology at the University of Edinburgh School of Law, where he teaches on the postgraduate M.Sc. in Global Crime, Justice and Security, and on the senior undergraduate course, Criminologies of Atrocity.

Annalisa Battista
has successfully defended her Ph.D. thesis at the University of Edinburgh School of Law. Her research topic is the widespread and systematic use of sexual violence as a means of genocide during the Yugoslav Wars of the 1990s. She teaches on the senior undergraduate course, Criminologies of Atrocity. She has taught on the criminology of atrocity at the University of Edinburgh, Saveetha Law School, and the University of Westminster.

Thijs B. Bouwknegt
is Senior Researcher at the NIOD Institute for War, Holocaust and Genocide Studies, and the Royal Netherlands Academy of Arts and Sciences (KNAW); and Visiting Research Professor at the University of Amsterdam (UvA).

Anne-Marie de Brouwer
is co-director at IMPACT: Center against Human Trafficking and Sexual Violence in Conflict, an expertise centre that focuses on how to prevent and address these two crimes. She is furthermore the chair of the Mukomeze Foundation and co-owner of Bèkske: Rwandan Empowerment Coffee.

Patrick Cammaert
Major General (ret.), had a distinguished military career in the Netherlands with the Royal Netherlands Marine Corps, as well as in the United Nations, where he served as Sector Commander in Cambodia (UNTAC), as Assistant Chief of Staff in Bosnia/Herzegovina (UNPROFOR), as Force Commander in Ethiopia and Eritrea (UNMEE), as Military Advisor to the Department of Peace Keeping Operations (DPKO), as General Officer Commanding (GOC) the Eastern Division in the Democratic Republic of Congo (MONUC) and, as a civilian, as Head of Mission of UNMHA in Hodeida in Yemen.

Koko Christiaanse
is a graduate of Utrecht University's LLM in Public International Law and Leiden University's M.Sc. in Law and Society, and was the research assistant for the 2023–2024 Global Justice Investigations Lab.

Marije Luitjens
is an assistant professor of peace and conflict studies (IR) at Vrije Universiteit Amsterdam and Amsterdam University College (AUC). In addition to lecturing at AUC, she conducts research in various conflict-affected settings, such as Medellín (Colombia), Kosovo and Srebrenica (Bosnia-Herzegovina). She has also developed an analytical tool called the 'Peace System Analysis', which can be used to unpack the complexities of peace and conflict processes and is subject to further research.

Brianne McGonigle Leyh
is Professor of Global Justice Studies at Utrecht University's School of Law, affiliated with the Netherlands Institute of Human Rights (SIM) and the Montaigne Centre for the Rule of Law and Administration of Justice. Her specializations include human rights law, transitional justice, victims' rights and the documentation of serious crimes. She is the Director of Masters Education of the Law School and a Senior Teaching Fellow, leading interdisciplinary education projects.

An Michels
is a clinical psychologist with an additional degree in family therapy. She specializes in the development of support strategies for conflict-affected populations. She has worked in Rwanda, Burundi and Indonesia for Médecins Sans Frontières and established the support unit in the Special Court for Sierra Leone in Freetown. Throughout her work, she has developed particular expertise in supporting victims of gender-based violence and children affected by armed conflict in their involvement in transitional justice mechanisms. She has advised numerous international organizations on these topics. She is the Psychologist/Trauma Expert and Team Leader of the psychosocial support team in the Victims and Witnesses Section at the International Criminal Court. In this role, she advises the Court on the development of survivor-centred and trauma-informed approaches. In addition, she authored a study on the integration of Mental Health and Psychosocial Support approaches in accountability mechanisms for atrocity crimes. She is a research fellow at the Human Rights in Trauma Mental Health Program at Stanford University and was nominated for a Rockefeller Foundation Bellagio Residency in 2024.

Caecilia Johanna van Peski
holds an M.Sc. Degree in Educational and Cultural Psychology from Tilburg University, an M.A. Degree in Civil–Military Interaction from the Helmut Schmidt University, University of the German *Bundeswehr* in Hamburg, Germany, and a Postgraduate Diploma in Integrated Border Security and Management for Senior Leadership from the OSCE Border Management College in Dushanbe, Tajikistan. She is a Commander in the Royal Netherlands Navy and a member of the UN Senior Women Talent Pipeline. In October 2010, she was appointed United Nations Special Representative for her country, in which capacity she addressed the 65th UN General Assembly in New York. She has worked for (inter-)governmental, multilateral organizations, amongst which are the Netherlands Foreign Office, the Netherlands Ministry of Defense, the United Nations (UNDP, UNDPO), the European Union (EEAS/EIDHR), the Organization for Security and Co-operation in Europe (OSCE/ODIHR), the North-Atlantic Treaty Organization (NATO), and the Geneva Centre for Security Sector Governance (DCAF-ISSAT). Since 2019, she has been appointed Fellow at the Baker Institute for Peace and Conflict Studies (US). She has worked in over thirty (post-)conflict countries in the Central and South Asian/Caspian Region, Russian Federation, Caucasus and the Balkans. Through her work on SDG#16, 'Peace, Justice and Strong Institutions', she actively contributes to the building of peaceful and inclusive societies for sustainable development.

Furtuna Sheremeti
is a criminologist who is researching the harms of crimes committed during wars and the needs of victims in these cases. She is from Kosova, and works and resides in Prishtina. She is a lecturer at the Faculty of Law in Prishtina.

Alette Smeulers
is a professor of international crimes at the University of Groningen and has recently published a book entitled *Perpetrators of Mass Atrocities – Terribly and Terrifyingly Normal*? (Routledge, 2024), which is based on doing more than 30 years of research on perpetrators of mass atrocities. The book has been published in Dutch under the title *Angtsaanjagend normaal* (Alfabet, 2025). She additionally hosts a podcast series together with Nicola Quaedvlieg called *Terribly and Terrifyingly Normal?*

Maartje Weerdesteijn
is an assistant professor at the Department of Criminology, Vrije Universiteit Amsterdam. She is on the board of the Peace and Conflict Studies Center and a researcher at the Center for International Criminal Justice.

Martin Witteveen
is an appeals prosecutor, specialized in international crimes and human trafficking, and works pro bono for NGOs. He works for Dutch & Detained in support of Dutch nationals detained abroad and works with the Minister of Justice and Human Rights of the National Unity Government of Myanmar and his staff, the National Unity Consultative Council, and various lawyers in and outside Myanmar to train on IHL/ICL and future accountability. He previously worked as an investigation team leader in the Office of the Prosecutor (OTP) of the International Criminal Court in The Hague, where he led the team investigating crimes in the situation of Northern Uganda. He also helped creating networks with investigators and prosecutors of international crimes in national jurisdictions and with international organizations such as Interpol and UN agencies. In 2008, he was appointed as an investigation magistrate for international crimes in the District Court of The Hague, the court in the jurisdiction of the Netherlands uniquely competent to adjudicate cases of international crimes. Between October 2012 and June 2014, he was seconded by the Ministry of Foreign Affairs in the Netherlands to the mission of the European Union in Palestine, where he advised the Public Prosecution Service. In 2014–2015, he was based in Kigali, Rwanda, where he served as an Advisor to the National Public Prosecution Authorities in Rwanda on international crimes, a program funded by the Ministry of Foreign Affairs of the Netherlands. In this capacity, he advised the Prosecution on their genocide cases. Between 2019 and 2021, he worked for International Bridges to Justice in Myanmar, supporting defence lawyers in criminal cases. In 2021, he advised the Ethiopian Human Rights Commission in Ethiopia, particularly on investigating the war in Tigray.

Introduction: Reflections on the Role of Emotions and Ethics

Maartje Weerdesteijn

1 Introduction

Emotions and ethics are inextricably bound together (Shaw & Baghramian, 2022, p. 193). Each is determinative of the other and together they help us navigate which path to take in life. Through feelings of shame, guilt and anger but also through gratitude and joy, we feel the boundaries of what is (un)desirable or (un)acceptable. Mass atrocities shock the consciousness of humanity (see the Preamble of the Rome Statute). When we stand witness to these horrible crimes – through the evening news, through a documentary, through the stories of our respondents, or by being there on the frontlines – our ethical compass is profoundly violated. Consequently, we may experience a wide range of powerful emotions.

Those working in the field of mass atrocities, however, have been expected to do so rationally and for many this, implicitly, means sidelining emotions. This is in line with broader notions on professionalism where in the work sphere formalism dominates in favor of cognition and reason, to the detriment of emotions (Kadowaki, 2015, p. 323). For a long time, emotions were treated as having no place in reason because, especially in the legal sphere, the two were seen as antitheses. However, this has started to change and over the last two decades, scholarship on the relationship between law and emotion has grown immensely (Maroney, 2021 Bergman Blix & Wettergren, 2024). It is increasingly acknowledged that emotions are actually a crucial component of how we enact our professional selves. That emotions are bound to impact how we conduct our research (Holland, 2007), how we teach and how we learn (Kaur & Harris, 2024; Nikisher 2019), how we position ourselves within our organizational environment and in relation to our colleagues; how we do our jobs. Even more so, "emotional labor" (Hochschild, 1979) is often a crucial and expected requirement in the execution of our jobs.

Emotional labor refers to the "way in which people manage and display their emotions in order to achieve the goals of their employment organizations" (Waters et al., 2020a, p. 1). Recent scholarship suggests that emotional labor is an important component in research (Waters et al., 2020a), teaching (Hagenauer & Volet, 2014; Roberts & Smith, 2002) and various areas of practice, playing a role for transitional justice judges (Nyseth-Nzatatira et al., 2023), civil society practitioners (Sarıaslan & Avetisyan, 2024) and soldiers at war (Godfrey & Bewis, 2018).

The consequences of emotional labor can be both positive and negative. Waters et al. investigated the impact emotional labor had on doctoral students and found that on the one hand, it can lead to increased gratitude and a sense of purpose (Waters et al., 2020b, p. 6). On the other hand, emotional labor may weigh heavily on people and may also lead to a sense of guilt, or the feeling of being overwhelmed (Waters et al., 2020b, pp. 6–7). As Yakren (2008, p. 141) argues, professionals tasked with emotional labor may "face substantial psychological risks."

A related and compounding factor is the traumatic material scholars and practitioners in the field of mass atrocities are exposed to. This puts them at risk for secondary traumatic stress, vicarious trauma, burnout and other psychological difficulties although the extent of this risk tends to vary and depend on, among other things, the degree of exposure, personal history, coping style and organizational factors such as supervision (e.g. Baird & Kracen 2006; Moran & Asquith, 2020; Hagan & Kay, 2011).[1] As a result, there is the risk, or at least the fear, of becoming numb (Nikisher, 2019).[2] An investigator at the International Criminal Tribunal for the former Yugoslavia (ICTY), used the German word *versteinen* (to become like stone) to describe her fear that she would become so good at taking the emotions out of her work, that she would "have no emotions left," and highlighted that she is always vigilant "that it doesn't happen to me" (Hagan & Kay, 2011, p. 291).

Thus, while emotions are inherent to our humanity, there is much versatility and nuance in the emotions that we experience. Our emotions are perhaps easily seen as inconsequential as the experiences of scholars, teachers and practitioners pale in comparison to that of the victims of the crimes. Yet, while there is no comparison possible, we believe the emotions of scholars, teachers, students and practitioners should be brought to the fore. As the chapters that follow highlight, being cognizant of our emotions, coping with our emotions, and even being forthcoming about our emotions, actually allows us to do our jobs better. The book, therefore, breaks open the taboos and exposes what was meant to stay private; the humanity of the professional.

1 For a more in depth explanation of these terms see the chapter of Michels in this book.

2 See also the chapters of Smeulers and Van Peski in this volume.

2 Emotions and Ethics

Emotions are hard to grasp, pin down or define (Scherer, 2005; Scarantino, 2016). A multitude of scholarly definitions abound, leading many to return to the adage "emotions are what people say they are" (Scherer, 2005, pp. 695–697). While understanding the adverse impact of such subjectivity for the advancement of the scholarly debate (Scherer, 2005), we have left our contributors free to determine what emotions mean for them. Their highly personal contributions reflect the more recent research which understands emotions as being "complex, diverse, and fundamental to human experiences" (Olson, 2023, p. 526). As such, a holistic and broad notion of emotions is reflected in this book. In doing so, it follows the approach of Goldie (2003, p. 1) who found emotions should not be studied in isolation from related phenomena such as "consciousness, thought, feeling, imagination, interpretation of action out of emotion and of expression of emotion, moods, and traits of character."

We, therefore, make no claim of universality. While we think the emotions discussed in the book are inherent in being human, of course, no human being is alike. Our book does not stand out because it is representative, but because it is personal. It includes unique reflections that only that author could have written. More generally it seems that the emotional reactions of those working with sensitive topics differs along the personality and background of the researcher, the work that they engage in or the methodology they employ in their research, and on the institutional context (Koning & Weerdesteijn, 2025; Nyseth-Nzatatira et al., 2023; Gebreslassie, & Irechukwu, 2023). In describing the emotional dimensions of their work, the authors in the present book generally reflect on several or all of these factors from their unique perspectives.

At the same time, this does not mean that there are no broader implications or lessons that can be learned from their experiences. Several of our contributors formulated advice for others based on their lived realities. These lessons are sometimes related to well-being, mental health and coping but also tie into ethical dilemmas related to the emotional experiences from their professional lives.[3]

Our ethical environment is shaped by our collective ideas without us even necessarily being aware of them and they determine what we find acceptable or unacceptable (Blackburn, 2021, pp. 1–2). Blackburn argues that our ethical environment shapes our very identities, as we need, or desire, our stories to be valued by others (Blackburn, pp. 1–2). The present book contains such stories

3 See for an overview of these general trends across the chapters, the conclusion of this book.

of identities. They are reflections of who the authors are, their place in the world and the manner in which it shaped their relationship toward their field. The chapters are a reflection of what they find important and how they cared for themselves and others, whether they are colleagues, research participants or students.

3 The Emotions and Ethics of Scholars, Teachers and Practitioners

Emotions associated with working in the field of mass atrocities can be positive and motivating, there are of course the joys of teaching and research, and of contributing to a sense of equality and justice. However, sometimes a sense of joy can feel inappropriate in the context of mass atrocities and, consequently, feelings of guilt may sneak in (Hagan & Kay, 2011, pp. 292–193). At other times being faced with the horrors of atrocities can be overwhelming.

Scholars may encounter perpetrators and victims of mass atrocity during field work, when conducting interviews or when following trial proceedings. They may face the legacy of the atrocities as it is recorded in archives and books.[4] While there are numerous works analyzing how researchers should engage in self-care, placing the responsibility solely on the scholar, raises ethical considerations. As Nikischer (2019, p. 913) argues "it is imperative that the responsibility for researcher protection goes beyond the individual researchers themselves" because universities and funding institutions are important stakeholders as well.

Ethics committees are established in order to prevent unethical research which can do harm to the researcher as well as research subjects/respondents. These committees, however, oftentimes overlook how to protect scholars from the emotional toll of talking to victims or perpetrators of mass atrocities, or from the impact that their research findings could have on them.[5] In addition, support facilities which could be used by scholars coping with research-induced stress, are often difficult to access, ill-equipped, or non-existent (O'Brien, 2021).

When academics teach students, it is the student who seeks out information, writes papers and thus takes up tasks equivalent to that of a researcher and is subsequently exposed to the emotional demands of working on this topic (Aydın-Aitchison, 2024). We know that emotions and learning are intertwined (Tyng, 2017) and O'Byrne argues the emotional dimensions of studying

4 See also the chapters of Smeulers, Luitjens and Sheremeti in this volume.

5 See the chapters of Luitjens and Sheremeti in this volume.

human rights are particularly important because the topic "is necessarily challenging to the humanity of the student" (O'Byrne, 2014, p. 66).[6]

Yet, the oversight ethical committees have when it comes to research, does not even touch the realm of teaching. As Lowe and Jones (2010, p. 1) point out, scholars researching sensitive subjects

> are required to take steps such as raising issues considerably with informants, allowing withdrawals at any time, and to have in place support services for informants.... Yet paradoxically, those of us who teach students about this topic have little or no institutional requirements along these lines, leaving us often unsupervised and under-resourced.

In addition, there is increasingly the knowledge and acknowledgement that emotions have a place in practice. Emotions have a place in international (criminal) law and legal practice (Saab, 2021; Sedgewick, 2011), emotions shape how humanitarian workers conduct their work (Sarıaslan & Avetisyan, 2024, pp. 19–20)[7] and how soldiers navigate conflict settings (Sutton, 2021). Practitioners are exposed to the consequences of atrocity crimes through interactions with the victims or perpetrators of the crimes. They may sit in sterile courtrooms that are filled with emotions as victims testify about what happened to them or perpetrators recount their gruesome acts.[8] Or they may be soldiers, exposed to violence as an inherent part of their job.[9]

This book explores the emotional impact of the work of scholars, teachers and practitioners who focus on, or are exposed to, mass atrocities and the ethical dilemmas that come with it. It will compare, contrast and synthesize the experiences of these actors, distill their needs and highlights what propels them forward to work on such heart-wrenching topics. It will, furthermore, explore how they cope with negative emotions that may stem from their work. It also aims to provide advice on how to best teach and study these subjects. It explores how to deal with them in a professional and ethical manner whilst acknowledging that emotions are a normal human reaction to these inhumane crimes.

---

6 See also the chapters of Bouwknegt, McGonigle-Leyh & Christiaanse, and Aydin-Aitchison & Battista in this volume.

7 See also the chapter of De Brouwer in this volume.

8 See also the chapters of Michels and Witteveen in this volume.

9 See chapters of Van Peski and Cammaert in this volume.

4 The Book

This book is the first to highlight the emotional and ethical dimensions of working in the field of mass atrocity as a scholar, teacher and practitioner. In the first part of the book, scholars open up about the role of emotions throughout their careers. Alette Smeulers interviewed a small sample of scholars about the emotional dimensions of their research into mass atrocities more generally, and perpetrators specifically. She underscores the need of being aware of our emotions as a way to be prepared for what we do and contribute to a broader effort to prevent such crimes. The chapter starts by investigating the motivational drives behind the work of scholars in the field of mass atrocities. These may be tied to personal backgrounds, when family members have been through war, or when scholars come from war-torn countries themselves. For others it is just interest, curiosity driven, for many it is a combination of both. Smeulers' respondents mention a wide array of negative emotions that stemmed from their research. In addition, the research of her respondents led to existential questions when the normalcy and kindness of (some of the) perpetrators became apparent. However, it also often changed their perspectives and who they are for the better. There is a sense of purposefulness that propels many of the interviewed scholars forward.

In the chapter that follows, Marije Luitjens takes an anthropological perspective as she examines the emotional dimensions of her work. She argues that the growing body of work within anthropology on the emotions of the researcher is meant to contribute to the objectivity of the research as a reflexive practice. The impact of the work on the emotions of the anthropologist as such, is still rarely the central focus. Based on her own experience, Luitjens also contrasts her experiences with ethnography in the field with digital ethnography, the impact of the latter being often underestimated. She offers suggestions for better coping mechanisms before, during and after the research. In doing so, she advocates for more institutional attention for the impact of the work on scholars, stresses the importance of supporting one-another within the research community and argues that it is important to take the time to process emotions during the research process.

In a personal account, Furtuna Sheremeti tells the story of how she navigated her complex emotional landscape when she fled her country as a child and returned as a scholar on a quest to understand the violence that caused her fear and plight in her early youth. Sheremeti highlights the struggle to stay objective when her research brings her back to Kosovo to interview people who have lived through serious human rights abuses and mass atrocities. Next to recognizing the personal biases that are inherently present because of personal experiences, she argues that methodological rigor, peer review, reflective practices, trying to maintain some emotional distance and being extra vigilant to proceed ethically are all crucial to maintaining objectivity. In doing so, Sheremeti bridges the gap between scholarly literature that has long underscored the difficult nature of doing research in a post conflict setting and the practice itself where this literature is largely ignored.

The second part of the book is devoted to teaching mass atrocities. Thijs Bouwknegt analyzes who he is as a teacher, scholar, a "homo academicus" and "homo emoticus." He reflects on how he teaches and perceives his responsibility toward his students. He reflects on his personal background and how it has propelled him forward on his professional path as a historian. Tracing his family's background to WWII and his grandfather's military service in the Dutch East Indies (contemporary Indonesia), Bouwknegt's curiosity in violence was at least partly triggered by the silence his family kept on the topic and the serendipitous encounters he had with people who were touched by war during his childhood and university studies. He speaks of the responsibility we have toward ourselves, our colleagues and our students. His teaching, he explains, is therefore guided by conscientiousness and cautiousness, in particular regarding the manner in which biases, politics, moralism and emotions might influence our work and the importance of being aware and forthcoming about them.

The two chapters that follow describe how courses can be set up to take into account, acknowledge and mitigate the negative emotions students may experience because of the gruesome nature of the topic. Brianne McGonigle Leyh and Koko Christiaanse first shed light on their digital open-source investigations lab which they taught using a trauma and resilience informed approach. On the basis of survey results and student reflections logs they stress the need to start thinking early about which elements of a trauma and resilience approach match the learning environment. These can be implemented initially and appropriately adjusted as the course continues.

Andy Aydin-Aitchison and Annalisa Battista explore the interplay between ethics and emotions in relation to their course "Criminologies of Atrocity." Through a survey, student focus groups and reflective meetings with staff, they analyzed the emotional reactions and ethical reflections of students in relation to the work they conducted on perpetrators and victims of atrocity crimes in the archives of the ICTY. Aydin-Aitchison and Battista emphasize the importance of developing a course that is "grounded in ethics and open to emotions."

The last part of the book explores the dynamics of emotions and ethics for practitioners. Starting in the legal sphere, with appeals prosecutor and former investigation magistrate Martin Witteveen who delves into some of the emotions he felt throughout the years. Witteveen describes frustration as a powerful motivator but also as a treacherous emotion, potentially leading to feelings of hopelessness and exhaustion. Trauma, fear and stress, shame and disillusionment all marked his long career. They were present within himself but also in witnesses, defendants and colleagues he worked with. Importantly, Witteveen also describes moments where there was humor and laughter. All these emotions, he acknowledges, might very well have impacted his decision-making possibly resulting in biases. He concludes that a person should always maintain a certain amount of skepticism about their ability to be truly independent and objective. The emotional challenges also led to organizational change to ensure the well-being of witnesses and staff. Fortunately, Witteveen concludes that while negative emotions are often present, a sense of gratitude prevails.

Staying in the legal realm, An Michels focuses on the emotional toll the work of psychosocial professionals working with victims and witnesses of mass atrocities may take. After recounting her own experiences and the need to be attuned to one's own emotions, Michels argues that there is a need to use precise terminology and highlights several risk factors and protective factors to provide a roadmap that strengthens the protection of professionals in the field. In doing so, Michels argues that lessons from the work of psychologists can be drawn to help other professionals working in the field of mass atrocities.

In the following chapter, Anne-Marie de Brouwer allows us insight into her multifaceted career as a researcher, practitioner, entrepreneur and teacher in support of women and men who survived sexual violence in Rwanda. She does so against the backdrop of broader developments in the field, narrating how ethical guidelines within international criminal justice to protect victims/survivors of conflict-related sexual violence (CRSV) have become more sophisticated. While De Brouwer is upfront about the emotional costs of working on such a difficult topic throughout her career, and stresses the importance of self-care, she also emphasizes the tremendous inspiration, strength and energy she drew from the resilience of victims/survivors of genocidal CRSV. Next to the interactions with the victims/survivors themselves, her work with local organizations, such as Solace Ministries, were particularly formative and inspirational.

Thereafter, Caecilia van Peski highlights how those who are deployed in the field of international crisis response can become better professionals when they are attuned to all the ways they were wounded over the course of their lives and careers. Doing so can turn the professionals into "wounded healers" where their wounds are embraced as signs of personal and professional growth. They can be cherished as wounds that make the professionals more caring and more capable of helping others.

In the final chapter, Patrick Cammaert takes the reader to several conflict situations where he served as commander of a UN Peacekeeping force. From Yemen to Cambodia, to Ethiopia and Eritrea, to the DRC, South Sudan and Gaza, Cammaert lets us into his life as commander where he not only needed to manage his own emotions when faced with starving children in Yemen but also the emotions of his troops amid a dangerous security situation in Cambodia. He stresses the importance of relying on support from others, on friends and family. He also emphasizes how important it is to be open about ones feelings, not repressing them and ensuring sufficient time for rest.

References

Aydın-Aitchison, A. (2024). Teaching Atrocity Criminology with ICTY Archives: Disciplinarity, Research, Ethics, *Journal of Criminal Justice Education*, 35(3) pp. 528–546.

Bergman Blix, S., Wettergren, Å. (2024). Integrating Rationality and Emotion in Legal Institutions. In: H. Flam (Ed.). *Research Handbook on the Sociology of Emotion*. Edward Elgar Publishing, pp. 173–197.

Blackburn, S. (2021). *Ethics: A very short introduction*. Oxford: Oxford University Press.

Baird, K., Kracen A. (2006). Vicarious traumatization and secondary traumatic stress: A research synthesis. *Counselling Psychology Quarterly*, 19(2), pp. 181–188.

Godfrey, R., Brewis, J. (2018). 'Nowhere else sells bliss like this': Exploring the emotional labour of soldiers at war. *Gender, Work & Organization*, 25(6), pp. 653–669.

Goldie, P. (2003). *The Emotions: A Philosophical Exploration*. Oxford: Oxford University Press.

Gebreslassie, D. Y., Irechukwu, E. N. (2023). Compassion Satisfaction, Burnout and Secondary Traumatic Stress among Humanitarian Workers in Gashora Emergency Transit Mechanism Rwanda. *Journal of Sociology, Psychology & Religious Studies*, 5(2), pp. 160–181.

Hagenauer, G., Volet, S. (2014). 'I don't think I could, you know, just teach without any emotion': Exploring the nature and origin of university teachers' emotions. *Research papers in education*, 29(2), pp. 240–262.

Hagan, J., Kay, F. M. (2011). The Emotional Toll and Exhilaration of Human Rights Activism: Gender and Legal Work at the Hague International Criminal Tribunal. *Queens Law Journal*, 37(1), pp. 257–301.

Hochschild, A. R. (1979). Emotion work, feeling rules, and social structure. *American journal of sociology*, 85(3), pp. 551–575.

Holland, J. (2007). Emotions and Research, *Int. J. Social Research Methodology*, 10(30), pp. 195–209.

Kadowaki, J. (2015). Maintaining professionalism: Emotional labor among lawyers as client advisors. *International Journal of the Legal Profession*, 22(3), pp. 323–345.

Kaur, M., Harris, L. (2024). *How to Account for Trauma and Emotions in Law Teaching.* Cheltenham: Edgar Elgar Publishing.

Koning, A., Weerdesteijn, M. (2025). De mens achter de onderzoeker: Emotioneel gedoe bij criminologisch onderzoek, *Tijdschrift voor Criminologie*, 67(1), pp. 70–86.

Lowe, P., Jones, H. (2010). Teaching and Learning Sensitive Topics, *Enhancing Learning in the Social Sciences*, 2(3), pp. 1–7.

Maroney, T. A. (2021). Lay Conceptions of Emotion in Law. In: S. A. Bandes, J. L. Madeira, K. D. Temple (Eds.). *Research Handbook on Law and Emotion.* Cheltenham: Edward Elgar Publishing Limited.

Moran, R. J., Asquith, N. L. (2020). Understanding the vicarious trauma and emotional labour of criminological research. *Methodological Innovations*, 13(2), pp. 1–11.

Nikischer, A. (2019). Vicarious trauma inside the academe: Understanding the impact of teaching, researching and writing violence. *Higher Education*, 77(5), pp. 905–916.

Nyseth-Nzatatira, H., Gertz, E., Uggen, C. (2023). Judging Genocide: Emotional Labor During Transitional Justice. *Law and Social Inquiry*, 48(4), pp. 1210–1231.

O'Brien, M. (2021). Coping with Trauma from Research Content: Conducting Genocide Research. *Voices of Academia*, retrieved 25 January 2023 from https://voicesofacademia.com/2021/07/16/coping-with-trauma-from-research-content-conducting-genocide-research-by-melanie-obrien/

O'Byrne, D. (2014). The places and spaces of human rights education. *Enhancing Learning in the Social Sciences*, 6(1), pp. 66–74.

Olsen, R. E. (2023). Emotions in human research ethics guidelines: Beyond risk, harm and pathology, *Qualitative Research*, 23(3), pp. 526–544.

Roberts, A., Smith, K. I. (2002). Managing emotions in the college classroom: The cultural diversity course as an example. *Teaching Sociology*, 30(3), pp. 291–301.

Sarıaslan, K. Z., Avetisyan, A. (2024). Local Meanings of Peace: The Politics of Words and Emotional Labor among Civil Society Practitioners in Armenia and Turkey. *Caucasus Survey* (published online ahead of print 2024).

Saab, A. (2021). Emotions and International Law, *ESIL Reflections*, 10(1), pp. 1–10.

Scarantino, A. (2016). The Philosophy of Emotions and Its Impact on Affective Science. In: L. Feldman Barret, M. Lewis, J. M. Haviland-Jones (Eds.), *Handbook of Emotions.* New York: The Guilford Press.

Scherer, K. R. (2005). What are emotions? And how can they be measured? *Social Science Information*, 44(4), pp. 698–729.

Sedgwick, J. B. (2011). A People's Court: Emotion, Participant Experiences, and the Shaping of Postwar Justice at the International Military Tribunal for the Far East, 1946–1948. *Diplomacy & Statecraft*, 22(3), pp. 480–499.

Shaw, A., Baghramian, M. (2022). Ethics and Emotions: An Introduction to the Special Issue. *International Journal of Philosophical Studies*, 30(3), pp. 193–201.

Sutton, R. (2021). How the Emotions and Perceptual Judgments of Frontline Actors Shape the Practice of International Humanitarian Law. In: S.A Bandes, J. L. Madeira, K. D. Temple (Eds.). *Research Handbook on Law and Emotion*. Edward Elgar Publishing, pp. 477–491.

Tyng, C. M., Amin, H. U., Saad, M. N., Malik, A. S. (2017). The influences of emotion on learning and memory. *Frontiers in psychology*, 8, 1454, pp. 1–22.

Waters, J. Philips. J., Westaby, C., Fowler, A. (2020a). The emotions and emotional labour of criminological researchers. *Methodological Innovations*, Aug.-May, pp. 1–4.

Waters, J., Westaby, C., Fowler, A, Philips, J. (2020b). The emotional labour of doctoral criminological researchers. *Methodological Innovations*, Aug.-May, pp. 1–12.

Yakren, S. (2008). Lawyer as emotional laborer. *University of Michigan Journal of Law Reform*, 42(1), pp. 141–184.

PART 1

Reflections from Scholars

CHAPTER 1

The Challenges of Studying Mass Atrocities and the Perpetrators thereof

Alette Smeulers

1 Introduction

The images of the mass destruction and human suffering in Gaza make me nauseous. How can this ever be right? Why does this happen? How can we stop this? Who is doing this and why? I look away and see my bookcase with all my books on genocide, war, terrorism and especially perpetrators. My analytical mindset takes over: I know who does this and I know why. I am all too familiar with the motives of perpetrators. I studied them for over 30 years and came to understand their mindset which causes them to see the world in black and white. I studied the conflict in Israel and Gaza. I read about the trauma and fear of the Israelis, but also about the way the Palestinians were treated and about how despair can lead to hatred and terror attacks. I read Netanyahu's autobiography, I read about Hamas and religious fundamentalism. I understand the dynamics, the social-psychological mechanisms; I came to understand how people can commit the most horrendous crimes while still believing they are the real victims, the good guys. I learned how perpetrators can trick themselves in believing they do the right thing while committing genocide but it doesn't help. Today I don't want to understand, I just want to cry and run away.

In general I am passionate about my job. I believe it is important to understand – to do research and to teach but on some days I just hate what I am doing. Seeing all of today's violence in Gaza, Ukraine, Syria, Sudan and many other places of the world is depressing. For the first time in my life I seriously consider the possibility of a Third World War. Then what was the point of doing all this research? I feel sad but then manage to pull myself together. Research and knowledge can help us understand and help to prevent. It is a long shot but at least I should try – try to make people understand, try to make people see. Make them see that perpetrators aren't born bad and that we aren't born good but that each one of us is capable of good and bad – that each one of us is capable of horrendous crimes and that our best chance of preventing this is to understand that. I glance back at the television with the horrible images and go back to work. I force myself to convert my anger, frustration and fury into the determination to understand how this can happen and in finding ways to get my message out there. I need to know that at least I tried. It is all I can do.

Doing research on mass atrocities and perpetrators is not easy but important. I strongly believe that it is not enough to merely find and imprison the current perpetrators: we need to understand why they did what they did in order to prevent and deter future crimes and to make sure that no one will ever commit such crimes again. Since the start of my career 30 years ago I was always convinced that we need to teach our students about mass atrocities and that we need scholars to do this research. However, in the last few years, I became much more aware of the fact that we need to take positive action and also need to look after the students and scholars studying mass atrocities because the lessons we learn and teach are emotionally challenging, and we need to face that. It is something that I gradually became more aware of thanks to my former Ph.D. student and the co-editor of this book, Maartje Weerdesteijn. In this chapter, I will share what it was like for me to do this type of research and what it was like for a number of other scholars and friends who have been doing similar research (studying mass atrocities in general and perpetrators more specifically) over the years. I hope to provide inspiration to young scholars who study mass atrocities while at the same time caring for them and helping them to find the ways and means on how to cope with this type of research.

2 Structure and Methodology

For this chapter, I interviewed seven distinguished scholars in an open interview. The scholars were Jessica Stern, Pieter Nanninga, Olivera Simic, Mina Rauschenbach, Kjell Anderson, Barbora Holá and Adina Nistor.[1] In each case, I started off with a list of questions, but sometimes the conversation went into a specific direction, and I let this happen. The analysis below reflects both my

1 Stern interviewed many terrorists and the Bosnian Serb leader Radovan Karadzic who was responsible for genocide, see Stern, 2004, and 2020, but also – as to her background and a personal motivation – Stern, 2010; Nanninga studied suicide terrorists, see Nanninga, 2019; Simic interviewed Biljana Plavsic and Esad Landzo, see Simic, 2020 and 2025, but see also on her personal background (Simic, 2014); Anderson interviewed many perpetrators of genocide, see Anderson, 2017; Rauschenbach interviewed suspects who were convicted or acquitted by the ICTY (Rauschenbach et al., 2017); Holá studied informers in Czechoslovakia (Drumbl & Holá, 2024) and Nistor studied Ongwen, see Nistor, 2023.

own experience, and the answers I received from the interviews, in combination with what I have learned over the years from studying perpetrators and talking to fellow scholars.

The findings are not meant to be representative, and the research was based on a convenience sample as I sought to present an explorative and reflective study that investigated what made these scholars get involved in this type of research; what emotions it triggered, and how they dealt with them. It also aims to provide advice for young scholars. The sections below will reflect a number of issues discussed with the interviewees. I deliberately chose not to indicate exactly who said what, as I believe this is far less relevant than what has been said in general. I want the emphasis to be on the take-aways from the inspiring and thought-provoking interviews and conversations I had. Indicating who said what would, I believe, merely distract. On top of that, I also used the many things scholars over the years told me in order to give a broad picture of what doing research in this field can be like.

3 Getting Involved in Research on Mass Atrocities

Scholars decide to do research on mass atrocities and the perpetrators thereof for various reasons. For me, it was sheer curiosity: I wanted to understand why some people could be so cruel. I had been reading novels on resistance fighters in the Netherlands during the Second World War, and these brave men and women became my childhood heroes. They were the good people fighting evil, and I could only think: If I ever lived through a war, I hope that I would be as brave as they were and will actively fight oppression. But then I started to wonder: wouldn't everybody want to be the good guy? Who, then are the bad guys and why are they bad? Who are they and why do they do what they do? These questions came up for the first time when I was probably 11 or 12-years old, but ever since have triggered my curiosity and led me to study the people who were the bad guys in the novels I read: the perpetrators of mass atrocities. These questions have never left me and are the red thread throughout my career.

During the many conversations I had over the past 30-years with fellow scholars and from the interviews I conducted for this chapter, I realized that some other scholars were also driven by sheer curiosity. One respondent told me: "I was always interested in the dark side of humanity." The interest of some of my respondents was triggered by a book or a movie, an inspiring teacher, a fascinating lecture or a great course at school or university. In some cases, a major event like 9/11 was crucial. This terror attack was a watershed event for many people, some radicalized because of it, others like one of my respondents, started to do research on terrorism and terrorists.

In addition, there can be more personal and compelling reasons, as one of the respondents noted:

> I felt a psychological compulsion to understand violent men.

This can be the case when the scholars themselves, their families or their group, lived through a period of war or were the targeted group but survived. Many of the early genocide and Holocaust scholars were from Jewish origin and had fled Nazi Germany, like, for instance, Ervin Staub who wrote the book *Roots of Evil,* or survived concentration camps, like Eugen Kogon who wrote the classic *Der SS-Staat*. Similarly, one of my respondents, who lived through a war stated:

> I was very young, running for survival… I was a refugee and started to ask questions when I stopped running.

This respondent explained that she was "frozen and had symptoms of PTSD" and thought she would never want to deal with mass atrocities again, but then ended up in a career doing research on mass atrocities:

> I had a nervous break-down and was in hospital for weeks… then I started to write. I wanted to understand. It was a means to cope.

In this case, writing was a means of coping and a form of healing. This respondent's research initially focused on victims and only later on perpetrators. Doing research on mass atrocities becomes way more personal for scholars who got interested because of these personal experiences than it is for scholars who merely study this out of curiosity.

A family history can also trigger an interest. Unanswered questions, doubts, rumors, which are met with silence, can all play a role. One of the respondents interviewed a family member who had been a war veteran in WWII and a prisoner of war for a school project. While doing so, she realized that he didn't say everything and that there was some ambiguity. It became clear that some things were left unsaid, which made this respondent wonder: was he a perpetrator too? There must be many families in which these kinds of questions start to make the younger generation wonder.

Chance can also play a role: sometimes people get caught up in a situation which strongly affects them. I met someone who, by pure chance, was in Rwanda in April 1994 when the genocide started; others saw horrendous crimes as journalist or while being part of peacekeeping missions. All these experiences can trigger the motivation to study mass atrocities, sometimes by studying the law but sometimes to support the victims and sometimes to better understand the perpetrators. One respondent stated:

> I wanted to know: who are these people?

Over the years motives can also get mixed and it becomes harder to pinpoint one single motivating factor:

> It is a mix of altruism, curiosity, the psychological need to stop violent men.

An interest in mass atrocities and the perpetrators thereof might also be triggered by having been the victim or witness of an ordinary crime. Being a victim oneself, being on the run or being faced with family members who have been traumatized or killed can all trigger questions such as: why did this happen? How can I explain this? Who are these people who did this to me, my family, my people? And why did they do that? Researching mass atrocities is then based on a strong internal drive to understand, a compulsion almost and for these scholars, studying mass atrocities is more closely linked to their personal and emotional well-being than for those who are merely driven by curiosity. It might be a means of coping and of healing to study mass atrocities. Past experiences related to mass atrocities might make these scholars more resilient, but it might also make them more vulnerable because memories can come back.

What becomes clear is that, no matter what the origin was, all scholars I talked to and met over the years are passionate about their work. They have a strong desire or even need to know, to understand and subsequently use that knowledge to do something about it. It is not a topic that one can study with total emotional indifference, as also becomes clear from the following quote:

> My need for knowledge and understanding is stronger than my pain and fear.

4 Emotions Triggered by Research on Mass Atrocities

Doing research on mass atrocities is difficult. Not all the time and not always, but there are definitely difficult moments. For me, reading the diary of a woman who was imprisoned and sexually tortured stood out as one of the most horrendous things I ever read. The book is called *Requiem for a Woman's Soul* (Rivabella, 1986). It made me sick. On asking my colleagues the question what emotions were triggered during the research they conducted, I got a vast array of answers and the following emotions were mentioned: shock, horror, disgust, strain, anxiety, anger, stress, discomfort, embarrassment, guilt and shame. The answers also included the following phrases: "emotionally and psychologically challenging or even draining"; "upsetting"; "baffling"; "disturbing and traumatic"; "it made me feel numb almost sick"; "I felt pain"; "it made me feel restless or uncomfortable"; "I couldn't sleep"; "I had nightmares"; "I was stunned, perplexed"; "I cried"; "I felt totally depleted and exhausted." These emotions and effects show how tough doing such research can be. In comparison, in a quantitative survey by GNET on 95 well-known scholars studying terrorism, the following emotions were found to be the most common: sadness (28.4%); irritation (20%); anger (15.7%); fear (15.7%). Other emotions experienced, but less common were: a sense of failure; loneliness; resentment; helplessness; emptiness; disgust; uneasiness; but also (although rarely) indifference. The respondents in this bigger study reported also: having dreams (71.5%); memory loss (39%) and increased devotion to food, alcohol or smoking (57.8%). Also found, but less common: headaches; stomachaches; problems with sleeping; problems with concentration; losing hope for the future; growing distance from family and peers; unable to trust others; agitation (Lakomy & Bozek, 2023, pp. 16–17).

In their book, *Perpetrators – Encountering Humanity's Dark Side*, Alex Hinton admits: "It's not easy. And while doing perpetrator research, I have had awful, violent dreams" (Robben & Hiton, 2023, p. 25). Robben had no nightmares but saw his therapist three times a week (Robben & Hinton, 2023, p. 26). One of my interviewees, Olivera Simic has always been very open about the emotional costs and effects of doing this type of research. In earlier publications, she had already explained how it is sometimes impossible to not become overwhelmed by emotions when interviewing victims:

> Although I know that it is terribly unprofessional, I have held hands with my interviewees and wept openly with them – if a woman is talking about her experience being gang-raped, or about her child being abducted, how can I remain passively un-engaged? I know there's a fine line about emotional engagement in this kind of work, but I can't figure out where that line is and how to properly negotiate it.
>
> SIMIC, 2017, p. 134

> I see a lot of pain and suffering. The oftentimes very gruesome stories these individuals share evoke a variety of emotions in me: sadness, anger, frustration, hopelessness to name but a few … I also have a lot of very bad dreams in which I re-live the stories people tell me with me experiencing their stories first hand…
>
> SIMIC, 2017, p. 151

Sometimes these feelings and emotions are un- or subconsciously put on hold, as one of my respondents, who also extensively interviewed victims, explained:

> It hit only once I was back home – I was in a daze for weeks, it might have been a very mild and temporary form of PTSD.

What can add to the stress are the conditions under which interviews are conducted, especially if the interviewees are victims. One respondent said he had to interview victims from 8 AM till 10 PM, which is obviously emotionally draining and exhausting, and certainly not the way it is supposed to be done, but sometimes you just don't have a choice. So, the logistics can be hard – the waiting and then the jumping on the opportunity, when it presents itself. When talking to victims, many scholars also felt the need and responsibility to listen, they intuitively cared and then felt the strong commitment to write down their stories: to be their voice, as so clearly expressed by Simic in her earlier work.

> I owe it to the women who trusted me with their stories.
>
> SIMIC, 2018, p. 161

Just reading interviews (rather than interviewing oneself) can be difficult at times as well, especially if it somehow overlaps with someone's personal life. One of my respondents explained:

> What you read or hear can unravel things in you or make you discover things in your own or your family's history. It can also trigger memories – from a past and sometimes of something of which you only later understand the significance.

When interviewing perpetrators, there can also be issues with safety. There are many known cases where scholars have been threatened or discouraged from doing the work they do. One respondent states: I was told, things like: "I know where you live … that isn't that far from here." Others also experienced that their work was met with threats, negative reactions and warnings. Robben and Hinton also note that they were sometimes intimidated:

> I once interviewed an officer who opened the drawer of his desk and silently put a pistol on top of the table while looking at me.
>
> ROBBEN & HINTON, 2023, p. 74

One scholar describes a scene "in which she was pretty sure that the people she was interviewing were – in her presence but in a language she was not familiar with – discussing whether or not to kidnap her" (Quoted in Smeulers, Weerdesteijn & Hola, 2019, p. 317).

Doing research on mass atrocities also sometimes means going to sites, memorials or commemorations, and this can be tough too. The one in Srebrenica, which I witnessed myself, and the one in Rwanda, which some of my respondents witnessed, are extremely emotional and very tough to watch and process: the pain of those left behind is so clear, it can be overwhelming. Doing research can also mean that you have to watch videos in which violence is shown, and this can be very hard too. Within terrorism studies, there is now more attention to the potential trauma-related effects of terrorist propaganda on researchers, as such propaganda is "extremely distressing, as its intent is [meant, AS] to upset viewers" (Lakomy & Bozek, 2023, p. 6). In the report from GNET already mentioned above, it was concluded that "most surveyed terrorism researchers experienced mental harm from exposure to violent extremist content at least once in their careers. There is a broad spectrum of reactions they have experienced. Terrorist propaganda frequently triggers sadness, irritation, anger and fear. Problems with concentration, headaches, dreams related to the analyzed content or even memory loss are also quite common. Many of these reactions are considered symptoms of trauma or mood disorders" (Lakomy & Bozek, 2023, p. 1).[2] Another report by REASSURE, which stands for researchers security, safety and resilience project, and which was written by a group based at Swansea University, concluded that "two-thirds of the respondents experienced harm whether an external threat to security, such as being trolled or receiving a death threat; or an

2 One of the findings was that: 75.7% of respondents agreed or strongly agreed (33 and 39 respondents, respectively) that long-term exposure to online visual and audiovisual terrorist content can negatively affect the researcher's mood' (p. 14). Another disturbing figure is that 13.6% "admitted to always or often being traumatized by exposure to violent extremist materials on the internet" (p.15).

internal emotional harm such as depression or anxiety; withdrawal or nightmares" (Pearson, 2023).

In all the above cases, scholars can at least try to prepare themselves, but this is not always possible. As became clear from the interviews I conducted, sometimes it is the element of surprise that shocks the scholar. One respondent explained that when she reads transcripts, she can sometimes and suddenly get touched by something, like the testimony of a child who was forced to kill his friend and who subsequently had a nightmare in which his friend appeared and asked him: "why did you kill me?" Things like that can "catch me off guard and make me wonder: what kind of world are we living in?"

I myself vividly remember that I studied the motives of the many Chechen Black Widows involved in the Moscow theatre hostage crisis in 2002, while at that very moment, Russia was invading and committing horrendous crimes in Ukraine. This made me realize that the same scenario as what had motivated these Chechen women (Russia's interference in another country and the use of extreme violence in the process) was unfolding once again and in a few years, we might once again, see a similar terror attack as the one in the Moscow theatre. It suddenly made knowledge of past crimes extremely topical. For this very reason, my work frustrated me more than it usually does and made me wanting to shout: haven't we learned anything from the past?

5 The Particular Difficulties of Doing Research on Perpetrators of Mass Atrocities

What can cause extra stress is to study perpetrators, as it makes that you as a scholar have to try and see the world through their eyes, and will inevitably be exposed to their way of thinking. It makes you see their very different motives: sometimes the hatred, but also sometimes their indifference; it shows how they can ruthlessly profit or how they genuinely try to make the world a better place (while in reality making it so much worse with their crimes). It can show their evilness, their normalcy or their weakness. Studying perpetrators means that you have to get close to people who have done horrendous things, and this is not always comfortable. Intuitively, you want to distance yourself from them and their crimes, and yet as a scholar you want to understand, and when you do, this might be even more horrifying. It would be so much easier if you would find that they are very different from us, from you and me, but the reality is that they are very similar to us; and studying perpetrators thus also means – in a way – studying your own potential for evil. It can hardly get any more personal than that.

In their book called *Perpetrators – Encountering Humanity's Dark Side*, Robben and Hinton noted that:

> there is a psychological cost to studying the ruins of perpetration [...] it dirties you and makes you abject. Perpetrator research invites the "black sun."
>
> ROBBEN & HINTON, 2023, p. 144

All my respondents agreed that it is, at least at times, difficult or even very difficult to study and especially to interview perpetrators. A few quotes:

> It was very difficult – I didn't know how difficult it was... I exposed myself to evil ... I sometimes had to recover for months... It is psychologically dangerous work.

> It is very dark.

> It is deranging one's own sense of morality.

Jessica Stern, who interviewed many terrorists and also Radovan Karadzic, one of the leaders in the conflict in the former Yugoslavia and held responsible for the genocide in Srebrenica, explained in an interview:

> This is dangerous work, the work I do, studying violent men or men who incite violence. I have to listen without judgment. I have to yield, if only temporarily, to their image of themselves. I can often hover above myself in my imagination, monitoring my reactions. But that doesn't mean I'm never afraid of falling in or losing myself.
>
> STERN, 2020

What struck me most in my own research was the extremely matter-of-fact and cold reports of torturers on what they did to their victims. It made me shiver, while the mind-boggling ability of perpetrators to rationalize and justify their crimes, or rely on the excuse that they merely followed orders, made me at times sad and angry. I was once, several decades ago and still a student, in a library, where I couldn't get the printed article that I needed so badly because the library was about to close, and I didn't have the right coin. The librarian was very strict in sticking to the official rules and not allowing me to borrow the much-needed coin, when it would have been so easy for her to be flexible, as she had the coin and I was the only guest in the library. Sticking to the rule in this case defeated its purpose, and I couldn't run out to get a coin elsewhere as the library was about to close. It was very frustrating and almost made me blurt out: "you are no better than Eichmann!" It showed me how allergic I got to a mindset in which people just stick to rules. Losing sight of the broader picture.

Just like perpetrators get used to the violence they commit, most scholars somehow get used to studying violence: "you have to, otherwise you cannot do the job," one respondent explained. Most respondents confirmed that in the beginning it is more difficult but that it gets easier and "you can handle it," at least to a certain extent. However, this is not always the case, as traumatizing research can also accumulate. One of the respondents indeed said:

> I can't say it gets easier – every story is unique – every pain is unique. Becoming indifferent or numb is not good.

To the latter (becoming indifferent and numb), all other respondents would agree. What it takes is a professional approach and good ways to cope.

> I found a way to do the interviews – used techniques to protect myself.

Others found ways, but these are not always healthy as they indicate themselves:

> I learned to deal with it. Put myself in a dissociative state but this is not a healthy thing.
>
> I get into a zone – I have a task to do ... it's a functional thing ... I block empathy and do a job.
>
> When doing research you are in a tunnel vision but don't stay there too long. That is not healthy.

Ideally, you would get a training on how to interview people and what situations you can get into, but most respondents are of a generation that didn't get any and had to learn how to do the research and conduct interviews, as well as learn how to cope with the emotions of conducting the research, themselves. They noticed that they started to develop a skill. Several interviewees explained that they could stay very focused, composed and professional during the interview, but later, when leaving the room, checking their notes or discussing them with others, the horror fully hit them. They then could feel burdened or even contaminated and dirty:

> I have the capacity to empathize in the moment but the minute I leave the room the horror comes crushing down on me … I can't read the notes right away. I get into an extremely dissociated state. I feel physical revulsion and get into a very uncomfortable mental state… I couldn't get clean … there is an element of contamination.

When talking to perpetrators, it matters a lot what kind of perpetrators they are. They could be leaders, administrative staff, bureaucrats or hands-on perpetrators. It also matters what made them commit their crimes. For some, that might have been obedience, fear or ideology, but for others, it could be sheer lust for power and sadism. One respondent explained:

> I talked to psychopaths – someone who said he enjoyed killing people.

This is scary and chilling, and a moment when you look evil straight in the face, but this, of course, is not always the case. Interviews with perpetrators are not always and not by definition upsetting, as many perpetrators just try to narrate their story to make you understand, as I also know from my own experience interviewing perpetrators. Robben and Hinton write in their book:

> Most wanted to be acknowledged as fellow human beings, and we, as researchers, may afford them that space of humanity.
>
> ROBBEN & HINTON, 2023, p. 51

Many perpetrators are eager to talk; they seek understanding and validation. One respondent explained:

> a lot of people wanted me to see them as good – that they are a good person which shows that when doing an interview, there is a relational aspect to it – it is an interpersonal exchange … they try to construct reality and take a moral distance which makes it easier. You get the sanitized version.

When comparing conducting interviews with perpetrators and victims, some concluded that interviewing victims is harder as "the victims open their hearts and talk about the harm," while the accused were self-presenting. Interviewing perpetrators, however, makes that you have to make sure not to be manipulated. This could especially happen if the perpetrator is a psychopath, Machiavellian or charismatic leader. It is hard to find the balance between being open (in order to understand) and sufficiently critical (in order not to be seduced).

6 Face-to-Face with the Perpetrators

All respondents who conducted interviews with perpetrators stated: the aim of an interview is to understand the motives and drives of a perpetrator, not to judge them. They all stressed that you have to stay professional and detached, and always treat people with kindness and respect. During the interviews, there is no place for moral judgement as that wouldn't serve the purpose. An interview can't be confrontational (see also Robben & Hinton, 2023, p. 75).

The researcher has to build rapport with the perpetrator and show empathy, and this can be hard.[3] Especially, Olivera Simic, who extensively interviewed Biljana Plavsic, who was the second in command to Radovan Karadzic during the war, in the former Yugoslavia and president of the *Republika Srpska* from 1996 to 1998, explains that in quite some detail in her written work and stressed the importance of:

> building an atmosphere of trust, familiarity and friendliness.
>
> SIMIC, 2018, p. 148

This is crucial to then get them to talk and trust you with their story as another respondent noted:

> The aim is not to set the record straight or correct them but understand how they give meaning to their own behavior. Understand their narrative.

The interview is conducted by the scholar to understand the perpetrator, but it is also a meeting and interaction between two people and a possible clash of characters. Jessica Stern described in an interview with the New York Times how she interviewed Radovan Karadzic, for many hours in an attempt to try and understand his mindset. She described what happened then:

3 Hinton and Robben (2023, p. 63) note a potentially important nuance here: "rapport and trust are not required when interviewing perpetrators. Etnographers can put themselves in their place without having a close bond because empathy doesn't require trust."

> Mr. Karadzic looked straight at me. "Would you like me to show you how it works?".
>
> I was startled, unsure how to respond. I thought: If I say no, he will have won. He would see that I was afraid of him and of his claim to mystical power. But saying yes meant exposing myself to his touch. Not just his touch, but his "healing" energy. He was still looking at me, indicting me with his gaze. It came to me that he wanted me to sense his power, maybe to frighten me.
>
> I reminded myself that although convicted of genocide, he has never been suspected of committing violent acts himself. I did not think he would strangle me. But I knew that the guard on duty, who was supposed to be monitoring us and keeping me safe, was sitting at a desk, idly flipping through the pages of a magazine.
>
> STERN, 2020

To stay neutrally detached while also trying to fully understand the person you are facing is not always easy. Sometimes you meet a perpetrator who committed horrendous crimes, and you expect to meet the devil but are suddenly faced with a friendly, kind and polite human being who warmly shakes your hand. Several scholars have described this confrontation and paradox in their books on perpetrators. Gobodo-Madikizela, for instance, in her book on Eugene de Kock, the leader of the death squad Vlakplaas during the Apartheid era, recounted: "The embodiment of evil stood there politely smiling at me" (Gobodo-Madikizela, 2003, p. 6). Olivera Simic, likewise acknowledges in her book on *Plavsic* (Simic, 2025) how she was warmly greeted and embraced, which made her freeze:

> How are you supposed to react? It is so easy to judge

To see someone in the dock and feel their pain, can also have an effect. One of the respondents stated that during trial observations she:

> saw a broken person who was not helped until too late. I felt empathy for him (the perpetrator, AS). It made me feel bitter – it was a bitter pill.

One of the respondents said he felt guilty when he asked questions and realized he had upset a former perpetrator he interviewed by probing into a dark and difficult period. Sometimes perpetrators become upset or angry when interviewed. This is understandable, as perpetrators might have done horrible things and can suffer from trauma too (Mohamed, 2015).

Some scholars note that they got upset because they feel empathy for the perpetrator (see, e.g., Koning & Weerdesteijn, 2025). Is this wrong? It raises theoretical and ethical questions but also has a lot to do with natural human instincts and feelings of empathy. Speckhard, who studied Palestinian (would-be) suicide killers, wrote: "I keep feeling strong waves of emotion welling up inside. Somehow, the overwhelming sadness and trauma we listened to today has hit hard … I just want to scream and perhaps explode emotionally at all the injustices Palestinians suffer" (Speckhard, 2012, p. 236).

One of the most compelling documented testimonies of this struggle is from Gobodo-Madikizela who interviewed Eugene de Kock and then while listening to his story, very briefly put her hand on his shaking hand to console him but she was surprised and shocked by her own intuitive and empathetic response and later in her book stated:

> I felt guilty for having expressed even momentary sympathy and wondered if my heart had actually crossed the moral line from compassion, which allows one to maintain a measure of distance, to actually identifying with De Kock.
>
> GOBODO-MADIKIZELA, 2003, p. 33

She described the two sides of De Kock: one that was evil and "had penetrated my defenses" which made her feel "invaded, naked, angry," while the other "the one I was more afraid of confronting" was "a human being capable of feeling, crying, and knowing pain" (Gobodo-Madikizela, 2003, p. 39). The reverse can also be true. One respondent felt shame because she "allowed" perpetrators to "say certain things." The need to stay neutral while being overwhelmed by disgust can be very hard.

Another respondent explained how, while on a research stay conducting interviews with perpetrators, was caught off guard when someone totally unexpected and outside of an interview setting started to explain that he had been involved in mass atrocities. This happened twice:

> Once I was in a bar with a guy who said he strangled people to death – just like that because they were a nuisance … he told me very casually, it was very intimidating. He had very big hands.

> A guy who worked for an NGO suddenly told me he had been a torturer. He was a pleasant guy and his sudden admission upset me. The guy felt ashamed.

7 Is Looking into a Mirror the Hardest Part?

Doing research on perpetrators often leads scholars to conclude that the perpetrators are not deranged or disturbed but very ordinary people, even people with whom the scholar can relate to or even come to like if the circumstances would be different. A sentiment often heard is the one expressed by Rosenberg, who did research on perpetrators in Latin America:

> I would have preferred them to be monsters. Coming to understand that this is not the case was disturbing – for what it taught me about these people, and ultimately, about myself.
>
> ROSENBERG, 1991, p. 17

One of the respondents agreed and stated:

> the most difficult part was to admit that they were human... it bothers me.

The most telling quote I came across in literature was from a doctor cited by Hannah Arendt in her book *Eichmann in Jerusalem – The Banality of Evil*. He was one of the doctors who examined Eichmann, the man who in Nazi Germany had been responsible for the transportation of the Jews from their homes to the concentration and death camps. The doctor could only conclude that Eichmann was normal, but then tellingly added: "more normal, at any rate, than I am after having examined him" (Arendt, 1964, p. 25). The problem is that perpetrators are, as Arendt noted, so "terribly and terrifyingly normal." I myself fully agree and used this phrase as the subtitle of my most recent book on perpetrators of mass atrocities (Smeulers, 2024).

The reason why we find it terrifying that the perpetrators are terribly normal is because we intuitively want to qualify them as very different from us. We want to see ourselves as good and the perpetrators as evil. We want to demonize them. For me personally, studying perpetrators also meant looking in the mirror and knowing that under certain circumstances, I could be a perpetrator too. I realized that it wouldn't be consistent to conclude academically that all people can become perpetrators, and then make an exception for myself and my loved ones. To me, it was the most difficult part of my research over the last 30 years to accept that everyone could become a perpetrator, and it was something I have struggled with for a while. I asked my respondents if they had similar experiences and what it did to them to look evil in the face.

The answers of my respondents were very personal and vastly different. It also depended very much on the situation and the types of perpetrators they studied. One respondent clearly realized that not all perpetrators are ordinary people and stated:

> I looked evil in the face. [...] I didn't believe in evil – I do now.

Whereas another explained

> For me understanding made it easier – these people did horrible things but after my research I understood they are also just boys like me – that made it less scary.

The finding that everyone can become a perpetrator can also become a driving force behind the research, as Maartje Weerdesteijn confessed in an article:

> I became fascinated by the subject during my studies because I realized that I would probably be an excellent perpetrator; because of my sense of duty, respect for authority and the urge to do everything right. These disturbing thoughts have always motivated me to find out more. It continues to fascinate me endlessly how I could come to that conclusion, while I couldn't hurt a fly.
>
> WEERDESTEIJN, in KONING & WEERDESTEIJN, 2025, p. 73

One of the respondents also realized that what she was studying could be her and said:

> I would probably do the same ... I got to know myself a lot better.

Several of the respondents were struck by the complexity of it all: "It is not black and white but more complicated." There is a lot of grayness and people can be many things in the same conflict: perpetrators and victims.

> They are human not evil and there is a wide and diverse range of emotions that can bring them there ... emotions that are familiar to which I can relate. It shows how complex it all is.

Others said that people are not evil but weak.

> I learned how weak people are – how they choose the path of the least resistance.

This coincides with my own conclusions in my research on perpetrators.

8 The Lack of Understanding and the Difference between Being an Outsider or Insider

Many scholars, myself and most respondents included, have been faced with the question as to why they would want to study perpetrators. Some have faced blunt criticism or comments such as "what do you know?" or "who are you to say something about this?" or "you can never understand." Not everyone understands why it is necessary to try to understand perpetrators rather than merely condemn them. Many were also confronted with criticism as to their findings that perpetrators are also just ordinary human beings. This is not a popular finding, and scholars have been accused of the weirdest things. Two female scholars who tried to understand perpetrators (of very different conflicts) were both accused of having fallen in love with the perpetrator. In both cases a painful and ridiculous accusation. Many people want to keep seeing perpetrators as very different from us, ordinary people. They want to demonize them, want to see them as evil as, that is, emotionally easier. They want them to be sent to prison without any chance of parole or even executed. Scholars are often critiqued for giving perpetrators a platform to speak. They are confronted with questions like: Why do you even talk to them? Some people just don't understand. Don't want to understand (see also Browning, 1992, xx; Gobodo-Madikizela, 2003, 16 and Robben & Hinton, 2023, p. 20ff).

Scholars who are from the same country they study, or worse, even from the same group as the perpetrators they study, have an additional set of challenges to meet. Simic, who is an example of such an insider, has discussed this extensively in her written work so far and explains how hard it sometimes is, and how it can be an extra motivation to do her work well:

> I have always been driven by feelings of personal and academic responsibility to account for the crimes committed by what is consistently perceived from the outside as "my own group."
>
> SIMIC, 2018, p. 154

To come from the same background and culture, to speak the same language, being familiar with the traditions and prevailing norms, values and customs has clear advantages:

> as an insider I have a strong understanding of the dynamics and the interplay of social relationships that inform the situations in my home country.
>
> SIMIC, 2018, p. 149

One of the respondents agreed that doing research on mass atrocities and perpetrators in one's own country makes it way more personal:

> It is very personal [...] it is close to home. When they talk about customs, or places, pubs, food. There are so many things I am familiar with [...]. You just get things faster. You get more profound insights. You just get it. [...] It makes it more alive. I saw myself [...] I would probably do the same. It was very confrontational.

It, however, also helps to understand, to associate, as Simic wrote: it was easier to connect.

> I am no longer simply a Bosnian woman. I am a Serb woman.
>
> SIMIC, 2018, p. 148

Doing research on your own country is a lot of things at the same time: "It is interesting, emotionally draining," "more intense" but also "more fulfilling [...] more fruitful." The same respondent continued:

> the people were apathetic. I am like that. It is the way I am. I don't like it. It is lame.

This respondent continued to say that the research is "tied to what I do and who I am." Publishing the findings of research can have a huge impact, and even more so when the scholar is an insider. One can be seen as a traitor when talking about (in this case) Serb perpetrators. It can lead to ostracization, something Simic has experienced herself (Simic, 2018, p. 157). That is not easy but in her case it strengthened her determination (Simic, 2018, p. 160). She also experienced that it can also easily be turned around. This happened when she wrote about a Serb victim in the book *Lola's War* (Simic, 2023).

However, insiders who no longer live in the country can also be seen as outsiders: "who are you to tell us?" was one of the reactions a respondent received. To publish the research findings or book in the native language is kind of scary they admitted.

9 The Impact of This Type of Research on the Scholar

I wondered whether doing this type of research changed any of my respondents; changed their attitudes or behavior as it did for me. I became much more aware of the danger of a number of character traits such as obedience, conformism and being very hierarchical but also elitism and arrogance; the danger of the lack of empathy and absence of critical reflection; the danger of power, but also of being very authoritarian both as a leader and as a follower. I very strongly became aware of the need to take responsibility for one's actions. I don't think I was ever very authoritarian, but studying perpetrators made me speak out more often. My research taught me how dangerous it can be to look away and stay quiet and this affected and changed me. This was also true for some of the others, but not for all. One respondent admitted that studying violence had the opposite effect on him:

> I became less vocal probably because I saw the danger in being very vocal.

The research also made me very aware not to judge too quickly and to constantly be mindful of the choices I make. It made me realize that I could never sit back, confidently believing that I am a good person, and that, therefore, all I do would be, by definition good. I realized, I just didn't know how I would respond to certain circumstances. This sentiment was very much reflected in what one of my respondents said.

> If I hear people say: if there is a war, I'll be a hero, I can only think that, that is a very presumptuous thing to say.

I totally agree. I will never say that perpetrators are just bad people and that I could never do anything like that, and many of my respondents would agree with that. One respondent told me that, because of the research, she realized that whether you become a perpetrator or not can be "a matter of luck being born in the right or the wrong place." She continued to explain: "This gave me a sense of privilege. It is a privilege not to have to fight for survival." It made this scholar aware that not living in constant fear but in freedom and safety is something that needs to be treasured. Here too, I very much agree.

While studying mass atrocities and perpetrators, some of my respondents said that they also found unexpected kindness and goodness shown by others. They learned that not everyone acts the same, and this struck them in a very positive way:

> I also saw how heroic people can be.

Or they feel more touched by kindness and goodness since they started doing research on mass atrocities:

> I am moved by goodness. In my ordinary live there is goodness. It is moving to see how high we can go.

And some consciously try to show more kindness and goodness. Other effects reported by my respondents were that they became: a better listener; more empathetic; more compassionate; more aware that we often know just one part of the story. Some said it ensures that they always pay critical attention; it sensitized them and made them aware of what is happening. One respondent said: "it affected me in how I think of banal things." Several said they reflected upon the research and their findings a lot; asked themselves how they would have responded and understood better how and why they, like me, react negatively to authoritarianism. Several said they became more critical and that the research made them cherish critical reflection even more. Several reported that they don't take things for granted or at face value anymore. Remarkably, some also became more optimistic and hopeful:

> If I wouldn't be hopeful, I wouldn't do it. My hope is that it will change and my hope keeps me going. […] knowledge is power – knowing can protect you.

One of the respondents strongly admired the resilience of children and people who have gone through a period of mass violence: "I am amazed that people could go on with their lives. That they moved on. I found it impressive."

Some said their perspectives changed, and this helped in life, but there were also some of my respondents who said that they didn't really change because of the research.

10 The Importance of This Research

Despite the noted difficulties, all respondents were happy they engaged in this type of research. Some saw it as an important task:

> It is a public service.

And felt that it was their responsibility, their role:

> Someone needed to do it.

It was, however, not just a sense of obligation. The research can also be scientifically challenging and satisfying:

> It can also be interesting and exciting – it sounds paradoxical but to discover things is exciting.

At least as important are the lessons learned as a human being on human behavior and violence. The lessons learned from staring evil in the face:

> I am happy I did it. I learned a lot. It helped me to grow.

> I found a lot of answers and don't feel the compulsion anymore. [...] It made me a bigger person. Who understands more variance, more empathetic, less shocked, more familiar.

> to understand gave me more peace. It made me hopeful.

Most importantly, however, and with the exception of one, all respondents seemed to agree on that hope that their and other's research findings would help to change the world and make it a better place. What almost everyone said was that they wanted to understand in order to prevent:

> We can draw important lessons from this which can help to prevent these horrible things.

To give an example, research showed that many, if not all perpetrators suffered trauma – undigested trauma and humiliation, which then turned into violence (see for, instance, Gilligan, 1996). This knowledge teaches us that we should try to prevent or mitigate trauma and humiliation if we want to prevent violence. Such concrete findings can have practical consequences and can be seen as a major achievement. Ultimately, all respondents wanted to help make the world a better place. It is probably telling that several scholars who studied the dynamics which make people do bad things, at some point, refocus their research and study mechanisms and dynamics that can help people to be a better person. Well-known examples of scholars who shifted their focus are Ervin Staub, who shifted his from perpetrators to bystanders and from bad to good (Staub, 1989, 2011); while also Philip Zimbardo re-shifted his research interests: after studying atrocity-producing situations, such as the prison environment (Zimbardo, 2011), he refocused on the question as to how to become a hero, and even set up training programs on how to be a hero.[4] The one respondent who was not motivated by the aim to change the world but more so by sheer interest said it was more realistic not to expect to be able to change the world.

One of the respondents stated that to work on prevention is easier but not necessarily more satisfying. I totally agree: We need to learn from the past and pass on our knowledge – teach people to be more critical; to self-reflect; to listen to each other and show more empathy. These are just some of the many things that we can pass on to the future generations that might help them do a better job. As one respondent stated:

> I place a lot of hope in young people. The mentality is changing. I can see more clearly now that it takes another generation. It takes an effort but the next generation will be more peaceful.

11 Recommendations for Future Students and Scholars

All respondents were happy to share some advice for younger scholars. This is important because the earlier-mentioned study by GNET also showed that experienced researchers on terrorism are much more aware of the risks involved in doing this type of research and more careful in their approach than younger scholars are (Lakomy & Bozek, 2023, p. 31)[5] and there is no reason to believe that this is less true for scholars on genocide, crimes against humanity and war crimes. So, some advice and recommendations for future scholars are well in place here.

My respondents agreed that young scholars need to carefully think about whether this type of research is really what they want to do and whether they believe that they can cope. But if they can, and this is what they want, then the advice is: do it. Go for it. Not a single respondent regretted doing this type of research. They were all glad they did it. One, however, did also add the advice:

---

4 Hero imagination project, see https://www.heroicimagination.org/ (retrieved January 8, 2025).

5 What is very troublesome is that REASSURE states that especially junior scholars, scholars of color and women are affected and that the harm suffered from doing research on terrorism can have a negative effect on their careers (Pearson, 2023).

"but do it for the right reasons as it is tough." Do it when it moves or inspires you, when there is a strong urge and drive to know or to understand. When it triggers your curiosity. But also be aware: "don't glamorize the job. Approach it in a simple way. The job can be very tedious and be sensitive to the consequences" of what you say, to who you say it and in what way. An important aspect of the latter is to be sensitive to the audience. A reaction some of the respondents got was: "What do you know?" or "who are you to tell us what was right and what was wrong?" So always make sure that what you say about some else's conflict is not experienced as incorrect, insensitive or condescending. Don't become someone who only studied it from books and then starts telling the people who went through it what it is like. It doesn't work and is not appreciated, and it is perceived as arrogant and condescending, rightfully so.

If you decide to go for it, then make sure you are prepared to take a professional approach and don't make it too personal. One respondent further clarified: "Only do what you need to do for your work. So, only watch gruesome things if you have to watch them and then turn the sound off or look away at the most explicit violent parts." The advice is further to ensure that you have a clear division between home and work. Ideally, do the most difficult work only at the office rather than at home. Don't contaminate the home space by watching horrible videos there or transcribing interviews. Most respondents also admitted that this cannot always be prevented, and individuals can be very different in how to achieve the work-private balance, but a certain amount of self-care is key. Stay true to yourself was another piece of advice.

In her article on the challenges of doing research in the field of transitional justice, Simic (2017, p. 153) found that some scholars are afraid to share their emotions because they fear to be disqualified for doing so: "fear for their reputation: that they are undermining their competency and objectivity; that their research is not 'real' and denounced as subjective." Yet, all respondents agreed that as a scholar you need to make sure that you feel protected and don't break apart while being exposed to evil. Figure out what helps you: meditation, yoga, arts, therapy, counseling, sports, watching silly romantic comedies or trash TV or do some other kind of research for a while. Make sure you have a balance between work and private life; between dealing with tough issues and relaxation and protect your boundaries. These boundaries might be different for each and every individual though.

Some advised not to bring the horrible stories from the research on mass atrocities to the dinner table, so as not to traumatize anyone:

> I can't share this with my family or friends, I would traumatize them. So I don't get the validation from them. I hide it. It is lonely.

This loneliness needs to be tackled, and most are also strongly advised not to isolate, although that is not easy. You need to make sure that you talk to other people about it. Ideally, colleagues who do similar research because they know best: then you can discuss your experiences together (see also Pearson, 2023). It can be close colleagues at your own university but also colleagues you meet at conferences. Some of the respondents said they had a bunch of colleagues with whom to discuss these issues, while others went to see therapists to talk about it and yet others have a good friend or partner with whom they discuss these issues and find comfort. But whatever you do, self-care is the key here.[6] Universities offer little support, but amongst scholars and certain organizations, there is more attention for the topic nowadays, which is a good thing.[7]

We do, however, also have to be cautious of self-indulgence, as several respondents warned. Firstly, because we study this topic by choice, while victims do not become victims by choice. And secondly, because our pain in studying this is far less than the pain of those living through it, and we are in the very fortunate position that we can more easily seek help compared to those who survived a genocide or live in a war-torn country. One respondent said:

> I feel a slight discomfort discussing this in public because the focus should be on the victims and their suffering [...] drawing sympathy to yourself. I don't like it. What scares me most is when it is carried as a badge of honor.

Hinton and Robben also discuss this unease:

> Perpetrator research can take a toll. It somehow feels unseemly to talk about it (or write about it, as I am doing now) given the enormous

6 Lakomy and Bozek (2023, 19), found the following coping mechanisms used by their sample: distracting oneself (44.2%); humor (42.6%); seeking advice (36%) which often included therapy sessions. They also (pp. 33–34) enlist the following solutions: selective attention (only watch what is needed for analytical purposes); reduce screen time; take a break; physical exercise; talk about challenges with family, friends and partners; making jokes; "adopt a mindset that enables mood disorders to be avoided or mitigated" and lastly regularly attending sessions with a psychotherapist.

7 See also report of GNET by Lakomy and Bozek (2023, pp. 2 and 14) in which they conclude that 83, 1% said that there institution "never provided training or support to study violent extremism." They note: "Many universities managers remain unaware of the potential risks involving in terrorism research. A generally unhealthy workplace culture in academia is also a significant factor at play" (2023, p. 32). This is confirmed in the REASSURE report as concluded by Pearson (2023).

> suffering, past and present, experienced by the victims and relatives of the victims [...] While acknowledging their much greater psychosocial burden, researchers also need to recognize their own abjection and process their ruin as they pass through the ruins of perpetration.
>
> HINTON & ROBBEN, 2023, p. 149

That is very true, of course, and we most certainly don't ever want a victim to point a finger at us and say: "our tragedy is your career." We should always be very much aware that we are in a privileged position and generally a safe environment. And yet: the better we are prepared dealing with the horrible nature of what we study, the better we are able to objectively and scientifically analyze what is going on. Scholars need to become resilient too, and most importantly of all: the better we are able to do so, the better we will be able to show the victims that we care about them. We will not, and never will, be able to undo what happened to them, but we can at least try our best to study this in order to never let this happen to them, or anyone else, again but in order to do so, we need to be able to continue doing the research ourselves, hence, the importance of paying attention to the challenges of studying mass atrocities and the perpetrators thereof.

References

Anderson, K. (2017). *Perpetrating genocide: A criminological account.* London: Routledge.

Arendt, H. (1964). *Eichmann in Jerusalem: a report on the banality of evil.* New York: Penguin Books.

Browning, C. R. (1992). *Ordinary men – Reserve Police Battalion 101 and the final solution in Poland.* New York: HarperCollins.

Drumbl, M., Hola, B. (2024). *Informers up close: stories from communist Prague.* Oxford: Oxford University Press.

Gilligan, J. (1996). *Violence – Reflection on a national epidemic.* New York: Vintage Books.

Gobodo-Madikizela, P. (2003). *A human being died that night: a south African story of forgiveness.* Boston: Hoghton Mifflin Company.

Kogon, E. (1974). *Der ss-Staat – das System der Deutschen Konzentrationslager.* München: Wilhelm Heyne Verlag.

Koning, A., Weerdesteijn, M. (2025). De mens achter de onderzoeker: emotioneel gedoe bij criminologisch onderzoek. *Tijdschrift voor Criminologie*, 67(1), pp. 70–86.

Lakomy, M., Bozek, M. (2023). *Understanding the trauma related effects of terrorists propaganda on researchers*, Global network on extremism & technology, executive report, retrieved 17 December 2024 from https://gnet-research.org/wp-content/uploads/2023/05/GNET-35-Researcher-trauma_web.pdf.

Mohamed, S (2015). Of monsters and men: perpetrator trauma and mass atrocity. *Columbia Law Review*, 115, pp. 1157–1216.

Nanninga, P. (2019). *Islam and suicide attacks*. Cambridge: Cambridge University Press.

Nistor, A. L. (2023). Culture and the illusion of self-evidence: spiritual beliefs in the Ongwen trial. *International Criminal Law Review*, 24, pp. 3–28.

Rauschenbach, M., Staerkle, C., Scalia, D. (2016). Accused for Involvement in Collective Violence: The Discursive Reconstruction of Agency and Identity by Perpetrators of International Crimes. *Political Psychology*, 37(2), pp. 219–235.

Rivabella, O. (1986). *Requiem for a woman's soul*. New York: Random House.

Robben, A. C. G. M., Hinton A. L. (2023). *Perpetrators – encountering humanity's dark side*. Stanford: Stanford University Press.

Rosenberg, T. (1991). *Children of Cain: violence and the violent in Latin America*. New York: William Morrow and Comp. Inc.

Pearson, E. (2023). Who's protecting the researchers? REASSURE report findings on identity and harms for online extremism and terrorism researchers, retrieved 17 December 2024 from https://icct.nl/publication/whos-protecting-researchers-reassure-report-findings-identity-and-harms-online.

Simic, O. (2014). *Surviving peace: a political memoir*. Spinifex press.

Simic, O. (2017). Research note – "doing the research I do has left scars": challenges of researching the transitional justice field. *Transitional Justice Review*, 1(5), pp. 134–168.

Simic, O. (2018). *Silenced victims of wartime sexual violence*. New York: Routledge.

Simic, O. (2020). Traumatized war criminal? Documenting the case of Esad Landzo. *International Criminal Justice Review*, 32(4), pp. 357–373.

Simic, O. (2023). *Lola's war – rape without punishment*. Singapore: Springer.

Simic, O. (2025). *Madam war criminal – Biljana Plavsic, Serbia's iron lady*. London: Hurst Publishers.

Smeulers, A., Weerdesteijn, M., Hola, B. (2019). *Perpetrators of international crimes – theories, methods and evidence*. Oxford: Oxford University Press.

Smeulers, A. (2024). *Perpetrators of mass atrocities – Terribly and Terrifyingly Normal?* London: Routledge.

Speckhard, A. (2012). *Talking to terrorists – understanding the psycho-social motivations of militant Jihadi terrorists, mass hostage takers, suicide bombers & "Martyrs"*. McLean: Advanced Press.

Staub, E. (1989). *The roots of evil – the origins of genocide and other group violence.* Cambridge: Cambridge University Press.

Staub, E. (2011). *Overcoming evil – genocide, violent conflict and terrorism.* Oxford: Oxford University Press.

Stern, J. (2004). *Terror in the name of God – why religious militants kill.* New York: HarperCollins Publishers.

Stern, J. (2010). *Denial – a memoir.* New York: HarpersCollins Publishers.

Stern, J. (2020). *My war criminal – personal encounters with an architect of genocide.* New York: Harpers Collins Publishers.

Stern, J. (2020). Why did I let a convicted war criminal practice energy healing on me? My 48 hours alone with Radovan Karadzic, *New York Times*, retrieved 8 January 2025 from https://www.nytimes.com/2020/01/16/opinion/sunday/radovan-karadzic.html

Zimbardo, P. G. (2011). *The Lucifer effect – how good people turn evil.* New York: Random House.

CHAPTER 2

An Anthropological Perspective: Dealing with Emotions when Conducting Ethnography in Conflict-Affected Areas

Marije Luitjens

1 Introduction

An earlier draft of this introduction started with a quote from Catalina, a young woman from Medellín (Colombia) that remained with me years after the interview had taken place. Catalina explained in detail the horrors she had witnessed as a kid, specifically during the *Operacion Orion* in Medellín, a military offensive that aimed at removing the left-wing guerrilla from the area.[1] While it was certainly not the first time I had interviewed severely traumatized people, and I had even heard similar stories before, this time it felt different. Due to the COVID-19 pandemic, I had been 'forced' to conduct my research using digital methods from home, almost 9,000 kilometers away from Medellín. Due to the time difference with Colombia, most interviews took place in the evening, after which I found myself in my, by now dark, living room. Time to go to sleep.

Reading my first draft again, I wondered why I would have to share Catalina's horrors here if only for the urge to share what I had heard, what I had witnessed second-hand. While at that time I did not acknowledge the emotional impact that the research had, the stories and information influenced my dreams, my overall mood, and towards the end of the research I felt drained. These are all signs of indirect traumatization (Figley, 1995; Močnik, 2020; Pearlman & Saakvitne, 1995), which I was still oblivious to at the time; I refused to see it as such, I had no right to it. It was, after all, the people I worked with and spoke to who had gone through these horrors, not me. It was only when Maartje Weerdesteijn invited me to speak at a round table event focusing on the role of emotions that I started to reflect more thoroughly on these and similar experiences. In line with existing anthropological literature (e.g., Glynis, 2013; Davies & Spencer, 2010), I mostly thought about

1 The Inter-American Court of Human Rights (IACHR) has since convicted the Colombian state of human rights abuses during the operation (Gill, 2017).

emotions in relation to reflexivity; I reflected on the potential impact of personal emotions on the validity and reliability of the obtained ethnographic data. While this remains crucial, I am pleased to discover a slowly growing body of literature on the emotional impact of conducting ethnography (e.g., Močnik & Ghouri, 2024; Hummel & El Kurd, 2020; Robben & Hinton, 2023). Building on this work, this chapter focuses on the emotional toll that ethnographic research within contexts of trauma and suffering can have and offers insight into potential coping mechanisms, thereby arguing for the need for both institutional attention and support from within the research community. To do so, this chapter draws on personal experiences and existing literature. To moreover provide a good overview, the chapter is divided into three main parts in line with different phases of conducting ethnography: I first discuss the role of emotions before fieldwork, followed by a section detailing the emotional toll research can take during fieldwork, and, lastly, the aftermath of research is discussed. In doing so, and considering the increasing use of online research methods, I highlight the difference between the emotional toll of being physically in the field and of using digital methods to conduct ethnography. Before doing so, the next section presents an overview of the existing literature on secondary and vicarious trauma, followed by the role of emotions in anthropology.

2 Dealing with Emotions before, during and after Ethnographic Fieldwork

It was roughly three decades ago that the possibility of traumatization through working with traumatized individuals made its way onto the research agenda. Since then, research has surged, focusing on the effects of indirect exposure to trauma on the professional or researcher (Figley, 1995; Hammerslough, 2015; Močnik & Ghouri, 2024; Branson, 2019; Pearlman & Saakvitne, 1995). Now, there is general agreement among mental health researchers that secondary or indirect exposure to trauma from, for example, detailed descriptions of memories, feelings, or behaviors, can deeply impact the person hearing these (Evces, 2015; McCann & Pearlman, 1990; Pearlman & Saakvitne, 1995; Močnik, 2020; Moran et al., 2020). This form of traumatization has been conceptualized as secondary traumatic stress (STS) or vicarious traumatization (VT). While the two concepts appear similar and are often used interchangeably or simply referred to as *compassion fatigue* (Pearlman & Saakvitne, 1995), various scholars agree that STS occurs as an immediate reaction to exposure to indirect trauma. It appears similar to Post-Traumatic Stress Disorder (PTSD), with related symptoms such as unwanted mental images, avoidance, and oversensitivity to trauma-related stimuli (Figley, 1995; Jenkins & Baird, 2002; Močnik, 2020; Devilly et al., 2009; Kiyimba & O'Reilly, 2016; Branson, 2019). Where STS can occur after a single exposure, VT develops over a longer period and is a process of accumulation (Aparicio et al., 2013; Branson, 2019; Jenkins & Baird, 2002). The conceptualization of VT, as introduced by Pearlman and Saakvitne (1995), remains widely agreed upon and refers to a permanent cognitive change within an individual's view of the world in five key areas: trust, safety, control, esteem, and intimacy (Branson, 2019, p. 423; Pearlman & Saakvitne, 1995; van der Merwe & Hunt, 2019; Močnik, 2020). Regardless of the differences between STS and VT, it is evident that, in the words of Hammerslough (2015, p. 38), "working with the traumatised can lead to trauma." There is, however, no blueprint or set-in-stone path to traumatization: what is experienced by the researcher as traumatic is, logically, also dependent on the researcher. Traumatization, in any form, is a complex process depending on a wide variety of factors (e.g., Vachon et al., 2016; Elwood et al., 2011). Despite the surge in research, a significant knowledge gap remains regarding the risk factors and the (long-term) effects of working in contexts of traumatization or with traumatized populations (Vachon et al., 2016). On top of that, most of the existing research continues to focus on the prevalence of STS or VT among healthcare professionals and social workers (Močnik, 2020). In line with the overall objective of this book, and this chapter in particular, I believe it is crucial to broaden the focus to include researchers from social sciences and humanities working within contexts of traumatization.

It is almost ironic that within anthropology, where a strong focus is placed on the broader role of emotions, the debate on the emotional impact of conducting ethnographic fieldwork remains largely undiscussed. Anthropology has always been subjected to critique regarding the objectivity and validity of obtained data, and it is therefore not surprising that most of the existing literature concerning the role of emotions is situated within that context. First and foremost, the 'reflexive turn' in anthropology in the 1980s[2] marked the start of broadly reflecting on the ethnographers' position in the field and the way that this influences the (collection of) data (Zadrożna, 2019; Davies & Spencer, 2010; Fort, 2020). This focus on positionality largely centers around the understanding of the ways in which 'fixed' (e.g., culturally ascribed traits such as gender, skin color, nationality) and 'fluid' (e.g., political views, personal life-

2 The origins of the reflexive turn can be found in the crisis the discipline found itself in, mostly (but not only) regarding to the strong links between colonialism and anthropology within the founding of the discipline.

history, experiences, etc.) aspects of the researcher influences their position in the field (Davies & Spencer, 2010; Močnik & Ghouri, 2024). Interestingly, Jean Briggs (1970, p. 6) offers an alternate view, arguing that reflections on her personal feelings and emotions within certain situations were crucial to her research, as "I was an intrinsic part of the research situation." However, it still took roughly three decades before the focus on emotions became a more mainstream aspect of conducting ethnography (Davies & Spencer, 2010; Robben & Hinton, 2023; Concetta Lo Bosco, 2021; Beatty, 2014). Despite this, emotions are still largely understood as an object of analysis, which can increase the rigor of the research process.

Another way in which emotions are already discussed within anthropology is that empathizing with the emotions of your research community is considered an important tool when conducting fieldwork (Ajebon et al., 2021).[3] In the words of Antonius Robben and Alexander Hinton (2023, p. 70), "ethnographers put themselves emotionally in the other's place and then imagine how that person experiences the world." Empathy is hence crucial to ethnography, as it is through the process of sympathetic engagement that in-depth, rich data become available, for example, through the establishment of rapport (Hinton; 2023, p. 70; Sahdan, 2021; Branson & Bixby Radui, 2018). Interestingly, empathy is also considered a leading cause in the development of vicarious or secondary trauma (Sahdan, 2021, p. 120; Hansen et al., 2018; Močnik, 2020). The British Medical Association (2022) even defines vicarious trauma as "a process of change resulting from *empathetic engagement* with trauma survivors." Recognizing this, it becomes even more surprising that the emotional impact of conducting ethnography has not received more attention within the discipline and, at the same time, is important to further expand the slowly growing debate (o.a., Maček, 2016; Močnik & Ghouri, 2024; Fort, 2020). For example, a recent book published by Antonius Robben and Alexander Hinton (2023) on working with 'perpetrators' touches upon the "strong negative emotions" that fieldworkers working within contexts of trauma and suffering can experience. This chapter hence falls into this growing body of work reflecting on the *personal emotional impact* of conducting fieldwork within traumatized contexts. The purpose of this chapter is hence to raise awareness of the risks for secondary and vicarious traumatization in order to, in the words of Nena Močnik (2024, p. 2), "avoid compassion fatigue, burnout and emotional vulnerability in all phases of research." Reading Močnik's reference to *all phases* of research made me smile in recognition, as in the process of planning this chapter, I

3 At the same time, however, the degree of emotional involvement of a researcher within the field remains a topic of discussion (DeWalt & DeWalt, 2011; Bernard, 2011).

realized I experienced different emotional challenges in the three main stages of research: preparation, fieldwork, and the aftermath. The following sections are therefore organized per research phase, where I discuss both the experiences and the lessons learned during my ethnographic fieldwork in Medellín,[4] Kosovo, Honduras, Lebanon, and Bosnia and Herzegovina.

2.1 *Fieldwork Preparation*

While conducting any type of research involves a significant amount of preparation, preparing for (long-term) fieldwork requires a specific engagement with the field before arriving (see for reference: Robben & Sluka, 2012; Okley, 2020; Blommaert & Jie, 2020; DeWalt & DeWalt, 2011). This does not imply that you can be fully prepared for any sociopolitical occurrence that might happen, but with the various streams of information available to most researchers right now, there is often plenty of knowledge available to get 'familiarized' with the field.[5] For me, this type of desk-research involves both reading academic and non-academic (news) articles and reports, as well as an in-depth search for documentaries, podcasts or social media output.[6] My first experience conducting fieldwork in a setting where trauma and suffering had become part of the everyday was in Tegucigalpa, Honduras. As part of my research master's program, I decided to conduct an ethnography on gang-dominated neighborhoods in the capital of Honduras, which I could only enter when accompanied by the NGO Save the Children. In preparation for this research, I watched documentaries, read articles, books and NGO reports on 'gang-life,' scoured the internet, and spoke to a Honduran friend I had made during previous research in Barcelona.

While I was very excited to go to Honduras, and I understood to a certain extent the dangers that I would face, I was also very nervous. I realized this as I experienced a growing number of violent dreams and an overall bad feeling that I could not quite shake off. I thought nothing of it; it did not seem alarm-

4 Due to COVID-19, this ethnography took place online using digital tools.

5 I am aware that there is an ongoing discussion within anthropology about what the distance of the ethnographer to the field should be, arguing that researching too 'close to home' might blur objectivity. In line with the argument of 'going native', I believe it is much more important to use solid research techniques (such as triangulation, or thorough data analysis) than to refrain from doing research in familiar settings. That being said, I do believe that for those doing research in already familiar contexts, it is crucial to prepare well and to re-familiarize oneself with the research setting through a similar process of desk-research.

6 While I prepared in a similar manner for each research, the number of potential sources of information have certainly increased since my first field experience in Barcelona in 2011, which in turn has an effect of the level of engagement with the field. More on this when I dive into my experience conducting fieldwork in Medellín.

ing yet, and it certainly made sense given the topic I was focusing on. In addition, the information sources available to me confirmed I was well prepared. DeWalt and DeWalt (2011), for example, argued that "researchers doing social research must be prepared to deal with emotion and tears" (p. 154), and because of this, I needed to know "when and how to conclude an interview" (p. 156). During our research training at the university, we had qualitative interview training and discussed the ethics of conducting research on 'sensitive topics.' I would like to note that this was, in comparison to other programs, quite a thorough preparation for the field. Despite this, the only advice in relation to coping with personal emotional reactions to fieldwork that I remember was a teacher half-jokingly advising us to "go somewhere sunny, somewhere you like being." This type of avoidance is indicative of the broader mindset in anthropology, especially at that time; while some anthropologists would want to integrate emotions into the language of anthropology, they are, in the words of Robben and Sluka (2012, p. 98), "fearful of criticism, of not being taken seriously." In hindsight, this certainly applied to me. Although I felt prepared for the field, the lack of awareness concerning secondary forms of traumatization made me more vulnerable going into the field.

2.1.1 Lessons Learned

Based on my experience, both with preparing the research in Honduras and from research that followed afterward, I have deduced three 'lessons learned' for the preparation phase. First and foremost, while I have dealt with a number of ethical approval applications at different universities, none of these included a focus on the mental health of the researchers themselves. During my last ethics approval process, there was a strong focus on the potential for retraumatizing the people I spoke to. While I remember being pleasantly surprised reading this, I simply clarified how I aimed at minimizing this risk and included a list of potential actions (such as a list of aid providers) that the interlocutors could take if they wished to do so. Almost ironically, there was no request for similar strategies for the researcher, and as a result, it did not occur to me to do so either. In this preparation process, there was a clear "lack of attention to, and acknowledgment of, the emotional labor involved in fieldwork" (McGarrol, 2017, p. 437). Various researches agrees that being well prepared for what is to come is key to lowering the risk of experiencing secondary traumatization, specifically secondary traumatic stress (Močnik, 2020; McGarrol, 2017).

Besides improving the ethics approval process, institutions can also provide a better overview of the help available within institutions. For example, by providing the details of the in-house trauma experts or psychologists available, by setting up a network of researchers who conduct similar type of research, or by providing a lecture (series) concerning these topics in preparation of fieldwork. This aligns with the outcome of the workshop, "The Cost of Bearing Witness: Secondary Trauma and Self-Care in Field-Based Social Research," organized in 2018 by, among others, Močnik (2020), where various participants argued that institutions need to provide training and ensure access to counseling services. These actions help with both normalizing the request of emotional support, and at the same time advocate for the importance of 'taking care of yourself' as a researcher.

Finally, besides institutional support, it can be of great help to learn from others, as by examining how others have dealt with similar situations and emotions, researchers can become more resilient in the field. There is a general agreement in the literature that there is an overall lack of preparation and training before conducting research within contexts of trauma and suffering, which significantly increases the risk of traumatization (Bell et al., 2003; Cunningham, 2004; Knight, 2010; Bryman, 2016). My experience aligns with this, as none of my fieldwork preparations included a focus on my mental well-being. It is crucial to prepare as well as possible, and while the field is often unpredictable, and therefore difficult to really prepare for, there are certainly ways to limit the risks of traumatization. And, as learning from the experiences of others can help oneself to be better prepared, the next section will focus on experiences (both mine and others) while being in the 'field.'

2.2 *During the Fieldwork*

In the summer of 2019, I, together with Esther Schoorel, conducted research on memorialization and resistance practices during the Mars Mira (peace march) in Bosnia and Herzegovina. The Mars Mira stretches over roughly 100 kilometers and retraces the steps of the victims of the Srebrenica genocide that took place in 1995 (Luitjens & Schoorel, 2022). It was not my first time being in the area, and not even my first time walking the Mars Mira, as I had been part of the Srebrenica project team when I worked for the NGO Pax for Peace. I knew the situational context, I had worked with various survivors of the Srebrenica genocide, and I had been in the area several times. I not only felt well-prepared, but the people and place had become close to my heart. Over the course of the three days, we held (walking) interviews with participants (either genocide survivors or relatives), all of whom shared their feelings and thoughts that arose while walking the march. We stayed in Potočari (Srebrenica) for the annual Memorial Day on July 11, after which we left for Sarajevo for a couple of days. I remember vividly how we were sitting in one of the capital's cute restaurants, discussing our notes and wondering what we felt. We tried to evaluate, to reach our feelings, but it was not until we arrived at the airport back home that all the emotions poured out. This wave of emotions lasted for some days, which, in combination with the intensity of it, surprised me.

On the one hand, this is because of my assumption that I was well-prepared due to my familiarity with the context, but on the other hand, I realized that once I assume my position as the ethnographer, I take an emotional distance to the topic, to be able to do thorough data collection and analysis. This is in line with anthropological fieldwork training, whereby young anthropologists learn that fieldwork is, in the words of Sluka and Robben (2007, p. 2), "based on participant observation, which hinges on the dynamic and contradictory synthesis of subjective insider and objective outsider." While anthropologists generally agree that striving for 'full objectivity' is impossible, Sluka and Robben refer to the necessity of a rigorous analysis of the ethnographer's thoughts, feelings, and emotions to secure the reliability and validity of the obtained data. In line with this, influenced by the reflexive turn in anthropology, it is generally agreed upon that keeping a record of feelings and emotions in a field diary is key to being able to reflect on the impact that these emotions have on the research process, which is crucial to the rigor of the research (Fort, 2020; Davies & Spencer, 2010; Blommaert & Jie, 2020; Carstensen-Egwuom, 2014; Singleton Jr. & Straits, 2005). As a result of critically analyzing personal emotions, researchers automatically distance themselves from their emotions, viewing these as merely analytical objects that impact the research process. Ghassan Hage (2020), for example, explains about his research into 'political emotions' generated by the Arab-Israeli conflict that while he was constantly experiencing hatred and anger, he was "trying to recover some sense of emotional detachment and objectivity […]" (p. 150). I now realize that I have also learned to emotionally detach as soon as I enter the field as a researcher. In other words, I have my 'anthropology glasses' on and therefore regard emotions as analytical objects instead of feelings that personally affect me. As a result, I am not fully aware of the emotional impact that the research has on me during data collection in the field. This is in line with the experience of Émilie Fort (2020), who (also) conducted fieldwork in Kosovo and had been trained to critically *analyze* her emotions and not how to *cope* with them, and as a consequence, she explains that even "when being back home, my mind was trapped in my research site" (Fort, 2020). She had not processed her emotions well, and as a result, remained stuck, unable to move forward. These experiences demonstrate the importance of taking off our 'anthropological glasses,' process and cope with the emotions caused by fieldwork as a person rather than as a professional. Learning how to do so will specifically help with lowering the risks of vicarious trauma, as VT occurs through a process of accumulation and thus tends to develop over a longer period of time.

There are various factors that play a role in the development of either secondary traumatic stress or vicarious traumatization, and as such, not every research has the same emotional impact. One of these factors is the research methodology. A relatively new method that was recently added to the 'toolbox' is the use of digital methods to conduct ethnography. I, therefore, feel it is important to reflect on the risks of traumatization and the lessons I learned during this type of remote fieldwork.[7] During my fieldwork period in Kosovo, COVID-19 spread rapidly across the globe. As a result, I was forced to shorten my stay in the field from 6 months to about 4 months and conducted interviews online once back home. At this stage, it was still impossible to imagine the world would be 'closed' for roughly 2 years, and I remained fully convinced I would go to Medellín (Colombia) for the second half of my fieldwork. This never happened, and I ended up conducting remote fieldwork through the use of digital methods for the remainder of my Ph.D. research. Over the course of about 4 months, in the spring of 2021, I conducted over 80+ interviews, used social media as Instagram or WhatsApp to obtain data, watched numerous documentaries and self-made videos, and walked the streets of Medellín using Google Maps to familiarize myself with the context. I aimed to obtain as much first-hand data as possible while stuck at home behind my laptop. Luckily, I had already been in Medellín before, which helped me to understand the context. In hindsight, however, due to a variety of factors,[8] this research took a higher mental toll than I had anticipated. Especially towards the end of the research, I had difficulty sleeping, had horrible dreams and was highly emotional. It is important to discuss this, as I believe these symptoms were (also) linked to the type of methods used for this research. Due to the online nature, the discrepancy between the research 'field' and 'real life' became more difficult to deal with over time. While I mentally lived in Medellín and conducted research within a context of suffering (due to the focus of my research), I remained connected to my everyday life at home, where my life continued as normal. Next to that, I felt I had to compensate for not actually 'being in' Medellín. As soon as my network expanded, I tried to schedule as many interviews as possible and spent the rest of the day scouring the internet for other useful data. Due to the time difference and the availability of the

7 I want to clarify that I refer to the use of digital methods to conduct remote ethnographic fieldwork, not 'digital ethnography', whereby a digital society/group is studied online.

8 While of course the spreading of COVID-19 can be seen as a factor, I will not discuss this here specifically. This is mostly because by the time my research took place; vaccinations had just appeared and at least in my surroundings life as 'normal' seemed to pick up again a bit.

interlocutors, most of the interviews were scheduled in the evening, which meant I often went to bed straight after. Near the end of the research, I realized the number of interviews was too high, and I tried to limit this to a maximum of two interviews a day, preferably not right before going to sleep. While reflecting on this, I realized it was not just the number of interviews but also the remote and digital nature of the research that made it emotionally difficult to cope with; processing the information and disconnecting from my research after an interview was not easy, which furthermore made it difficult to fall asleep shortly after being done. It is therefore important to discuss this type of research separately, to better understand and consequently prepare for the risks it holds of developing STS or VT. While I do not discuss it as a separate lesson learned, it is important to realize the specific impact conducting digital ethnography might have. The next section highlights three general reflections of being in the field, which all consist of lessons learned and practical tips.

2.2.1 Lessons Learned

Derived from my own experiences, as well as those of others, the first reflection discussed in this section links to the analytical position that emotions have within anthropological fieldwork. Taking off these analytical glasses to be able to focus on the processing of emotions, however, involves breaking down the hidden taboo concerning personal emotions, which is discussed in the second reflection. Lastly, the contradicting role of empathy in both ethnography and traumatization is reflected upon.

As discussed previously, an anthropologist is trained not to ignore personal emotions but to reflect on the impact that these emotions might have on the research process. The way these experiences affect *you*, outside the scope of your research, does not receive sufficient attention. As such, it has become normalized to distance yourself from your emotions and to look at your emotions through the analytical glasses you put on during the research process. Doing so, however, increases the risk of vicarious trauma, which can go unnoticed for a long period of time as its symptoms accumulate and consequently affect a persons' world view in relation to trust, safety, control, esteem, and intimacy (Aparicio et al., 2013; Branson, 2019; Jenkins & Baird, 2002; Branson, 2019, p. 423; Van der Merwe & Hunt, 2019; Močnik, 2020). Creating awareness of this accumulation process can thus limit the risk of vicarious traumatization. Based on my own experiences, and through reading those of others, I deduced two practical tips to counter the development of vicarious traumatization: share or express your experiences and create time to sit with/feel your emotions. While both seem straightforward, I will explain each in more detail, as they are usually not part of existing anthropological fieldwork training.

First, there is a consensus that sharing internal emotions caused by traumatic experiences is crucial for reducing negative psychological consequences (Kinsler, 2017; Calhoun & Tedeschi, 2013; Nolen-Hoeksema & Larson, 1999; Saltzman et al., 2018). According to Palmer et al. (2016), this is particularly true when sharing experiences with others who have gone through similar traumatic experiences. This is not only confirmed by the success of various peer support groups for people going through hardship (see for example: Yearwood, 2019; MacNeil & Mead, 2005), but also rings true in my own experience. In the early spring of 2020, my partner and I moved to Kosovo for my Ph.D. fieldwork. This was the first time I spent time in a context of trauma and suffering with someone who was not part of my field of research. Consequently, I had the opportunity to share some of my experiences with someone who did not assume an ethnographer' position. On International Women's Day, March 8, we visited the house of Ferdonije Qerkezi (Bami 2022), whose three sons and husband were abducted and killed by the Serb paramilitary during the 1998–1999 war and who has turned her house into a museum dedicated to remembering her loved ones. My partner told me afterwards how emotional the visit had made her and asked me how I *felt* about it. While I would normally rehash the visit, explaining what interesting analysis I obtained from it, she took me out of this researcher position, which provided a space for me to process my own emotions.

Stepping out of the researcher position links to another lesson learned: create opportunities to process your own emotions. The average ethnographer is used to writing in a diary, where daily notes are taken that reflect on the researcher's feelings, emotions, and thoughts of that specific day (see, e.g., DeWalt & DeWalt, 2011; Bernard & Gravlee, 2016). While I do believe it is crucial to reflect on your positionality and your emotions (generated by) the field, it is equally crucial to also let the 'feelings in.' Doing so, however, links to the second reflection: there is a hidden taboo on discussing the personal impact that conducting ethnography might have on the researcher. While anthropology is highly reflexive, this reflection excludes the personal impact that conducting ethnography in trauma contexts has. On top of that, a researcher makes a (voluntary) decision to situate their research within trauma contexts. In other words, there seems to be an unspoken agreement not to allow oneself to feel these emotions, as the situation of the researcher is never as horrific as that of the interlocutors. I feel this struggle too, especially while writing this chapter, but I also realize that understanding signs of STS/VT helps to limit its risks,[9] which in turn helps to improve the quality of research.

9 This goes for both the researcher and the interlocutors, but that is not the topic of this chapter, for more information on this, see Howe (2022).

In line with this, in order to 'share experiences,' it is, of course, crucial to first acknowledge (or at least be open to acknowledging) the negative impact that these experiences may have on you. When one can accept that it is okay to feel a personal impact, and it does not negate or 'take over' the experiences of others, it then becomes possible to reflect better on this personal impact.

This brings me to the following: there is a growing body of literature that argues secondary traumatic stress experiences can also be catalysts for positive change, referred to as post-traumatic growth (PTG) (Calhoun & Tedeschi, 2013; Cohen & Collens, 2013). This is, for example, visible in the form of improved relationships, a greater appreciation for life, or a greater sense of personal strength (Henson et al., 2021). Similarly, there is a growing focus on vicarious posttraumatic growth (VPTG) (Nuttman-Shwartz, 2014; Arnold et al., 2005), which argues that those affected by vicarious trauma can also experience similar growth, including an increased positive self-esteem or feelings of self-efficacy (Močnik, 2020). Interestingly, being able to share negative emotions is considered an important factor in the realization of posttraumatic growth (Ogińska-Bulik & Kobylarczyk, 2015; Dirik & Göcek-Yorulmaz, 2018). This brings me back to the necessity of breaking the 'emotions taboo': in order to process experiences from the field and the accompanying emotions to potentially grow from this, it is crucial to first acknowledge and allow their presence.

Lastly, I want to discuss a reflection specific to anthropology, which relates to the role of empathy in both fieldwork and the development of STS/VT. The realization that empathy is considered to play a leading role in the development of vicarious or secondary trauma (Sahdan, 2021, p. 120; Hansen et al., 2018; Močnik, 2020; British Medical Association, 2022; MacRitchie & witz, 2010) led me to reflect differently on my experience researching the Marš Mira. I believe the unexpected emotional toll that the fieldwork had is linked to the important place of empathy within the research. In our conclusion, Esther and I wrote (Luitjens & Schoorel, 2022) that the "participatory nature of the Marš Mira enables participants to more fully empathize with the commemorated victims." My lack of awareness concerning the link between empathy and secondary traumatization left me unprepared for the emotional impact in the aftermath of this research. While I am not suggesting (at all) that researchers should become less empathetic, creating awareness of the relation between empathy and STS/VT helps with finding ways to lower these risks. Following this, Močnik (2020) suggests researchers should aim for *compassion*[10] instead of empathy during fieldwork in traumatized contexts, which

10 This is moreover in lines with the term 'compassion satisfaction', which Figley (2002) introduced as a contrary to 'compassion fatigue', as described above.

links to the notion of vicarious posttraumatic growth (Tsirimokou et al., 2022). Compassion literally means 'to suffer together', but within this context, it refers to the motivation felt to relieve this suffering, even if only slightly, and the satisfaction that comes from being able to do this effectively, something that is not immediately connected to being a scholar (Figley, 2002; Močnik, 2020; Craig & Sprang, 2010). While it seems that 'relieving this suffering' makes more sense in trauma therapy settings, it can certainly be beneficial in relation to ethnography as well. I feel that this is true when reflecting on my experience during the last day of the Marš Mira: each year on July 10, the march enters Potočari, where alongside the road many people, mostly genocide survivors and their children, greet the participants while passing. Thinking back to this moment indeed brings me relief, due to the feeling of connection with this community when locking eyes or shaking hands, to be able to 'suffer together' for just a bit. While this experience cannot be generalized to every fieldwork setting or experience,[11] I agree with Močnik (2020) that thinking in terms of compassion instead of empathy helped shift my feelings toward this moment from despair to solidarity. While it is not black and white and does not work in each setting, a researcher can find strength in reconceptualizing their frame of thought: instead of merely taking in the others' perspectives and feelings without being able to give anything back, it helps the researcher to focus on momentarily relieving the suffering, for example, by being there and listening, or by writing about it.

Concludingly, I believe there is a necessity for an overall switch in mindset to better learn to cope with the emotional impact during fieldwork. First, it is important to approach emotions as *feelings* that need to be felt, instead of mere analytical objects that impact your research outcome. Taking off these 'anthropological glasses' is, however, extra difficult due to the presence of the *hidden taboo* on emotions. Acknowledging the personal impact research has does not impact your stance toward those traumatized, but it does allow you to better process the emotional impact of the research. Learning how to do this well, in turn, makes you a better researcher. Lastly, it is important to understand the role that empathy plays within secondary traumatization processes and, consequently, to reframe this focus on empathy to compassion. Switching this mindset during time in the field potentially helps to ease the aftermath of fieldwork. In order to provide a more comprehensive overview of the three fieldwork stages, the next section focuses on the period after coming

11 Of course, there are situations in which the frame of compassion is not as appropriate. For example, when researching perpetrators the focus on compassion is more complicated, or when conducting research within the setting of your own community.

back from the field. Based on this experience, I will present two lessons learned.

2.3 *After the Fieldwork*

So far, this chapter has focused on the lessons learned from the preparation stage and the period in the field. First and foremost, as has become clear throughout this chapter, the preparation for fieldwork is crucial to minimize the emotional impact of the research afterwards. Had I known the previously discussed lessons learned before conducting fieldwork in Honduras, the aftermath would have been significantly different. In early February of 2015, I returned from Tegucigalpa (Honduras) after a stay of about seven months. Despite the security limitations, I had loved living there because it felt as if I, and what I was doing with my career, seemed to actually matter for the first time. Through building a network with the Ministry of Education, I had moreover secured a job I could return to after I finished my Master's. With that in mind, I returned home satisfied, eager to write my thesis.

Once at home, this altered rapidly: I stayed at my parents' place, who lived in Belgium at the time, away from my social life back in the Netherlands. I did not feel many emotions, I was rather numb; my sleep was distorted (longer than the jetlag period), I did not do much during the day and spent most of the day on the couch. I remember my parents asking if I was okay, which I thought I was: it made sense to me that I was tired and just needed to relax. Besides that, I did not feel much, which I interpreted as 'I'm doing fine.' It was not until I really had to go back to university that I realized I was not fine; I was overly nervous and experienced high anxiety levels: the thought of leaving the house made me emotional. When finally making the trip back to my own home, I cried for most of the three-hour trip. The realization that I, for example, walked in the streets with my phone in my hand would give me a minor panic attack. I did understand this had to do with the normalization of violence and fear that I had experienced living in Honduras, but I felt guilty because I lived in a safe country where I could walk the streets and not have to be continuously afraid. Hence, I did not allow myself to feel this and tried to shake it off. Living with these taboo emotions, of course, did not help me to process them, and while Honduras was likely all I spoke about with my friends and family, it was difficult to share with peers, as most of them had conducted very different research. It took time for me to adjust again, and I must admit that after months of being back at home and having picked up my routine, I did not mind it too much when I heard my position at the Ministry of Education in Honduras had fallen through.

Of course, no matter what preparations I would have made, living in this context of fear and suffering would have taken a toll. I am fully aware of that, and I do not argue that such an emotional impact can be completely prevented. But, in line with the previous sections, raising awareness about the processes of traumatization and implementing the lessons learned and shared by other researchers can significantly lower the risks of STS/VT. When no preventative measures are taken, as in my case in Honduras, there are still important lessons learned that can make coping in the future easier and potentially help foster vicarious posttraumatic growth. In line with this, I will present two final reflections in the lessons learned section of this chapter.

2.3.1 Lessons Learned

It is important to reiterate that, even if prepared well, it is highly likely that researchers coming home from trauma-filled contexts will experience some kind of an emotional impact. What is important, however, is to learn how to support researchers well in this process in order to minimize the (long-term) impact. With that in mind, there are two general lessons learned that are presented in this section. In line with the lessons from the preparation phase, it is, first and foremost of importance that institutions provide the necessary care in the aftermath of fieldwork. The following advice is, hence, directed towards institutions. In line with the lessons learned presented in the preparation phase, it would be helpful if someone from the institution (who would depend on the structure of the institution) could 'check in' with people coming back from fieldwork. This provides the researcher the opportunity to share emotions. In addition, it is important that researchers are made aware of the options that are available within the institution for guidance or support, without forcing anyone into anything. These options could range from no action at all to talking with peers through a network set up by the institution or directing someone to an in-house psychologist with specific expertise on STS/VT. When there is no institution to provide support, it becomes even more important to recognize the symptoms of traumatization, such as unwanted mental images, strong feelings of anxiety or rage, or trouble sleeping, and to seek help if needed. Even when not seeking professional help, it remains beneficial to seek peer-support, preferably from people who have had similar experiences, but any support from peers is beneficial when processing fieldwork experiences.

Lastly, as it is clear, ethnographers (as are most humans) are not robots; it is impossible to eliminate all emotional impact. Coming home from a tough period in the field without taking time to recover a little is also not healthy. When a researcher has taken precautions, it is possible to prepare relatively well for what to expect when coming home from the field. I would, therefore, suggest calculating this as extended research time, allowing for a bit of personal time before diving back into work and social life right away. This does not have to be a long period. Depending on the length and content of the fieldwork, a weekend might be sufficient to unwind, process your feelings, and simply share time with loved ones who are aware of and understanding of your situation.

3 Conclusion: Institutional Responsibility

Having reintegrated into my familiar routine after coming back from Honduras, I decided I wanted to continue working in the field of peace and conflict. During my time in Honduras, I felt that I had successfully proven to be able to live and work in a context of conflict and violence. This is how I ended up working for the Dutch NGO Pax for Peace, where I focused on the Balkans and Colombia. Secondary traumatic stress or vicarious traumatization was not part of the NGOs vocabulary, and my time there gradually numbed me; I soon crystallized a perspective that 'this is just what the world looks like.' I carried this with me when teaching about the subjects of conflict, trauma, and violence at various universities afterwards. In my classes, I often used visual material, like the documentary *Sri Lanka's Killing Fields,* which details the horrors of the Sri Lanka genocide in 2009. I never thought of providing any disclaimers, other than a short introduction, as I believed it was important to share 'this part of reality.' While I still teach similar topics (though with a larger focus on peace and peacebuilding), I do provide disclaimers and specifically ask if students have personal ties to the context of the material. This is because I now understand that my attitude arose from my incapacity to deal with my own experiences. Interestingly, while writing this chapter, it became clear to me that I was also part of the system that needs changing: my mindset needed to change as well to provide a healthier working environment for myself and my students.

In this chapter, I have presented various lessons learned that I believe can help with changing the current status quo. These lessons learned have been divided into three main sections linked to three research phases: the preparation phase, the time in the field, and the aftermath of fieldwork. While each of these phases brings forth different lessons learned, they are largely interconnected and lead to two main conclusions. First, a large part of the responsibility for change lies with the institutions. This links to my second point that we need an overall change of mindset, break existing taboos, and normalize experiencing an emotional impact. Regarding the former, there are a number of specific steps that institutions can take in order to improve the support of researchers: first, the ethics approval process should include a section that focuses on the impact of research on the mental health of the researcher, and at the same time, offer information on conducting fieldwork in these settings. Institutions could, for example, organize specific (interdepartmental) seminars based on need and create a network of peers who have conducted similar research to promote the sharing of experiences and, thereby, the opportunities to learn from each other. It is, moreover, important to provide clear opportunities to seek professional help, for example, by providing the opportunity to visit an (in-house) trauma-therapist. At the same time, however, a larger shift in mindset is needed. To do so, the taboo on emotions needs to be broken first: there is a need to normalize the fact that conducting research in contexts of trauma and suffering takes an emotional toll. It is, therefore, important to remember that acknowledging this does not minimize or negate (and never should) the lived experiences of traumatized communities. To break this taboo, anthropology should not just understand emotions during fieldwork as analytical objects that potentially impact the research process, but space should also be created to feel and process emotions. Removing these 'anthropological glasses' that are used to analyze emotions is an important step for improving mental health while in the field.

Over the course of writing this chapter, I have come to realize that learning about secondary traumatic stress and vicarious traumatization has helped me to grow as a researcher and has led me to be better prepared to cope in the future. I believe it is essential to share this knowledge that could hopefully help (young) researchers minimize the risk of having similar adverse experiences. At the same time, I also want to continue my learning process, and I remain curious to learn from the experiences of others.[12] Because being able to grow as a peace researcher makes it possible, in that capacity, to continue to strive for a more just and fairer world.

References

Ajebon, M. O., Kwong, Y. M. C., Astorga de Ita, D. (2021). *Navigating the Field Postgraduate: Experiences in Social Research*. Cham: Springer Nature.

12 If you feel like sharing or want to provide feedback, please feel free to reach out to me at m.r.luitjens@vu.nl

Aparicio, E., Michalopoulos, L. M., Unick, G.J. (2013). An examination of the psychometric properties of the Vicarious Trauma Scale in a sample of licensed social workers, *Health and Social Work*, 38, pp. 199–206. http://dx.doi.org/10.1093/hsw/hlt017

Arnold, D., Calhoun, L. G., Tedeschi, R., Cann, A. (2005). Vicarious Posttraumatic Growth in Psychotherapy. *Journal of Humanistic Psychology*, 45(2), pp. 239–263.

Bami, X. (2022). Mothers' Stories Highlight Tragedy of Kosovo's Disappeared, *Balkan Insight*, 10 January 2022, retrieved 9 September 2024 from https://balkaninsight.com/2022/01/10/mothers-stories-highlight-tragedy-of-kosovos-disappeared/.

Beatty, A. (2014). Anthropology and emotion. *The Journal of the Royal Anthropological Institute*, 20(3), pp. 545–563.

Bell, H., Kulkani, S., Dalton, L. (2003). Organizational Prevention of Vicarious Traumatization. *Families in Society*, 84(4), pp. 463–470. doi:10.1606/1044-3894.131.

Bernard, R. (2011). *Research Methods in Anthropology*: Qualitative and Quantitative Approaches. New York: AltaMira Press

Blommaert, J., Jie, D. (2020). *Ethnographic Fieldwork: A Beginner's Guide*. Bristol: Multilingual Matters.

Branson, D. C. (2019). Vicarious trauma, themes in research, and terminology: A review of literature. *Traumatology*, 25(1), pp. 2–10. https://doi.org/10.1037/trm0000161

Branson, D. C., Bixby Radui, M. (2018). Do Qualitative Researchers Experience Vicarious Trauma? And, Does It Matter? *Journal of Sociology and Social Work*, 6(1), pp. 12–22. doi:10.15640/jssw.v6n1a3.

Briggs, J. (1970). *Never in Anger*. Boston: Harvard University Press.

British Medical Association (2022). Vicarious trauma: signs and strategies for coping, *British Medical Association*, 17 January 2022, retrieved 9 September 2024 from https://www.bma.org.uk/advice-and-support/your-wellbeing/vicarious-trauma/vicarious-trauma-signs-and-strategies-for-coping.

Bryman, A. (2016). *Social Research Methods*. New York: Oxford University Press.

Calhoun, L. G., Tedeschi, R. G. (2013). *Posttraumatic growth in clinical practice*. New York: Routledge.

Carstensen-Egwuom, I. (2014). Connecting intersectionality and reflexivity: Methodological approaches to social positionalities. *Erdkunde*, 68, pp. 265–276. Doi: 10.3112.

Cohen, K., Collens, P. (2013). The impact of trauma work on trauma workers: A metasynthesis on vicarious trauma and vicarious posttraumatic growth. *Psychological Trauma: Theory, Research, Practice, and Policy*, 5(6), pp. 570–580.

Concetta Lo Bosco, M. (2021). Feelings in the Field: The Emotional Labour of the Ethnographer. *Anthropology in Action*, 28, pp. 8–17.

Craig, C.D., Sprang, G. (2010). Compassion satisfaction, compassion fatigue, and burnout in a national sample of trauma treatment therapists. *Anxiety, Stress & Coping*, 23(3), pp. 319–339.

Cunningham, M. (2004). Avoiding Vicarious Traumatization: Support, Spirituality, and Self-Care. In: *Mass Trauma and Violence: Helping Families and Children Cope*, N. B. Webb (Ed.). New York: Guilford Press, pp. 327–346.

Davies, J., Spencer, D. (2010). *Emotions in the Field: The Psychology and Anthropology of Fieldwork Experience*. Standford: Stanford University Press.

Devilly G. J., Wright, R., Varker, T. (2009). Vicarious trauma, secondary traumatic stress, or simply burnout? Effect of trauma therapy on mental health professionals, *Australian and New Zealand Journal of Psychiatry*, 43, pp. 373–389.

DeWalt, K., DeWalt, B. (2011). *Participant Observation: a guide for fieldworkers*. Plymouth: AltaMira Press.

Dirik, G., Göcek-Yorulmaz, E. (2018). Positive Sides of the Disease: Posttraumatic Growth in Adults with Type 2 Diabetes. *Behavioral Medicine*, 44(1), pp. 1–10.

Elwood, L. S., Mott, J., Lohr, J. M., Galvoski, T. E. (2011). Secondary trauma symp- toms in clinicians: A critical review of the construct, specificity, and implications for trauma-focused treatment. *Clinical Psychology Review*, 31(1), pp. 25–36.

Evces, M. (2015). What Is Vicarious Trauma? In: M. Evces, G. Quitangon (Eds). *Vicarious Trauma and Disaster Mental Health: understanding risks and promoting resilience*, New York: Routledge, pp. 9–24.

Figley, C. (1995). Compassion fatigue: Towards a new understanding of the costs of caring. In: B. Stamm (Ed.). *Secondary traumatic stress: Self-care issues for clinicians, researchers, and educators*. Lutherville, MD: Sidran Press, pp. 3–28.

Figley, C. R. (2002). *Treating compassion fatigue*. Brunner-Routledge

Fort, E. (2020). Acknowledging the long-lasting effects of fieldwork experience: emotions and the writing process. *LSE blog*, 28 September 2020, retrieved 9 September 2024 from https://blogs.lse.ac.uk/fieldresearch/2020/09/28/acknowledging-the-long-lasting-effects-of-fieldwork-experience/.

Gill, S. (2017). Human Rights Court convicts Colombia for Medellin war crimes. *Colombia Reports*, 12 January 2017, retrieved 9 September 2024 from https://colombiareports.com/amp/human-rights-court-convicts-colombia-medellin-war-crimes/.

Glynis, P. (2013). Ethnography and reflexivity: Emotions and feelings in fieldwork. *Nurse Researcher*, 10(3), pp. 28–37.

Hage, G. (2020). Hating Israel in the Field: on Ethnography and Political Emotions. In: Davies, J., D. Spencer (Eds.). *Emotions in the Field: The Psychology and Anthropology of Fieldwork Experience*. Stanford: Stanford University Press, pp. 129–154.

Hammerslough, J. (2015). What are the Barriers to Addressing Vicarious Trauma? In: M. Evces, G. Quitangon (Eds.). *Vicarious Trauma and Disaster Mental Health: understanding risks and promoting resilience*. New York: Routledge, pp. 37–42.

Hansen, E. M., Eklund, J. H., Hallén, A., Bjurhager, C. S., Norrström, E., Viman, A., Stocks, E. L. (2018). Does Feeling Empathy Lead to Compassion Fatigue or Compassion Satisfaction? The Role of Time Perspective. *The Journal of Psychology*, 152(8), pp. 630–645. doi:10.1080/00223980.2018.1495170.

Henson, C., Truchot, D., Canevello, A. (2021). What promotes post traumatic growth? A systematic review, *European Journal of Trauma & Dissociation*, 5(4), pp. 1–34. https://doi.org/10.1016/j.ejtd.2020.100195.

Howe, K. (2022). Trauma to self and other: Reflections on field research and conflict. Security Dialogue 53(4), pp. 363–381.

Hummel, C., El Kurd, D. (2020). Mental Health and Fieldwork. *Political Science & Politics*, 54(1), pp. 121–125.

Jenkins, S. R., Baird., S. (2002). Secondary Traumatic Stress and Vicarious Trauma: A Validational Study. *Journal of Traumatic Stress*, 15(5), pp. 423–432. doi:10.1023/A:1020193526843.

Kinsler, P. (2017). *Complex Psychological Trauma: The Centrality of Relationship.* New York: Routledge.

Kiyimba, N., O'Reily, M. (2016). The Risk of Secondary Traumatic Stress in the Qualitative Transcription Process: A Research Note. *Qualitative Research*, 16(4), pp. 468–476. doi:10.1177/1468794115577013.

Knight, C. (2010). Indirect Trauma in the Field Practicum: Secondary Traumatic Stress, Vicarious Trauma, and Compassion Fatigue Among Social Work Students and Their Field Instructors. *Journal of Baccalaureate Social Work*, 15(1), pp. 31–52.

Luitjens, M., Schoorel., E. (2022). Commemorating by Marching: Memorialization and Resistance Practices of the Srebrenica Genocide. *Nationalities Papers*, pp. 1–18. doi:10.1017/nps.2021.68

Maček, I. (2016). *Engaging Violence: Trauma, Memory, and Representation.* New York: Routledge.

MacNeil, C., Mead, S. (2005). A Narrative Approach to Developing Standards for Trauma-Informed Peer Support. *American Journal of Evaluation*, 26(2), pp. 231–244, https://doi.org/10.1177/1098214005275633

MacRitchie, V., Leibowitz, S. (2010). Secondary traumatic stress, level of exposure, empathy and social support in trauma workers. *South African Journal of Psychology*, 40(2), pp. 149–158.

McCann, L.,, Pearlman, L. A. (1990). *Psychological Trauma and the Adult Survivor: Theory, Therapy, and Transformation.* New York: Brunner/Mazel.

McGarrol, S. (2017). The emotional challenges of conducting in-depth research into significant health issues in health geography: reflections on emotional labour, fieldwork and life course. *Area*, 49(4), pp. 436–442, doi: 10.1111/area.12347

Močnik, N. (2020). Re-Thinking Exposure to Trauma and Self-Care in Fieldwork-Based Social Research: Introduction to the Special Issue. *Social Epistemology*, 34(1), pp. 1–11, doi:10.1080/02691728.2019.1681559

Močnik, N., Ghouri, A. A. (2024). The Cost of Bearing Witness: Secondary Trauma and Self-Care in Fieldwork-Based Social Research. New York: Routlegde.

Moran, R. J., Asquith, N. L. (2020). Understanding the vicarious trauma and emotional labour of criminological research. *Methodological Innovations*, 13(2), pp. 1–11,https://doi.org/10.1177/2059799120926085

Nolen-Hoeksema, S., Larson, J. (1999). *Coping with loss*. Mahwah, NJ: Erlbaum.

Nuttman-Shwartz, O. (2014). Shared Resilience in a Traumatic Reality: A New Concept for Trauma Workers Exposed Personally and Professionally to Collective Disaster. *Trauma, Violence and Abuse*, 16(4), pp. 466–475.

Ogińska-Bulik, N., Kobylarczyk, M. (2015). Relation between resiliency and post-traumatic growth in a group of paramedics: The mediating role of coping strategies. *International Journal of Occupational Medicine and Environmental Health*, 28(4), pp. 707–719.

Okley, J. (2020). Fieldwork Embodied. *The Sociological Review*, 55, pp. 65–79. 10.1111/j.1467-954X.2007.00693.x.

Palmer, E., Murphy, D., Spencer-Harper, L. (2016). Experience of post-traumatic growth in UK veterans with PTSD: A qualitative study. *J R Army Med Corps*, 163(3), pp. 171–176.

Pearlman, L. A., Saakvitne, K. W. (1995). *Trauma and the therapist: Countertransference and vicarious traumatization in psychotherapy with incest survivors*. New York: W. W. Norton & Co.

Robben, A., Hinton, A. (2023). *Perpetrators: Encountering Humanity's Dark Side*. Stanford: Stanford University Press.

Robben, A., Sluka, J. (2012). *Ethnographic Fieldwork: An Anthropological Reader*. Malden; Blackwell Publishing.

Sahdan, Z. (2021). Recognising and Addressing Secondary Trauma: Stories from the Field. In: M. O. Ajebon,Y. M. C. Kwong, D. Astorga de Ita, (Eds.). *Navigating the Field: Postgraduate Experiences in Social Research*. Cham: Springer Nature, pp. 119–129.

Saltzman, L. Y., Pat-Horenczyk, R., Lombe, M., Weltman, A., Ziv, Y., McNamara, T., Takeuchi, D., Brom, D. (2018). Post-combat adaptation: improving social support and reaching constructive growth. *Anxiety, Stress & Coping*, 31(4), pp. 418–430.

Singleton Jr., R. A, Straits, B. C. (2005). *Approaches to Social Research*. New York: Oxford University Press.

Sluka, J.A., Robben, A. C. G. M. (2007). Fieldwork in cultural anthropology: An Introduction. In: A. C. G. M. Robben, J. A. Sluka (Eds.). *Ethnographic fieldwork: An anthropological reader*. Blackwell Publishing, pp. 1–28.

Tsirimokou, A., Kloess, J. A., Dhinse, S. K. (2022). Vicarious post-traumatic growth in professionals exposed to traumatogenic material: A systematic literature review. *Trauma, Violence, & Abuse*, 24(3), pp. 1848–1866.

Tsirimokou, A., Kloess, J. A., Dhinse, S. K. (2023). Vicarious Post-traumatic Growth in Professionals Exposed to Traumatogenic Material: A Systematic Literature Review, *Trauma, Violence, & Abuse*, 24(3), pp. 1848–1866. https://doi.org/10.1177/152483802 21082079

Vachon, M., Bessette, P., Goyette, C. (2016). "Growing from an Invisible Wound" a Humanistic-Existential Approach to Ptsd, In: G. El-Baalbaki, C. Fortin (Eds.). *A Multidimensional Approach to Post-Traumatic Stress Disorder – from Theory to Practice.*, pp. 179–204, London: IntechOpen, 10.5772/64290.

Van der Merwe, A., Hunt, X. (2019). Secondary Trauma among Trauma Researchers: Lessons from the Field. *Psychological Trauma: Theory, Research, Practice, and Policy*, 11(1), pp. 10–18.

Yearwood, K., Vliegen, N., Chau, C., Corveleyn, J., Luyten, P. (2019). When do peers matter? The moderating role of peer support in the relationship between environmental adversity, complex trauma, and adolescent psychopathology in socially disadvantaged adolescents. *Journal of Adolescence*, 72, pp. 14–22.

Zadrożna, A. (2019). Towards Reflexivity in the Sciences: Anthropological Reflections on Science and Society. In: J. Valsiner (Ed.). *Social Philosophy of Science for the Social Sciences*, Cham: Springer Nature, pp. 93–109.

CHAPTER 3

When Researching War Crimes and Genocide is also Personal

Furtuna Sheremeti

1 Introduction

In the haunting shadows of Kosovo, where historical tensions perpetually simmer, my research on war crimes and genocide is far from just an academic pursuit. It is a journey through a labyrinth of personal history and collective memory. Born into this turbulent backdrop, I have developed a unique form of resilience, profoundly shaped by the constant uncertainty and strife of my early life. The echoes of the war are not merely external noises but are woven into the very fabric of my being.

My academic path as a criminologist at KU Leuven and the University of Pristina has been deeply influenced by my personal experiences during the Kosovo war. Witnessing severe human rights violations through the eyes of a child has instilled in me a relentless drive to understand and work on these atrocities. Yet, this intimate proximity to my subject matter also poses significant challenges. Striving for objectivity while delving into the painful memories of war crimes and genocide in my homeland requires a delicate balance between personal engagement and academic detachment. However, I want to believe that my work not only contributes to academic discourse but also seeks to provide a voice for those silenced by violence, making my research a powerful bridge between scholarly inquiry and humanitarian advocacy.

This chapter explores that complex journey. It delves into the emotional aspects of conducting empirical research on such sensitive topics within Kosovo, a place I deeply love yet find profoundly scarred by past conflicts. Through my narrative, I aim to shed light on the often-overlooked emotional toll that such research can exact on scholars, especially those studying their own war-torn countries. Here, I offer insights into the struggle for objectivity amid the personal echoes of trauma and the vital importance of maintaining a rational approach in the pursuit of truth.

2 Researching Atrocious Crimes: The Theory

Studying horrific events in history – like genocide and war crimes – takes a heavy emotional toll on the scholars who research them. This summary brings together important writings about how investigating severe human rights abuses affect researchers. Overall, these works deepen our understanding of the secondary trauma and the complicated feelings that arise from this line of study.

Robert Jay Lifton (1986) offers a thoughtful examination of the psychological impact experienced by those who delve into the disturbing realm of medical atrocities committed during the Holocaust. Lifton (1986) explores the depths of emotional turmoil and ethical challenges that historians and psychologists encounter as they confront the grim details of experiments and killings conducted by Nazi doctors. Lifton's analysis sheds light on the concept of 'doubling,' a psychological mechanism wherein an individual creates an 'alter ego' to cope with participating in, or studying, morally reprehensible acts (Lifton, 1986). This phenomenon is particularly relevant to researchers immersed in the study of such dark subjects, as they must navigate the ethical quandaries and emotional distress that arise from exposure to these atrocities. The emotional complexities that Lifton discusses are not merely academic challenges; they represent significant psychological burdens that can lead to profound distress. Researchers often grapple with feelings of horror, sadness and anger, and these emotions can have long-lasting effects on their psychological well-being. Lifton (1986) emphasizes that engaging deeply with the material can cause secondary traumatic stress, similar to the experiences of trauma therapists and other professionals who work closely with trauma victims (Figley, 1995; Herman, 1992). Lifton also touches on the moral injuries that can occur when researchers confront ethical betrayals within the medical community, particularly those involving doctors who violated their ethical oath to 'do no harm' in such extreme and horrific ways. These betrayals challenge researchers' fundamental beliefs about the medical profession and humanity more broadly (Lifton, 1986).

In addressing these issues, Lifton (1986) calls for the development of support systems for researchers, including supervision, peer support groups, and therapeutic interventions specifically designed to address the unique challenges faced by those studying historical atrocities. He advocates for a more conscious approach to researching trauma, urging academic institutions to recognize and mitigate the potential psychological impacts on scholars. Lifton's work is crucial in understanding the burden carried by those who study the darkest aspects of human history. It highlights the need for greater awareness and proactive measures to support researchers' mental health and ethical integrity. By discussing these emotional and ethical complexities, Lifton (1986) not only contributes to our understanding of the Holocaust's medical crimes but also illuminates the broader implications for the field of historical and psychological research. This examination underscores the necessity for continued discussion and action to support the well-being of those who uncover and study humanity's most painful truths.

Judith Herman's influential book, *Trauma and Recovery* (1992), delves deeply into the psychological aftermath of trauma, with a specific focus on its pervasive impact not just on survivors but also on those who undertake the study of traumatic events such as war crimes and genocide. Herman (1992) articulates the profound need for a thorough understanding of trauma's mechanisms, which she argues is essential for researchers to process their experiences effectively and communicate the realities of these events with accuracy and sensitivity. In her exploration, Herman (1992) discusses the dual challenge faced by researchers: they must confront the horrifying facts of the atrocities they study while managing their emotional responses. This dual engagement with trauma can lead to what Herman describes as 'vicarious traumatization' or secondary traumatic stress, which can occur when individuals are exposed to the traumatic stories of others (Herman, 1992; Pearlman & Saakvitne, 1995). This condition highlights the emotional cost of empathy and the risk of trauma contagion among those deeply involved in researching traumatic histories.

Herman (1992) emphasizes that, to mitigate these risks, researchers need to develop a clear understanding of trauma's nature and its typical responses. This includes recognizing the symptoms of trauma in themselves and developing strategies to manage these symptoms effectively. Herman advocates for the establishment of routine self-care practices and the creation of institutional supports that acknowledge and address the emotional burdens carried by researchers in this field (Herman, 1992; McCann & Pearlman, 1990). Moreover, Herman (1992) points out the importance of maintaining a balance between detachment and engagement. This balance is crucial to preserve both the well-being of the researcher and the integrity of the research. Too much detachment can lead to dispassionate work that fails to capture the human suffering at the heart of these studies, whereas too much engagement can compromise objectivity and lead to overwhelming emotional distress (Herman, 1992; Figley, 1995). The strategies Herman suggests include structured debriefing sessions, where researchers can process their emotional experiences in a supportive environment, and training in trauma-informed research practices that equip researchers with the tools to understand and manage their reactions (Herman, 1992). She also recommends collaboration among researchers to foster a supportive community that can share the emotional load, reducing the isolation that often accompanies this type of research (Saakvitne & Pearlman, 1996). Ultimately, Herman's *Trauma and Recovery* (1992) serves as a seminal text that not only enhances our understanding of trauma's impact on individuals and communities but also extends this understanding to the realm of those who study traumatic events. Her work underscores the necessity of developing robust mechanisms to support researchers emotionally and professionally, ensuring that they can continue their important work without compromising their psychological health. This comprehensive approach ensures that the narratives of those who have suffered are conveyed with the utmost care and respect, facilitating a broader societal understanding and acknowledgment of these painful truths.

Shoshana Felman and Dori Laub (1992) explore the complex dynamics of witnessing and testifying to traumatic events. Their research is particularly insightful regarding the emotional and psychological challenges faced by those who study or work closely with narratives of trauma, such as historians, therapists, and researchers focusing on war crimes and genocide. Felman and Laub (1992) emphasize how the act of narrating or engaging with traumatic stories can sometimes lead to re-traumatization, both for the witness and the listener. Felman and Laub (1992) introduce the concept of 'secondary witnessing,' where the researcher or therapist becomes a witness to the trauma recounted by survivors. This process can have a profound emotional impact, as the trauma's narrative is not just passed on but can also be psychically transferred to the listener. The exposure to traumatic stories can trigger symptoms similar to post-traumatic stress disorder (PTSD) in researchers, a phenomenon often referred to as secondary traumatic stress or vicarious traumatization (McCann & Pearlman, 1990; Figley, 1995). The authors argue for the necessity of developing emotional resilience as a critical skill for those involved in this type of work. Emotional resilience refers to the ability to maintain psychological stability and adapt in the face of adversity or stress (Felman & Laub, 1992). Building such resilience involves both personal and professional strategies, including awareness of one's emotional responses, setting clear professional boundaries, and engaging in regular self-care practices (Saakvitne & Pearlman, 1996). Moreover, Felman and Laub (1992) discuss the importance of careful psychological management for researchers and therapists working with trauma narratives. They suggest that institutions and organizations provide support systems such as supervision, ongoing training in trauma-informed care, and access to therapeutic services for professionals. These measures can help mitigate the effects of secondary traumatic stress and provide a safer, more sustainable working environment (Figley, 1995; Herman, 1992). Felman and Laub

(1992) also stress the ethical implications of witnessing and testifying to trauma. They highlight that researchers and therapists must handle the stories of trauma survivors with the utmost care, ensuring that their practices do not inadvertently retraumatize the individuals whose experiences they are documenting or treating. This ethical consideration is crucial in maintaining the dignity and respect of trauma survivors and is fundamental to the integrity of the research and therapeutic processes (Felman & Laub, 1992).

Adam Jones (2008) delves into the complex psychological landscape that researchers navigate when they study the traumatic histories of genocide and war crimes. Jones (2008) meticulously examines how the constant exposure to accounts of severe human atrocities not only challenges researchers intellectually but also impacts them on a deeply personal level. His exploration into the topic highlights the phenomenon of secondary trauma, a condition commonly experienced by those who frequently interact with trauma survivors or their narratives (Jones, 2008). Secondary trauma, as Jones describes, results from the empathetic engagement of researchers with the victims' experiences, where the graphic and distressing details of genocide are internalized, leading to significant emotional distress (Jones, 2008). He argues that this is not merely an occupational hazard but a profound emotional and psychological ordeal that can affect the well-being of researchers' long term. The personal sacrifices involved go beyond the intellectual challenges of analyzing and presenting data; they involve a deep emotional toll that can manifest in symptoms similar to post-traumatic stress disorder (PTSD) (Jones, 2008). Jones (2008) supports his analysis by referencing studies that have documented similar experiences among mental health professionals, social workers, and first responders, who are also known to experience secondary trauma due to their work environment (Figley, 1995; McCann & Pearlman, 1990). He draws parallels between these professions and the field of genocide and war crimes research, suggesting that the mechanisms of trauma transmission are similar across these fields. Furthermore, Jones (2008) emphasizes the need for awareness and preventive strategies to mitigate these effects. He advocates for institutional support structures that include training in recognizing the signs of secondary trauma, regular psychological support, and the development of coping strategies tailored to those who are repeatedly exposed to traumatic content. He also suggests that creating a community of practice where researchers can share their experiences and support each other can be beneficial (Herman, 1992).

Jones' work is pivotal in bringing attention to an often-overlooked aspect of researching human rights violations. By highlighting the risks of secondary trauma among researchers, he opens a dialog about the importance of psychological resilience and support systems in academic settings where sensitive and traumatic subjects are studied. His insights contribute significantly to the discourse on the welfare of researchers, urging a re-evaluation of how academic institutions support their staff and contribute to sustainable research practices (Jones, 2008). This call for a more humane approach to academic research underscores the complex interplay between knowledge production and the emotional well-being of those who produce it.

The collective works of these academics not only contribute to our understanding of traumatic historical events but also call for a significant shift in academic practices. They highlight the urgent need for institutions to adopt a more compassionate approach that recognizes and addresses the complex interplay between conducting sensitive research and maintaining the well-being of researchers. This comprehensive perspective is crucial for enhancing research outcomes and ensuring the sustainability of scholarly work in fields that confront humanity's darkest episodes.

3 Doing Research in Kosovo: The Practice

Over the course of two years, I conducted intermittent research in Kosovo, structuring my schedule to allow breaks between stints not only to retain my connection to my homeland but also to manage the physical and psychological rigors that the fieldwork demanded. Each return to Kosovo was not just a geographical shift but also a profound psychological challenge, considering my childhood experiences there during the war. At the age of nine, the war's violence unfolded before my eyes from the safety of my apartment window, a stark and lasting image of brutality that prefigured the challenges of my research. My memories of escaping the war by train – without my mother, amidst the chaos of families torn apart – haunted me. These early traumas had already shaped a childhood steeped in turmoil.

Yet, despite this backdrop of personal suffering, the actual experience of conducting fieldwork was even more taxing than I had anticipated. I traversed rural Kosovo, visiting village after village, collecting stories of individuals who had endured extreme human rights violations – rape, torture, and the murders of loved ones. These accounts were not just data; they were intense, emotional exchanges that often left both the interviewee and myself in tears. One particularly intense day in Gjakova involved back-to-back interviews, each lasting about 2 hours and filled with such graphic and emotional narratives that, by the end of the day, I was emotionally and physically depleted. That evening, I managed the drive back to Prishtina, but the impact of the day's stories weighed heavily on me. The next morning, I found myself unable to leave my bed, initially attributing the paralysis to a possible flu. However, a visit to the doctor revealed no physical illness but pointed to stress and anxiety as the culprits.

The profound impact of these experiences came into sharper focus during a conversation with a colleague conducting similar research in another war zone. At that point, I had no idea about the work of any of the authors I mention above. It was only later, when reading Herman that I started feeling seen in his work. We shared feelings of being emotionally frozen, unable to move forward from the harrowing stories we had absorbed. This mutual experience underscored a significant gap in the support and preparation provided to researchers like us. Despite rigorous ethical preparation for fieldwork, which included protocols for engaging with vulnerable populations and safeguarding their stories, there was a glaring omission: no guidance had been given on managing our own emotional responses to such intense engagements. The toll was not just professional but deeply personal, challenging the notion that being a native or a survivor filled one with a natural resilience against psychological stress.

This experience illuminated the essential need for us working in war settings to be better prepared for the emotional challenges inherent in such work. It is crucial to recognize that the work transcends simple academic objectivity and delves into the realm of human emotion and connection. My interactions were not just with 'subjects' but with people, each with deeply personal stories of suffering that often mirrored my own experiences. The narratives I collected were of communities bound by shared tragedies, including instances of violence perpetrated within their own cities.

Understanding and preparing for the emotional aspects of research is crucial, not just for the well-being of the researcher but also for the integrity of the research. Striking the right balance between professional detachment and human empathy is essential, ensuring that researchers are effective in their work while being attentive to their mental health. Based on what I've learned, I would advise all researchers to acknowledge the challenging nature of this journey from the start, to educate themselves about both the theory and the lived experiences of others, and to establish a support system – whether it's a peer group, an online forum, or a therapist. The consequences of neglecting these emotional dimensions can be more significant and longer-lasting than many researchers might expect.

That is why, in this chapter, I have intentionally focused on earlier studies to highlight that knowledge about managing trauma's effects in research settings has long been available. Previous scholarship has emphasized the importance of understanding trauma and developing awareness and preventive strategies to combat secondary trauma among researchers. However, there appears to be a significant gap between the existing research and its practical application within academia. While I cannot make broad generalizations, my personal experiences reveal a notable discrepancy between theoretical discussions and real-world practices. This disparity underscores a broader issue – the divide between theory and practice. My lifelong goal is to bridge this divide, particularly between academia and policymakers. Reflecting on my experiences, it's intriguing to observe that this gap not only exists externally but also within the academic community itself.

4 Maintaining Objectivity: In Theory and in Practice

Conducting research on war crimes within the context of one's homeland presents unique challenges, particularly with respect to maintaining objectivity. When the researcher is also a native of the region being studied, the proximity to the subject matter can evoke strong personal biases and emotions, potentially skewing the analysis. The imperative to remain objective, however, is critical not only for the integrity of the research but also for the preservation of one's professional credibility and the respect of the academic community.

The way I see it, researchers must first acknowledge the inevitable presence of personal bias. This bias can stem from one's cultural background, personal experiences, and the emotional residue of living through the war. For instance, a researcher who has witnessed atrocities may find it particularly challenging to present an unbiased account of events or to empathetically portray perspectives that counter their own experiences. Recognizing these biases is the first step towards mitigating their influence (Brown, 2018).

Regarding strategies to maintain objectivity, the literature suggests various approaches, including methodological rigor, peer review and collaboration, reflective practice, emotional distance, and ethical considerations. While these strategies may not always be easy to implement, it is essential for any researcher dealing with these types of crimes to be cognizant of them and strive to apply them.

4.1 *Methodological Rigor*

Adopting rigorous methodologies is essential for achieving objectivity in research. This approach includes the meticulous design of study protocols to ensure they are free from bias and robust. Accurate data collection is critical, involving precise measurement and data-gathering techniques to guarantee the reliability and replicability of the data. This is followed by thorough analysis using recognized statistical or qualitative methods to impartially interpret the data. A fundamental technique in this approach is triangulation, which employs multiple data sources, researchers, or methods to cross-validate the findings. This comprehensive strategy helps protect against the possibility that conclusions may be influenced by the researcher's personal biases or one-sided data interpretation (Creswell, 2014).

In my research, this approach meant spending considerable time meticulously preparing topic lists in close collaboration with my supervisors, employing analytical methodologies that ensure objectivity through their detail-oriented systems, such as QUAGOL. QUAGOL, also known as the Qualitative Analysis Guide of Leuven, is a structured method for analyzing qualitative data that emphasizes iterative reading, coding, and interpretation of textual material (Dierckx de Casterlé et al., 2012). By systematically refining emerging themes and engaging in reflective practice, this approach enables researchers to develop coherent, in-depth insights into participants' experiences and perspectives while maintaining methodological rigor (Dierckx de Casterlé et al., 2012).

Additionally, I did not rely solely on interviews with victims and stakeholders but also on analyzing reports, court judgments, and other pertinent documents that could substantiate the narratives derived from the interviews.

4.2 *Peer Review and Collaboration*

Collaboration and peer engagement are crucial for sustaining objectivity in research. Peer review acts as an external safeguard, identifying potential biases, questioning methodologies, and proposing different interpretations of data. Working with researchers from diverse backgrounds or those who are detached from the subject of the conflict can greatly enhance the research. These collaborators offer new insights that challenge subjective views and help mitigate any biases the primary researcher may have. Such varied perspectives strengthen the integrity of the research outcomes and promote a more thorough understanding of the issues being studied.

In my experience, the Ph.D. process was, regrettably, quite solitary. This isolation is often part of the research journey, as noted by many of the authors I mention above, but it was exacerbated in my case by frequent travel, making it challenging to establish a stable support network. It was an unexpected conversation with a colleague – one that happened purely by chance – that gave me a crucial breakthrough in my understanding. I realized that I wasn't getting sick merely because of the weather; my body was reacting to the emotional toll of handling sensitive, often heartbreaking data. In seeing that others had similar experiences, I understood that this was not just a personal issue but part of a larger concern. Without this conversation, I'm not sure how I would have continued my fieldwork. It motivated me to keep going and also made me recognize the importance of prioritizing self-care, because otherwise, I would have risked burning out and quitting altogether.

4.3 *Reflective Practice*

Reflective practice is an essential technique for researchers to control the impact of their personal experiences and emotions on their work. By engaging in regular self-reflection, researchers can gain a deeper understanding of their own subjective biases and the potential influence these may have on their research outcomes. Maintaining a reflexive journal is a valuable strategy in this process. In such journals, researchers record their thoughts about the research process, including their emotional reactions and any preconceptions they may have. This continuous record-keeping aids researchers in monitoring how their viewpoints and emotional reactions develop throughout the study, promoting increased self-awareness and enabling critical self-evaluation (Jones, 2008).

During my fieldwork, I maintained a journal where I recorded my personal reflections on the research process and the interviews. Initially, I was unsure whether this would be beneficial, but I continued to keep the journal as a way to gather and organize my thoughts. Over time, this practice proved to be significantly helpful.

4.4 *Emotional Distance*

While it may not be entirely possible or even advantageous to completely detach emotionally from one's research, it is essential to maintain a level of professional distance. Researchers should strive to strike a balance between their emotional engagement with the people and the need to preserve professional objectivity. To achieve this, researchers might consider adopting strategies like establishing firm boundaries between their professional and personal lives, taking regular breaks, or partaking in activities that facilitate mental disengagement from their studies. These methods can help researchers approach their work with a renewed, clearer, and more objective perspective (Brown, 2018).

I personally find that achieving emotional distance is among the most challenging aspects, and complete detachment may not be entirely attainable (nor preferable). However, this is not necessarily detrimental. The subjects we explore are inherently emotional, and as humans, our natural sensitivity, empathy, and emotions can enrich our research, adding depth and perspective rather than detracting from it.

4.5 *Ethical Considerations*

Upholding the highest ethical standards and reducing bias is essential, especially when dealing with sensitive topics like war crimes and genocide. In my research, ethical rigor involves several key components, including obtaining informed consent from all participants, which ensures they understand the nature of the study and the use of the data collected. In addition, I ensured confidentiality and the secure handling of sensitive information to protect the identities and privacy of participants. Moreover, I presented findings in a way that is truthful yet considerate of the potential impact on those involved. Researchers must be careful to avoid sensationalizing or trivializing the experiences of participants, which could lead to re-traumatization or exacerbate existing tensions. Adhering to these ethical guidelines helps maintain the dignity and respect of the subjects involved while ensuring the integrity of the research process (Israel & Hay, 2006).

Researchers also often need to take deliberate measures to reduce personal bias (Jones, 2008). In my case, this meant incorporating narratives from multiple ethnic groups to ensure a balanced perspective. The task of researching war crimes in one's own country demands a careful balance between engagement and detachment. While personal experiences can provide valuable insights, they can also introduce bias. It is the responsibility of the researcher to navigate this complex terrain with integrity, employing strategies that uphold objectivity while acknowledging the deeply human aspects of the research. By doing so, researchers not only contribute valuable knowledge but also honor the experiences of those who have suffered in these settings (Brown, 2018).

5 Conclusion

In this chapter, I have explored the deeply personal and emotionally charged journey of researching war crimes and genocide within the context of one's own country. The dual role of being both a researcher and a native of the region studied presents unique challenges, as it requires balancing profound personal engagement with the necessary academic detachment. Through a detailed examination of my experiences and the broader implications of such research, I have tried to uncover the psychological burdens and ethical complexities that accompany this type of scholarship.

The narratives presented in this chapter try to shed light on the emotional toll that this type of research can exact on scholars, particularly those like me who have a direct personal connection to the conflicts under study. These experiences highlight the necessity for academic institutions and professional communities to provide robust support systems, including psychological counseling and ethical guidance, to help researchers navigate the emotional and ethical challenges inherent in this work. Basically, to bring the theory to the table and put it into practice.

As I conclude this exploration, it becomes clear that the work of documenting and understanding war crimes and genocide is not only a professional undertaking but also a deeply human endeavor. It requires a careful balance of empathy and analytical distance, urging a reevaluation of how we support and conduct research in such challenging fields. It is my hope that this chapter contributes to our understanding of the psychological impacts of this type of research and works for a more humane approach to academic inquiry, one that acknowledges and addresses the profound emotional realities faced by researchers. This is essential not only for the advancement of knowledge but also for the healing and validation of communities that have been scarred by these tragic events.

References

Brown, P. (2018). Ethical challenges to research in the criminal justice system. *Crim. Behav & Mental Health* 28, pp. 5–12.

Creswell, J. W. (2014). *Research design: Qualitative, quantitative, and mixed methods approaches* (4th ed.). Los Angeles: SAGE Publications.

Dierckx de Casterlé, B., Gastmans, C., Bryon, E., Denier, Y. (2012). *QUAGOL: A guide for qualitative data analysis. International Journal of Nursing Studies*, 49(3), pp. 360–371.

Felman, S., Laub, D. (1992). *Testimony: Crises of Witnessing in Literature, Psychoanalysis, and History*. New York: Routledge.

Figley, C. R. (1995). *Compassion fatigue: Coping with secondary traumatic stress disorder in those who treat the traumatized.* New York: Brunner/Mazel.

Herman, J. (1992). *Trauma and Recovery: The Aftermath of Violence – from Domestic Abuse to Political Terror*. New York: Basic Books.

Israel, M., Hay, I. (2006). *Research ethics for social scientists: Between ethical conduct and regulatory compliance*. London: SAGE Publications

Jones, A. (2008). *Genocide, War Crimes and the West: History and Complicity*. London: Zed Books.

Lifton, R. J. (1986). *The Nazi Doctors: Medical Killing and the Psychology of Genocide.* New York: Basic Books.

McCann, I. L., Pearlman, L. A. (1990). Vicarious traumatization: A framework for understanding the psychological effects of working with victims. *Journal of Traumatic Stress*, *3*(1), pp. 131–149.

Pearlman, L. A., Saakvitne, K. W. (1995). *Trauma and the therapist: Countertransference and vicarious traumatization in psychotherapy with incest survivors*. New York: W. W. Norton & Company.

Saakvitne, K. W., Pearlman, L. A. (1996). *Transforming the Pain: A Workbook on Vicarious Traumatization*. New York: w.w. Norton & Company.

Wagner, S. E. (2008). *To Know Where He Lies: DNA Technology and the Search for Srebrenica's Missing*. Berkeley: University of California Press.

PART 2

Reflections from Teachers

CHAPTER 4

Concerning Mass Atrocity: A Personal Reflection on Studying and Teaching about Violence

Thijs B. Bouwknegt

1 Introduction: Fathoming Phantom Pain

> A civil war, a brutal repression, apartheid: it never dies completely. The unanswered questions and the sadness these events leave behind live on in the minds of those who experienced them. They are perpetuated as a 'phantom pain' in the bodies of those who come later, their children and their children's children.
>
> HUYSE, 2009, p. 15

Cruelty. Violence. We all know about it. Or we can imagine its sensations. The angst of civil war. The alarm of political revolt. The abruptness of ethnic rage. The scent of mass graves. The anguish of torture survivors. The imminence of a bomb attack. The shaking of hands with a *génocidaire*. Studying mass violence is exciting and challenging, both 'in the field' and in theory. Our line of scholarly and educational work ultimately exposes us to the rawness, unkindness and sadness of humanity. We deal with the emotive wildness of human-versus-human ferocity in tempestuous situations – that is, the extraordinary violence ordinary people so often get involved in (de Swaan, 2015). Machete-wielding Hutus chasing and hacking Tutsis in swamps and slopes in Rwanda in 1994 is just one example of such a context. As scholars and students, we have all experienced or encountered violence, or its consequences – each in our own ways, from our own perspectives, on our own terms. It can be 'live.' Or it can be channeled through secondary and tertiary information sources. We see it with our own eyes. We hear about it from survivors and eye-witnesses. We read testimonies, diaries, memoirs, books and archives. We see atrocity on television, social media and documentaries. We learn about violence from our colleagues' scholarship and in lecture halls. We immerse ourselves in libraries and archives. And of course, studying these matters of mass killing, torment and conflict rouses our senses – beyond our intellectual inquisitiveness. We cannot ignore the impact, or at times the (primary, secondary, tertiary) trauma. In what manners, then, do and can we – researchers and educators alike – traverse the poignant emotions, experiences and environments of distress, examine them and elaborate on them in classrooms? This chapter explores how we (can or cannot) relate to the human misery we study and teach. How do we deal, so to say, with our professional dealing with mass violence?

Coping and violence are two sides of the same coin. Psychology and its vernacular – or the actual psychologist's couch, for that matter – might aid our scientific and didactic thinking on the one hand, and possibly our private distancing from, or coping with, the phantom pains of mass atrocity, on the other. We seek armor, so as not to let others' sorrow become ours. Equally, writing and talking – the scholar's principal expressive conduits – about the risks of investigating and teaching about mass violence might be helpful too, even if it is just to share stories about our own navigation of our intellectual and emotional faculties and attitudes, both professionally and personally. I will give it a go here.

Communication is central in both research and education in the fields of the humanities and social sciences. I write here from the perspective of the historian. Why do we concern ourselves with violence? Why do we look at it? How do we – in the words of writer Susan Sontag (2003) – "regard" the pain of others? How do we study (consume) this delicate, sensitive, and unsettling topic? And how, then, do we connect to and communicate with those who have experienced it and convey it to students?

Cure and closure might not always be achievable, but they are desirable and thinkable. I promise not to provide answers or formulae for finding catharsis. I do not believe I have any – other than fostering profound and close companionships with people like us, who understand us, and whom we understand in return.[1] Instead, I can only offer a personal reflection on exploring and reporting on the myriad facets of 'affronts against humanity' (jurists would categorize such violence as genocide, crimes against humanity, war crimes, aggression, apartheid, torture, and enforced disappearances)[2] and their aftermath. I will begin by reflecting on the reasons (circumstance, confrontation, curiosity, conscience, chronicle, coincidence) why I study violence in the first place. I will contemplate the ways (compass, craft, conviction, consideration) and consider the contexts (contemporaneity) in which I have done so. I will chew over the purposes (cause) which have propelled me, comment upon the restraints (concern, caution) which have held me back. I will write about

1 Such are friendships, in my case particularly with Prof. Dr. Barbora Holá.

2 Also "international crimes," "atrocity crimes," "mass crimes." I will refrain from using the legal terms.

balancing (compartmentalization) between operating as 'a homo academicus', who has a professional impartial obligation towards factfulness and objectivity (career), and being a 'homo emoticus' – a human person with sentiments, morals and convictions (compassion). I will then try to bring these together by discussing how we educate promising researchers (curriculum), while also making students aware of (consciousness and care) the problems and pitfalls of studying mass atrocity violence – and to recognize the implicit biases we hold. Lastly, I will reflect on how joining forces (community, collegiality, conversation) could make studying violence more comfortable and careful – towards our science, and towards ourselves. Fathoming the plurality of phantom pains involved with the ferocious phenomena we study might enrich our cabinet of tools to deal with our dealing with violence.

2 Regarding Mass Violence

> Imagine life at its full peak
> Then imagine lying dead in the arms of your enemy
> Imagine peace on this earth when there's no grief
> Imagine grief on this earth when there's no peace.
>
> *I Have Seen a Man Die* (SCARFACE, 1994)

Why are we curious about violence that is so extreme and so massive? And why do we look at it? In one of my favorite books, *All Things Pass, Except the Past*, sociologist Luc Huyse (2009, p. 15) asks how he came to spend "roughly half a lifetime learning and writing about the aftermath of war and related miseries." After 25 years of examining mass atrocity violence and transitional justice,[3] it is a question I frequently hear too. It is always followed by, "and how do you deal with that?" Responding to the first is only seemingly simpler than answering the latter.

So, let us commence.

2.1 *Contemplating Cause*

Circumstances had it that I grew up in a post-war Dutch household, which, at weekends, relished the fragrances of my grandfather's homemade nasi gor-

3 'Transitional justice' is the historical phenomenon of societal and political (non-)dealing with historical injustices. Historians refrain from using neo-definitions coined by jurists, activists, and diplomats, who often see transitional justice as mechanisms or policy tools in service of liberal regime change.

eng – a culturally (mis)appropriated Indonesian plate of fried rice with marinated chicken, diced vegetables and oriental spices. Grandpa had mastered the fabulous recipe during his military service in the former Dutch East Indies (now Indonesia). Coming out of his teenage experience of the Nazi occupation of the Netherlands (1940–1945), he – and his brother – were, in their early twenties, conscripted and sent out to participate in a profane colonialist confrontation. Altogether, he lived through war for about nine years (May 1940–December 1949). First, he was standing by and witnessing. Then, he was drafted by an aggressor state (the Netherlands) and participating. Never did he speak about violence. Not once. Even while, as a young boy, I would ask him about guns and things. At times, yes, he would curse at Germans. "Moffen," he would call them. Sporadically, he would say that "things were terrible" or that "things were hard" during the Second World War (WWII). From his tropical years in Indonesia, my grandmother related later, he did not bring back bad memories into their home. Just cooking techniques and wajang dolls. And a medley of photographs. He showed me several when I was a child. Many portray him with a transistor. He was a radio officer, connecting central command to ground forces. He traveled much. He swam. He smoked. He idled. And he saw things. Only later, after he passed away in 1994, did I notice one particular photograph. In it, someone (I am quite sure it is not him) with a machine gun stands in front of what appears to be a burning kampong – a signature atrocity of the time.[4] What I know is that he had the photo in his possession, and that likely he took it himself. He even wrote a little text next to it: "the mess in Krawang, 1947." What I do not know is whether he did anything, and if so: what.

Curiosity about the human condition drives most of us. It is why we practice science. A smoldering question I had since childhood was only partially answered and probably only further stimulated my curiosity, perhaps not even consciously. Beyond my grandfather obviously knowing about outrages (Dutch inquiries talk about "excesses," "extreme violence," "war crimes"), what was my grandfather's role, if any, and how did he deal with it? If at all? What about my grandmother? I never really found out, mostly because I did not consciously endeavor to do so. But one question always itches at my conscience.

Conundrums of the past keep us in a grip in the present as we move into the future. What if one finds out their grandfather was a war criminal? To what extent, if so, would such cognition (re)character my research – and possibly

4 Also see Limpach (2016).

my teaching To this day, I cannot know. It remains outside the realm of my professional craft.

Chronicles about violence form the ways in which we perceive it. My grandfather's unrecounted chronicle is still on my mind. Perhaps more imaginatively than forensically. Certainly, it is still there academically. When I reflect here and now, I see the phantom story too as part of the forming of my inquisitorial compass. It pulls me into the field. But it also pushes me out of certain corners. Firstly, instead of probing direct family, I have spent the rest of my professional life inquiring about human(ity)'s affronts against humanity, particularly premeditated mass categorical murder (i.e., genocide) and war. I did so in places distant from my origins, mostly in Africa. I am always trying to comprehend the dynamics of human-to-human brutality. My way of dealing with family history, I came to realize, was partially through dealing with the stories and histories of others and from elsewhere. At a distance that was safe enough: in Liberia, Sierra Leone, Rwanda, Uganda, Sudan and Afghanistan. Only recently did I shift focus to my own country, the Netherlands – a former colonial power historically involved in much atrocity violence around the globe (Groen, 2021).

Commencing in this field, I made these attempts at comprehension while working as a researcher for Amnesty International (AI) in West Africa, the United Nations International Criminal Tribunal for Rwanda (UNICTR) and the International Criminal Court (ICC) – collecting and contending with (oral) histories and testimonies about brutality, mass murder and terror. Secondly – in a way like my grandfather, who became involved in local radio and media in the Netherlands – I dealt with violence as a journalist. For Radio Netherlands Worldwide (formerly Radio Orange, which broadcast over the BBC's airwaves during WWII), I traveled widely, covered and reported on cruel conflict, human rights outrages and people and their societies dealing with the past (transitional justice) in all corners of the globe. One quickly learns that violence and facing the misery of it concern us all; that it is much closer to us than we think – than we want to think, or than we dare to think. Because it is so human. Over the years, I have lost count of the many conversations and interviews I have had with people affected by violence: survivors, victims, bystanders, witnesses, perpetrators, accomplices, facilitators, informers, military, militia, ministers, humanitarians, journalists, academics, writers and artists – and sometimes their children, and their children's children. Together they constitute a choir that crescendos into a cacophony of gloom – chronicling mass violence. Furthermore, family history also steered and kept me away from certain research. As a natural reflex, I mindfully did not collaborate in a large-scale inquiry carried out by my employer (the NIOD Institute for War,

Holocaust and Genocide Studies) into the Netherlands' behavior and actions in its violent endeavor at recolonizing Indonesia (1945–1949).[5] This came too close to family. It was thus a topic that was too hot to handle. At least as of then, and still as of yet. Amongst private considerations, my concern was also that I might not be capable of remaining detached, dispassionate and diligent as a professional historian.

Coincidences, for a large part, guide us through life. As much as I believe in science and scholarly detachment (to the narrow extent that impartiality and objectivity exist and are achievable), I am still puzzled by certain chances – and they go beyond my grandfather and me sharing the same birthday. Writing this reflection, I returned to family archives. Browsing photo albums, I stumbled upon two more photographs. In May 1946 – 6 months before he left for Indonesia – my grandfather posed for a photo at a military barracks in The Hague. It is at the Nieuwe Frederikskazerne: the exact location from where I am currently conducting research for an inquiry into the Netherlands' military and diplomatic role in the international war against the Taliban and designated 'terrorists' and 'insurgents' in Afghanistan (2001–2021). In the photograph, I can see the building – once built by Nazi occupiers and currently housing the Netherlands Institute for Military History (NIMH) – which is very likely the place where, from 2023, I am spending most of my time reading military and political archives of war. Parts of this very piece are written there. I overlook the lawn where my grandfather once stood, preparing to go to war. But there is more history, more coincidence, more contingency. In the same month, May 1946, my grandfather also took a photo of the adjacent Alexanderkazerne barracks. These erstwhile garrisons stood precisely on the spot where the ICC is now. I worked as an analyst at that permanent atrocity crime court in 2006, researching violence against civilians – including the burning and looting of homes (reminiscent of the burning kampongs in my grandfather's photograph) by the Lord's Resistance Army (LRA) in Uganda and by the 'Janjaweed' militia in Darfur, Sudan. From its first hearing of an accused (Thomas Lubanga Dyilo) in March 2006 to January 2025 (Ali Muhammad Ali Abd-Al-Rahman), I have been observing all of its trials and studying the ICC's troubled pursuit of *atrocitaires*. Nineteen years since I worked at the ICC, now in 2025, my little walks during my work breaks are through the green dunes around the Court's premises. When I wander there, I sometimes won-

5 Independence, Decolonisation, Violence and War in Indonesia, 1945–1950 was a joint research programme of the Royal Netherlands Institute of Southeast Asian and Caribbean Studies (KITLV), the Netherlands Institute of Military History (NIMH) and the NIOD, see https://ind45-50.nl/en/node (retrieved September 30, 2024).

der about my grandfather. Together with his photo of the scorched village (possibly evidence of an international crime), these two photos, and the stories I gauge from them, are unusual discoveries. While they must be coincidental, the irony of it spiraled my curiosity back into a loop of self-reflection – reported on here.

Conversations and encounters, beyond family, likewise intrigued me further, fueling my craving to understand what draws and drags people – because it happens willfully and unwilfully, even serendipitously – into extremely violent situations, and what that does to them. Some encounters I remember very well. In high school (I must have been 12, maybe 13 years old), my Liberian classmate and friend often talked about his flight from 'childsoldierhood' in the two consecutive "uncivil wars" (his words, not mine) back home – and about his mother who, while fleeing, had to decide between taking him or his brother. His discordant happiness and sadness (and perhaps the "madness" – also his words – he found himself in later) I will never forget. Also in high school, I had a Surinamese history teacher. He told us about the long Dutch history of slavery (a crime against humanity) in the Americas and Asia. He narrated how his grandparents – and their parents and grandparents – suffered from their capture and forced displacement from Africa, their enslavement in the Dutch colonies and the apartheid and inhumane treatment under which they grew up. I realized later that, through generations, he too had suffered from these atrocities. In class, he played us songs by Bob Marley and The Wailers. They sang about dealing with slavery and the colonial past and obtaining (social) justice for the violence, oppression and trauma they had suffered from it. In a way, we got exposed to a genre of political music that, in the 1970s, already voiced the type of human rights discourse that would be weaponized by Western transitional justice advocates in the 1990s. Later, when I was a student and lived in a student house, I often overheard the drunken night cries of my neighbor, a young veteran who had served in Bosnia. In Potočari and Srebrenica, in July 1995, he had separated women and children from men. He had witnessed Bosnian Serb forces hunt for and shoot to death men and boys. In West Africa, while traveling there for my studies in 2003, I sensed the imminence of ethno-religious war in Côte d'Ivoire. I heard young Liberian refugees mimic the sounds of babies being smashed against a wall. In Ghana, I felt the political tensions sparked by the Special Court for Sierra Leone's (SCSL) issuance of an arrest warrant for Charles Taylor (Liberia's then-president), who was in Accra for peace talks. Such personal stories are massively imposing. They are influential. They infest, infect, almost. They stick with you. They spark a certain interest in humans, in humanity and in human stories – also when they speak about inhumanity and inhumane acts.

Chances (perhaps through choices – see below) in life had it that, over the years, I have heard probably several thousand people testify about gruesome violence – during investigations, in courts, and before truth commissions, for reportage, and for research. They paved a corridor of experiences that tested my capabilities. My first formal interview was in 2003, with a former Sierra Leonean child soldier only a little more than my age. As a former member of the 'small boys' unit' of a revolutionary force (the RUF), he had hacked off hands, arms, feet, legs and other body parts of his enemies. I could hardly imagine the trauma of his forced conscription (his victimization), what he had been made to do (him victimizing), and how he coped with all of that, if at all. My second interview was in 2004. She was an elderly Rwandan who was mass raped; her left breast was sliced off with a panga. I could hardly imagine what she had gone through. I had no training nor experience whatsoever, and I was upset. I must say that, professionally, one can get used to listening to testimonies about unimaginable atrocities through routinization (and forensic reimagination, seeing 'evidence'), but also that, personally, one never really does. After research, one ought to unwind (to 'chillout') from these stories, navigate what one can and what one cannot do. But stories also accumulate. Today, I find it more difficult than ever before to interview sufferers or to even hear their testimony. At times, I just choke. I have the privilege, however, to be able to choose not to – because my employer allows me that space to guard us from too much exposure to the pain of others.

Contemporaneity dictates our conditions, while the times we live in also condition us. There is a certain circularity, not only in our paths to, but also in our questions and perceptions of mass violence. We are all crops of our time, of the places and spaces in which we were nurtured, cultured and acculturated. Growing up in the liminal zeitgeist of the 1980s and 1990s, my generation (Xennials) lived through the global transition out of the Cold War into the Global War on Terror in the 2000s (a war that continued most visibly and tangibly in 2025 in the Southwest Asian region around Israel). It was also the spring of globalization and mass mediatization. Mass atrocity violence from elsewhere became almost palpably perceptible everywhere. It was televised; no longer in black and white but in color and in 'high definition.' For many (particularly of our generation, and in the 'West' or 'Global North'), comprehending mass violence ceased to become primarily an act of imagination. We went from conceptualizing violence to continuously seeing violence. We watched it, digested it, consumed it.

Context changed accordingly. Along the violence, paradoxically, the 1990s also saw the advent of the "era of human rights" and the "age of transitional justice" – a positivist and positive-minded, mainly idealist-activist movement that believed in 'truth and justice' as the saviors in the face of ferocity (Moyn, 2010; Adler, 2018). On television, we witnessed the world-historical events of the fall of the Berlin Wall (1989), the release of Nelson Mandela (1990) – and the subsequent ending of communist apparatuses in the Soviet Bloc, as well as Apartheid (an international crime with a Dutch name) in South Africa. Former secret services in Eastern Europe opened their archives. From April 1996, we heard testimony before South Africa's TRC. Only a month later, the United Nations' International Criminal Tribunal for the former Yugoslavia (ICTY) held its first war crimes trial. In July 1998, the ICC was established in sunny Rome. In September 1998, Jean-Paul Akayesu became the first person ever to be convicted by an international court (ICTR) for the crime of genocide. In the Western quarters of the world (particularly in the Netherlands, which even started to brand itself as the world's 'international capital of peace and justice'), there developed a zealous belief amongst diplomats, activists and even academicians that the world could and should be saved (Bouwknegt & Nauta, 2023) – and that in doing so, it should be molded (in Dutch the ideology of the "maakbare samenleving" could be best described and liberal regime change through social engineering). I must admit that, also for me, this sparkling humanitarian environment was contagious. Working for AI, the UN and the ICC, I also thought that the arc of the moral universe was bendable towards justice, open democratic societies and more truth than lies. Two decades later, I am more critical, skeptical perhaps, but not cynical. I have seen, by digging through states' archives, that realpolitik often wrestles *against* morality. The ICC's 'global justice' has not yet been global or inclusive at all – predominantly targeting the formerly colonized world and solely prosecuting Black men. International law's 'deterrent potential,' for that matter, is being murdered and buried as I write this – one crime scene is Gaza (also see Wintour, 2024), the other is Ukraine. As a concept, it appears to have been naïve. Unrealistic. Symbolic. Studying global history and reporting on violence and war crimes justice, one quite quickly sees and learns about the less compelling – that is, the dirty reality – stories, the controversies and the condition of humanity. The truth is that the reality is harsh. The idea that genocide can be comprehensively prevented is outdated. Wars and mass killings have been part and parcel of the history of humankind. Also, human rights are far from universal. International 'humanitarian' law, as the history of the Geneva Conventions shows, is just as often an à la carte menu available only to the powerful – rather than being primarily an armor of the 'wretched of the earth' it sometimes claims to serve (Schabas, 2023). And it was in the 1990s that the images of all this human atrocity (not least those from the war in the former Yugoslavia), for the first time in modern history, came to us raw and live.

Coverage in the news in the 1990s – I can only speak about the Netherlands – included no trigger warnings (cautions). The word did not exist yet. Generally, my generation grew up with quite explicit programming by public broadcasters. Raw images, sounds and texts were on the daily menus of television, radio and newspapers. The explicitness and wretchedness of warfare were omnipresent in the public sphere. We were saturated with it. Continuously. We got used to it. TV drew us into the Gulf War (1990–1991) as if it were a reality show. Operation Desert Storm was broadcast live. We saw U.S.-American 'peacekeepers' being dragged through the streets of Mogadishu, Somalia, in 1993. In 1994, magazines featured photos of macheted Tutsis on their covers. In 1995, the 'trauma of Srebrenica' – the genocidal mass murdering of Bosniak men and boys committed under the watch of Dutch soldiers like my former neighbor – lingered everywhere. Consistently. Distressing stories of Bosniak women survivors and the young Dutch military men and women who had not been able to protect them from Ratko Mladić's forces percolated into our societal fabric. Meanwhile, between 1993 and 2003, we saw the humanitarian hecatomb in the Democratic Republic of the Congo (DRC) unfold – during which nearly 5,000,000 people consequently died. Kosovo, Chechnya, Sri Lanka, East Timor and Sudan followed. The carnival of carnage was in full effect. We then felt the shockwaves of '9/11,' the (real and fabricated) fear of terror, the long wars in Afghanistan and Iraq, the rise of the Islamic State in Iraq and Syria (ISIS) and the insecurity in Mali. At the same time, however, with the same ease, we started to ignore it. We saw it as business as usual. Mass death was all around us. Today, it is all live-streamed to our mobile phones.

Culturally, the normalization of and accustomization to seeing violence in the public space also proliferated in the 1980s–90s. Realtime violence, around that time, was also mass-exploited and televised for commercial entertainment. When the news was not on, there was always some reality show about the US-America's 'war on drugs' – with white police pursuing and mass incarcerating young Black men. If not via television, narratives of racialized drug-violence in ghettoized urban areas entered pop culture via the genre of Gangsta Rap from NWA, Snoop Doggy Dogg and Tupac Shakur. The iconic black-and-white sticker on album covers, both LPs and CDs – stating "PARENTAL ADVISORY. EXPLICIT LYRICS" – we took as a sign of quality, not menace. We consumed much of it without critiquing the inhumanity it involved and narrated. Then the Internet bubbled up. Especially in the beginning, there were zero to few World Wide Web cautions about what gruesomeness one might pull up, view, see, download and share – and what alarm number to call if it caused distress. What was new, too, was that access to information was now available 24/7, and it came from all over the world. Many at the time saw the unredacted torturous footage of Nick Berg's beheading in Iraq in May 2004. It circulated everywhere. At a certain point, there was even a debate about 'atrocity fatigue.' Images of misery (the 'classic' African child with a fly in their eye, starving on posters) stopped having an impact – the shock effect that would trigger our humanitarianism. It was because they had become so much part of our everyday news intake. Dead bodies (particularly from 'other' areas of the world) became "unmournable" (compare Cole, 2015). A mass mediatized and unlimited stream of in-your-face violence was normalized when I went to university. We watched the second hijacked airplane hit one of the Twin Towers in New York City on 11 September 2001, live in the hallways of university. We stood around big televisions. Two years later, we saw the USA's full aggressive invasion of Iraq, in a classroom. Witnessing history unfold was no longer just for professional historians. That is even more true today. We all get to process it.

Communication with and about world events has changed comprehensively. By now, with speedy Internet and social media on our phones, laptops and smartwatches, we are conditioned to the mass exposure to atrocity. This exposure – through technology – is at times of 'higher quality' than ever before and, therefore, also more explicit, more direct, more impactful. It reaches us like uncontrollable wildfire. Moreover, we can see atrocity on demand, when we are ready, when we are prepared. It is at our fingertips. That is what is different today: the individualization and optionality of media (rather than the classically programmed television news and timed delivery of morning newspapers and the focused discussions on things we had all seen) arguably also give us a choice to not see violence (or, and the far more common option, I would imagine, to not see certain types of violence while seeing more of others) – to conceal it. To not engage. To be ignorant. To occupy us with us – no longer with others. Through our algorithms and social bubbles, we can protect ourselves from serendipitous exposure to anything, more than ever before. Paradoxically, for the forms of violence we do consume, we use this same technology to also increase and maximize our intake – using digital tools and apps to continuously keep up informed about and engaged with violence. We can follow revolutions – like the surprise toppling of Syria's Bashar Al-Assad in 2024 – minute by minute.

Counseling and comforting – and arguably shielding and curtailing ourselves from matters that upset – is only consistently offered to students in the last few decades. When all this was going on, I studied contemporary non-Western history – a broad mix of global history, anthropology and journalism focused on Africa, Asia, South America and Oceania. Research professors inspired and pressed us to read as much and as widely as possible. To follow the news. To browse the worldwide web. To travel outside the West. To talk to strangers. To always consider the past in the present. And to be wary of what the present and the future might possibly desire from us. To distrust the way power uses and abuses history and historical narratives – the unreliable information with which we are overloaded. Curtains were not offered to not see violence. Censorship of thought, debate and emotion was the supreme taboo at the faculty. We were not (to be) protected from what we might possibly read and learn. To the contrary: to see is to believe, to see is to comprehend, to see is to relate; that was the incentive. Nobody thought about what studying war and its aftershocks might do to students and graduates alike. Universities today cater to scholars and students much better than before. When I studied, the university (Groningen and Amsterdam) had possibly one student counselor. We did not know where they were or what they were there for. Libraries at the time had no safe spaces – or coffee corners, for that matter – to unwind, to chill, or to distract ourselves from the desolations of the shattered lives we studied. We had to find it ourselves. Through nightlife, dance and cigarettes and alcohol in cafés, bars and discos.

Choice and general interest are crucial too, but often forgotten. We should not essentialize too much that we study violence all the time, that we are all exposed to mass violence all the time, and that we do not study anything else. We once decided to do what we do. Many of my student peers simply decided not to focus on violence. It was not for them. They could not, or they would not, look at violence – and, of course, history has so much more to offer than violence. There are beautiful things to study too; what is destroyed was also once created and celebrated. Likewise, I curated my own curriculum and picked my own topics and courses from the academic list of options. For my first student paper, in 1999, I read the six volumes of the freshly printed report of South Africa's TRC (1998). They contained victims' testimony of cruel political abuse, murder and torture. Tears about the death, despair and defiance trickled from the pages. Later, I took courses in 'how societies confront historical injustices' (today that would be labeled transitional justice) and in 'genocide & mass murder,' and went on class excursions to see the trial of Slobodan Miloseviç in The Hague. Violence just became 'my thing.' On the side, in anthropology classes, we read Edward Said's *Orientalism* (1978) and learned about cultural relativism. Our training was professional (focused on the how), moral and ethical (focused on how not to), and always intellectual (focused on learning, analyzing, comprehending, explaining, debating). When I moved to Tanzania in 2004 for archival research for my thesis – and ended up doing investigations – the only real warning I got was to "not get bored," and 'to get the most out of it.' It was all part of our science and education. To a large degree, this is still the thinking at history faculties. I also studied 'International and European Law' and 'Holocaust and Genocide Studies' (HGS). Things were no different there, other than that the curriculum at the law faculty simply excluded the concrete exposure to, and the study of, the violence (i.e., the actual and the factual 'violations' themselves) international criminal courts and tribunals deal with. In HGS (a program I now teach myself), the only focus was on violence and its global history. The history of humanity, as I was told and as I now often (re)tell our students, is mostly the history of humankind's inhumanity to humanity during conquests, wars and exterminations. Fighting and colonizing is what *Homo sapiens* have done since their beginning. Indeed, there are few biologists who would argue against the observation that humans are the most violent, invasive and destructive species on Earth. We are, for example, the only species to mass 'produce' animals, to mass kill, mass butcher and mass eat them.

Cognition of ourselves requires us to look into the mirror. How can we study ourselves without facing ourselves? If we cannot see violence and death, we cannot study the Neanderthals, the Roman Empire, the Middle Ages, colonialism, history's revolutions (USA, France, Haiti, Russia, China), the two world wars, or the current conflicts in Ukraine, Gaza and Sudan. It is what it was. And it is what it is. What has drastically changed is students' awareness of their private positionality, their mental health and their vulnerabilities *after* they have chosen to study violence. Where absolute detachment had been the scholarly position over the past three decades (or at least at history faculties), now increasingly we involve our own selves in our research. Even this article I write in the first person. Some of us not only look anymore at what we can do for our field of study; they also look at what our field of study does to us. The answer, however, to the question of what guards us better from impact, I do not know – it depends on the person. I can only speak for myself.

2.2 *Contemplating Coping*

Configuring ourselves vis-à-vis our research topic so that we are comfortable with it is partially a matter of choice and partially a matter of trial and error. But studying violence also demands vocation (calling) and a bit of courage. One can get used to studying the contours, structures and dynamics of mass violence (on the macro- and meso-levels), but never really to the details—the micro-violence, the actual killing, torture, rape, blood, tears – which involves individuals and emotions. Some of us learn it the hard way. Some of us can prepare. My theoretical and library-based familiarity with mass violence as a student helped in understanding contextual and conceptual contours as well as the complexity of sources and processes of corroboration. My classes in cultural anthropology, oral history and journalism, to some extent, prepared me to approach and value the genre, procedure and significance of the 'interview' (communication). But that was it. This was the baggage I brought to my first field inquiries from 2003 onwards. Nothing (and at that time nobody at the university) could have ever properly equipped and prepared me how to interview drugged-up children, triumphant mass murderers, desperate refugees, rogue pirates and genocide survivors. The test then was to assess their credibility and reliability. To only focus on the forensics, not on the emotions behind them. Even while prepared, every first encounter with witnesses and other sources of violence is just hard. And it always remains hard. My path was only slightly softened by deep interest and having purpose.

Cause is crucial – no matter what it is: professional, private, or both. Nobody studies violence because it is 'just a job.' We all have our reasons, of which the personal (at least in my experience, also dealing with students from violence-ridden countries) could be the trickiest drivers – but when it turns into a passion, one might even call it a calling. I have had one colleague who wrote in their application letter that they "lived for genocide studies." Mine was, although once inspired by family history, driven by a craving to know. My goal has always been to get as close as possible to a probable reconstruction of the complex and truthful empirical reality of the root causes, courses and consequences of atrocity and core crimes – and ultimately, through multiperspectivity, understand and explain why things happen(ed). It is about comprehension. This requires looking at both the big and small pictures through various lenses, and it is where I think the most important balancing happens – as to what to study, why, how, when and where, to the effect that we can best cope with our topic.

Conviction is an important layer of cause. Even while always driven by the same fact-based purpose and goals, my professional research work – my craft – has had various objectives and drives. For AI, it was *documenting* human rights violations in Liberia, and *conceptualizing* transitional justice strategies, and *monitoring* SCSL trials. For the UNICTR, and later for the ICC, the focus was to contribute to the quasi-judicial (prosecutorial) process of *fact-seeking, fact-finding and fact-ascertainment* on mass violence. As an investigative journalist (2007–2012) *covering* human rights and international justice, it was often raw factual *reporting* on the ground (writing first drafts of history) and critically *observing* and *questioning* the power politics of history, truth and justice at play in the legal-humanitarian industries of international and transitional justice (i.e., the convictions of others). As a scholar, focusing on the (contemporary) history of mass violence and transitional justice, it is about further *unraveling* processes, dynamics and languages of violence and justice – and to *reflect* critically on the non-scholarly fields I had worked in previously. As a teacher, it is about *transferring* experiences. Regardless of the objectives, my orientation, or scholarly conviction, if you will, has always been to try and remain as observant of fact and behavior, impartial from anyone and anything, and critical towards everybody and everything as much as possible – without becoming unkind and cynical. Cynicism and unnecessary contrarianism, in my experience, are in no way helpful in our field and to our field.

Despite a clear investigative cause and conviction in our craft, which equally serve as pockets of compartmentalization, there are things you see, hear and feel that do not leave one cold. I have felt the tensions of imminent war in Côte d'Ivoire. I have covered ethno-political riots in Kenya. I have witnessed ethnic killing and persecution in Ethiopia. I have been spied on and intimidated during field work. In 2022, I crossed İstiklal Avenue in Istanbul, exactly at the point where, 2 hours later, a bomb attacker killed six people and injured 81 others. In various ways, I have felt the sensation of (imminent) violence. I have found that the best way to deal with this is conversation*:* to talk about experiences with friends, family, colleagues, professionals, students, graduates and strangers. At NIOD, we all study violence. It is thus not only common practice to discuss our work with colleagues but also to be given the opportunity to have a yearly professional mental check-up and counseling if necessary. It is easier to process and talk about my own experiences than to deal with the emotions of those people we regard, which, in turn, also requires processing. Over the many years, I have (over)heard – through interviews, conversations and in courtrooms – the personal stories of several thousand victims, survivors, bystanders, perpetrators, accomplices and even pirates. Some years ago, for example, I spent about 2 weeks sitting in a small courtroom in between a group of aged torture victims and their former (also aged, now troubled) tormentor. You cannot simply ignore all these people's floating emotions and pathos – wrath, agony, disheartenment, despair, defiance, anxiety, sympathy, repentance, resilience, clemency, guilt, regret, satisfaction, justness and many more. Situations like this weigh on your shoulders. Internalizing it might get us into trouble. Externalization can, in fact, be more helpful.

Creation is the uplifting antonym of destruction. What I do with experiences and emotions – my own, and those of others – is to include them in my writing. Doing so also commits the real atmosphere to paper. It is a process of externalization, finding words, looking for meaning and finding solace. To do so is to weave, to narrate: to create stories. Emotions are part and parcel of violence and of the study of the ecosystem of reckoning with violence. It makes absolute sense to include them in our scholarly exposure, whether that is *writing* books, articles and blogs, *presenting* papers, *discussing* findings, *debating* each other, or *talking* about our research on podcasts. This ordinary academic work might already be curative in itself, but we can further channel emotions too through other expressions – through our creativity, at home and at work. Cooking, for example, I experience as ultimately relaxing and distracting. As much as cycling, running and swimming. Additionally, for a while (and together with colleagues from the field, including former Nuremberg-prosecutors and criminologists), I have participated in theater plays about violence and (in)justices – using discourse, dialog and dance. These performances have even included war-affected comedians from war-affected countries (Burundi, Rwanda, DR Congo). Other colleagues, too, are involved in the arts or include the arts in their work. While such expressionism externalizes our sentiments (and invites emotive responses from audiences), we could also operationalize them in our scholarship. If you ask me, "using all our senses" is a methodological skill massively undervalued, underappreciated and underpracticed – and hence, also undereducated. Yes, it might be much safer to stay put in the armchair, hiding in books and behind computers in libraries and cosmopolitan coffee bars. But being 'in the field' not only gets us closer to a holistic perception and reception of violence and its aftermath, but we can also better relate to it. Whether we like it or not (or find it scary, which I often do), studying violence actually demands from us to really look at it, to hear it, to smell it, to feel it. This is what it takes. I say that not to offend or trivialize colleagues who do not. I do so, rather, to underscore that, as we know the perils of 'the job,' it also becomes easier to recognize for oneself what one can and what one cannot do. Not everything that comes with this job is for everybody. We therefore distribute our labor; share the grief we regard, discuss and process. I have reached a point where I know that, for me, the most uncomfortable area of our field is interviewing victims. And I have colleagues who are much better at it. When studying criminals against humanity, on the other hand, I find that I am much calmer, while others find it frightening. I am also most comfortable looking at violence through the lens of law. I find it the safest and most crystalline of lenses, as it allows for detachment from ugly facts and stories through the sanitization of juridical vernacular, legal arguments and formal technicalities and procedures.

3 Teaching Mass Violence

Correlations matter in our field. And studying and teaching go hand in hand. Over the past 15 years, as a research professor, I have designed and taught MAlevel courses on comparative genocide studies and transitional justice (the phenomenon of (not) dealing with the past). I have done so at several colleges: the University of Amsterdam (UvA), the National University of Rwanda (NUR), Utrecht University (UU) and Leiden University College (LUC). Since 2011, I have been a permanent member of the research and teaching faculty of a selective international master's program in 'Holocaust and Genocide Studies' (HGS), which is offered by the NIOD and accredited by the history department of the faculty of humanities at the UvA.[6] On the compulsory curriculum is a Core Course in Holocaust and Genocide Studies (18 ECTS) and a research thesis (18 ECTS). Our Core Course comprises concepts, methodologies, sources (historiography), perspectives, cases (roughly from mass violence in Congo Free State from the 1890s to Central and Southwest Asia in 2025), and varying topics. In 2025, major themes included slavery, colonialism, starvation, hunger, ecocide, perpetration and transitional justice. The research thesis is the student's largest project (stretching the entire academic year) and must cover a scholarly case or theme of mass violence. As the degree is in history, the thesis must be based on original and primary research sources (archives, fieldwork and/or interviews). On the side, students have been offered thematic electives (6 ECTS each), including: 'Topics in Holocaust Studies,' 'Topics in Comparative Genocide Studies,' 'Perpetrator Studies,' 'Topics in Transitional Justice,' 'Mass Violence in Africa,' 'Mass Violence in the Middle East,' and 'Mass Violence in the Balkans.' Our aim is to familiarize students, as much as possible within the restricted space of a year's study, with the causes, actualities and consequences of key historical cases of mass atrocity since the 1600s, key concerns in the field and the craft of studying mass violence. Amongst our group of graduates are professors, scholars and researchers, as well as international criminal lawyers, judges, war crimes police, intelligence officers, diplomats, politicians, parliamentarians, journalists, humanitarians, trauma counselors and museum curators. And off course, there are former students with no professional connection to the topic they studied (including chefs, tailors and artists). Not everybody wants to or can stay in the field. Our students also come from everywhere. Over the past 20 years, students came from all continents. And from a multitude of unexpected disciplines, such as (social) psychology, sometimes via personal experiences fleeing violence themselves, to equally unexpected professions, such as medical doctors.

6 See Holocaust and Genocide Studies, https://www.uva.nl/shared-content/programmas/en/masters/holocaust-and-genocide-studies-history/holocaust-and-genocide-studies.html?cb (retrieved February 20, 2025).

Comparison to similar programs is difficult. As a faculty of senior researchers based at an established specialized institute (operative since May 1945), we teach mostly about our own research and areas of interest, expertise and experience. As research professors, we are close to the topics we teach about. I have taught courses mainly on topics I work or have worked on as a researcher or journalist: (genocidal) violence, international atrocity crimes and justice in Africa. Such intimacy we also further seek to provide to our students – a select group with a maximum of 20. We have classes in our institute's main meeting room (a former cozy and intimate dining room, built in the 1890s, which in the 1940s also served as the courtroom of a Dutch war crimes tribunal). We take them on tours (through the former Jewish quarters in Amsterdam, around a former transit camp in Westerbork, and to the tribunals in The Hague). They meet with some of our institute's permanent and visiting specialists and scholars. We invite them to our conferences, workshops and film-symposia, and organize 'meet and greet' sessions with key people in the field. They work in our specialized in-house library, where they have immediate access to our archives and archivists. What we cannot offer, the University of Amsterdam provides – such as student counseling and study advice. But we do try to make our students part of a community.

Cautiousness is something that we provide by default because we also expect something from our students. Our program is so incredibly specific (in fact, our actual trigger warning is already in the name of our program: we deal with mass categorical murder) that we expect students to have made a conscious and realistic decision to join. They know what to expect, at least to the level that they will study violence and its consequences.

Coursework in our program is designed towards knowledge, skills and insight. But also, we train students to deal with complications, constraints and conflicts (of interest) in our field. In our first classes, we problematize that: (1) emotions might bias our forensic eye, (2) moral acting does not equal quality inquiry, (3) politics always diffuse all sources, and (4) law's orientation (which is quite dominant in genocide studies) is only determining individual criminal responsibility and meting out punishment – not, for instance, looking at motive. As research professors, we teach students how to research mass atrocity violence. In doing so, we substantively focus on global, regional and local historical contexts. In addition, we cover various concepts (what is mass violence?), theories (what possibly explains mass violence and its perpetration in culturally, economically and politically varying contexts?), and perspectives (history, sociology, anthropology, political science and law), as well as agency (perpetrators, victims, bystanders). We further focus specifically on the how: how to approach genocide, what do we know about genocide, what can we – and cannot – know about genocide, and to approach the complex plurality of documentary and human sources about genocide? This 'how' is crucial and determinative.

Colleague, friend and Professor of Holocaust and Genocide Studies Uğur Ümit Üngör has written about the positionality of the empirical scholar in genocide studies: what promises the field offers (empirically and conceptually), what pitfalls researchers face, and what problems to watch out for. His article, '*Studying Mass Violence: Pitfalls, Problems, and Promises*' (Üngör, 2012) is required reading for our students – and it informs and assists my discussion below. In short, we aim to make students aware that the scholarly study of mass violence (an inherently political and politicized topic) demands extreme vigilance regarding emotional, moral, juridical and political approaches, biases and engagements (of ourselves, of those we study and of the sources we use). I find them useful academically (as they protect our craft), but also personally. It offers tools and perspectives that help caution and protect us from getting into trouble professionally and personally.

Caution relates to our omnipresent politics. Among the most precarious ways through which we can perceive violence, Üngör writes, is through our own politics. Perhaps even more precarious is perceiving violence through the politics of others: how to deal, for example, with the work of lobby groups (such as Human Rights Watch), who also produce research work? Our task, and our biggest challenge, is not to confuse our science with our politics – and trickier: of those we sometimes rely on for information. Though the two may often be inextricably intertwined, a true understanding of the connections between them is a crucial element of robust scholarship when studying mass categorical violence. Mass atrocity violence is itself always, whether implicit or explicit, political: both on the macro- (e.g., governmental) and the micro- (e.g., household) level. Researching it is thus inherently very politically sensitive, as is dealing with its legacy. Studying mass violence sometimes requires that we disarm ourselves, as much as possible, from our inherent (and often subconscious) political, moral and legal views. That is a massive challenge in itself: it is easy to be against genocide and violence, to lobby for peace, and to condemn those doing violence – to say they are 'evil.' But studying violence deeply, and indeed teaching it, requires going so much further beyond these stances – often into less comfortable places and dealing with less comfortable emotions. Scholars also have to critically engage with actors that proclaim to 'do good,' or with those whom we might disagree with. We can warn our students that reliable scholarship – that is, looking deeply at a topic, trying to understand it and then explaining it – is at its most concrete when we can pinpoint where our opinions and politics lie within it, and, yes, in some cases, remove them.

Considerably easier, but equally crucial, is training students to at least identify and take into account the politics of others. Historians start our professional training by doing this most fundamental of tasks: 'source critique.' Everyone associated with mass violence politicizes, including many scholars and academics. State governments either deny, look away from, charge other states with genocide – or (occasionally) more subtly manipulate research into such issues through funding schemes. Victims or victim group activists demand recognition, justice and reparations. Perpetrators deny being perpetrators and blame others – including their victims. Bystanders, by definition, stand by on the side of violence: attempting (in good faith) or claiming (often in less good faith) to remain 'neutral.' Critics and opposition groups fight back, politically and at times violently. The 'international community,' if one can speak of any in this polarized world, condemns, approves, looks back, or intervenes when it deems it necessary – or opportune. Human rights groups, humanitarians and lawyers scandalize, lobby and promote or condemn. That they are 'non-governmental' does not mean that they are not political. Similarly, some academics and applied scientists theorize and recommend policy on how the violence could or 'should' be stopped, and who 'should' be held accountable. We can go on listing individuals and groups that politicize in one way or another. It is important that scholars challenge themselves to question political emotions by trying to treat every individual and group as political actors in a power struggle and, as such, include them as part of the analysis. What is most pertinent (and perhaps even more challenging) is for scholars to train their students to do so as well.

Caution, in the second instance, relates to our senses of justice, lawfulness and righteousness. Equally as detrimental to our perceptions of mass violence is to perceive mass violence too strongly, or exclusively, through the international legal lens and to describe it solely, or even primarily, using sterile legal jargon. Frequently, the lexicon of atrocity crimes is weaponized (by, *inter alia*, lobbyists, advocacy groups, critics, opposition groups and States) in service of political rhetoric, litigation, moral outcry, diplomatic interests and identity-politics. But the wanton allegation that mass atrocities are perpetrated through public scandalization does not always mean that there is unpolluted or unmanipulated evidence of crime, or that the argument is the only inference from the available evidence. If recent years have shown us anything, it is that the idea of international law as being uncontroversial and apolitical is a fiction. Take the very concept of genocide, for example. It was a Western neologism coined in the early 1940s by Raphael Lemkin to describe the historical phenomenon of the physical and cultural mass destruction of social groups. But international law – the outcome of an international power politics of negotiated consensus amongst elite empires – hollowed out Lemkin's original conceptualization, definition and meaning, rendering it useless as an analytical tool, and, as we are now seeing, by 2025, almost as useless as a legal one. Stripped out of the context of political structures and social collectives, while simultaneously subject to political strategies, it was mutilated into an individually punishable crime under international law in 1951. Individualizing the perpetration of a crime committed by masses exclusively against collectives, the Genocide Convention has proven to be ineffective as a prosecutable crime. That is precisely what many of its political authors foresaw: it was meant to express the core sentiment of the UN that a Holocaust should never happen again, but not to account for its own structures. It is also, in this way, exemplary of how atrocity law works: continuously straitjacketing and selecting focus. We can see this (non)focus in action through the post-Second World War's victor's justice at Nuremberg, colonial justice in Tokyo and non-justice for Italy's atrocities in North Africa.

Comparably, the long and mostly Western-stirred history of the *Geneva Conventions* (negotiated whilst its negotiator-states fought violent colonial wars against indigenous peoples, e.g., the Netherlands in Indonesia) shows that, in actuality, international humanitarian law is more political than humanitarian. Legalism, or a legalistic perspective, is not the same as a political gaze, but it is equally binding and blinding. Üngör – and many other historians and sociologists – tells us to avoid it and its lexicon, or at the very least to treat it with caution. Its end goals – namely judgment and punishment – are completely different from those of the scholar, and especially of the student: contextualization, comprehension and clarification. Indeed, lawyers often treat the past not as if it were history, but as if it were a crime. They criminalize history, perceive historical events as 'crimes,' see historical acts and categorize historical agents as 'criminal,' and orient towards criminal prosecution, judicial conviction and social exclusion of individuals from society as punishment. There are two fundamental problems with this: seeing history as something that is prosecutable and punishable is a bias that all too easily contradicts scholarly historical truth-finding processes – a holistic inquisitorial process aimed at explaining why certain things happen. Furthermore, in modern international law proceedings, any search for structures, causes and meaning of mass violence (the essence of researching violence) stops once an individual conviction is secured.

Caution, in the third instance, centers around our moral gaze on the world: perceiving the world with a sense of good versus evil. The legalistic downsides elaborated on in the previous paragraph do have methodological upsides: a legal perspective on mass violence creates a comfortable distance from reality, allowing space to sanitize, but also to compartmentalize and analyze. The law can step aside from emotions. Another scholarly and teaching pitfall is that it becomes too easy to moralize. Starting investigations on the moral premise that mass violence is bad, evil and inhumane is natural, even understandable. But, Üngör points out, it is not helpful in trying to understand the essence of humanity's violence among itself. A moralized view can all too easily render ahistorical, asociological and unsophisticated analyses and (re)presentations of the world as being unrealistically divided between good and evil, sane and insane, moral and immoral. This does not add any substance to our understanding of mass violence – other than recognizing it as a particular and problematic genre in historiography. Moralization, however, also serves as a tool to deal with the emotions tied to violence. Pretending that we ourselves are not inclined to violence creates a comfortable distance. But reckoning – as moral beings – with humanity's worst actions against itself also challenges us to deal with the difficult emotions that arise when studying it and to communicate our strategies for dealing with it to students.

Caution is also all about our emotions. Our morals are shaped largely by our emotions and passions, and to some extent, too, by those of the people around us. As humans, we act, react, and think emotionally. We are emotional creatures. It is through 'reason' – the history, philosophy and ethics of science have held for millennia – that we detach and disconnect from our emotions. Such rationalizing and rationalization provide a layer of protection. This is also what we tell our students: there is a fine line between involvement and detachment. Yes, our topic triggers emotions of anger, sadness, helplessness, uselessness, disgust, etcetera. And indeed, some of us see our topics pass by in our dreams – I remember dreaming about Liberia's (un)civil war when monitoring the trial of Charles Taylor, hearing witness after witness testify about how people were hacked, smashed and even eaten. Dealing with mass violence can be straining. But to what extent – beyond our basic human sympathy and our use of our emotional sensors as scholarly tools – do we serve society or individuals (through our research) with our sharing of personal feelings? Why confront a Rwandan genocide survivor with our personal feelings of guilt? What can forcibly displaced people in Syria buy from our apologies? What are the healthy emotional boundaries of our involvement – towards those whom we research, and towards ourselves? Referring to journalist Iris Chang's suicide (believed to be related to depression caused by studying Japanese war crimes in China), Üngör warns us about the perils of "excessive involvement" – to the extent that we might hurt ourselves. On another end of empathy, Üngör argues (by means of a personal example of researching the Armenian genocide in Turkey), looms the problem that the emotions of individual victims, or those valorized by victims' groups, might contaminate (by influencing and over-influencing) our scholarship. Thus, we can (unwittingly) fall into the trap of becoming entrenched in and, moreover, blinded by their relatable emotions but also implicated in their political causes. Lastly, our passions might also blur our field of study – through the enforced sacralization of suffering by victims – as if the very real and tangible violence against them is unfathomable (unimaginable), that they 'enjoy moral immunity,' and that there are inherent taboos on complex and ambivalent questions. Trivialization, concludes Üngör, looms at the other end of the spectrum and could be a trap into deliberate genocide denial – a highly particular emotion in itself.

Caution, finally, collects all the above and involves knowing ourselves and recognizing our positionality and the ingrained biases we hold – i.e., our intimate convictions. All the above classifications of fundamental biases may distort objective, neutral and meticulous investigation of mass atrocity violence – to the extent that objectivity or neutrality is even possible in the first place. Reflecting soberly, we could consider that scientific excellence is best secured if our research is carried out, as Üngör argues, in a dispassionate, amoral, apolitical and non-juridical way. However, our entire field (particularly genocide studies and transitional justice) is performed by many passionate agents, often based on a particular moral worldview and stirred towards achieving liberal political goals. The last pitfall is thus that, through our inborn biases, we risk becoming enemies of our own profession (Bouwknegt, 2020). In many ways, our field (particularly in the 'West' or 'Global North') is premised on a very particular *ideological bias*, which favors democratic values, Judeo-Christian-informed human rights and rule-of-law-type political systems in which we scholars feel most comfortable and secure. These are not epistemological tools but rather elements of a broader *universalist bias* – namely, the sentiment that our 'Western' way of doing things (including coping and reckoning with emotions triggered by atrocity) is globally applicable and appropriate. Other biases in our field include certain sentiments regarding justice, accountability and truth – namely, the sentiment that (doing) justice involves ascribing individual criminal guilt rather than collective reckoning (also see Mamdani, 2020). A final bottleneck may be *witness bias*: the assumption that traumatized victims and survivors of the most horrible atrocities do not lie and cannot be mistaken. Navigating our inherent biases – which certainly emotionally inform our intellectual approaches and perspectives – is hugely complex, and we cannot easily switch them off and turn into robots. How to deal with them (particularly across myriad cultural settings) cannot be taught, other than to insist that we work in full transparency and acknowledgment of our own biases (as much as our politics, morals and sentiments) and our own 'positionality,' for instance. It is not that we should not have emotions, convictions and predispositions. They are informed by an interplay between our mental faculties and senses (hearing, seeing, smelling, feeling, speaking). The crux is to be acutely aware of the sentiments that bias us – about the ones we hold ourselves as much as the ones held by our sources. A sense of cultural modesty and emotive honesty works best towards a healthy balance in simultaneously caring for our empirical research, the people we research, ourselves, our students and so forth – as a community.

4 Conclusion

I think experienced researchers have grand responsibilities (professional and personal) towards our subjects, towards ourselves and towards our students: young people who are usually coming in from the cold to a very heated and politicized field. This brings me back to the problem of empathy. As scholars of humanity (speaking as a historian, and from the field of the humanities), we ought to strike a balance between our subject (which is the human condition and humanity's violent nature) not leaving us cold and to absolute coldness – to not care at all. An immense pitfall to the human as scholar or the scholar as human, I find, is to either have too much empathy or to lose empathy entirely, because we are human – researcher and those researched. Through emotions, we relate to the emotions of those affected by violence (which, at its core, is an act of emotion – usually a mixture of fear and anger), and without having emotions ourselves, we cannot analyze, understand and explain them. Moreover, without empathy for our students, we cannot teach about violence. But how to carefully balance empathy for ourselves as scholars and persons, empathy (as much as our antipathy) for the themes, topics and people we study, as well as maintaining empathy towards the dispassionateness our sciences require? These are crucial questions, also raised in class, to which we have no crystal-clear answers. Even while we can never tame mass violence itself, we could aim at taming the phantom pains they cause. Care within our community is crucial. We have no standard cure. What we can offer and share, however, is a consciousness of the general promises, problems and pitfalls of our labor – and share with students our own established mechanisms of circumnavigating them. Our root responsibility – as professors, or as experienced experts who also teach – is to insist on carefulness: to train students to treat our scientific craft with care, but also to be careful while performing our science, and to be caring for those they research, for themselves and for their peers. Studying mass violence logically requires both conscientiousness and cautiousness. That is, admittedly, very difficult, if not impossible, to teach. But we can extend our hand – including by telling our own stories and bringing stories together. I hope to have added to this conversation, which continues in this volume and elsewhere.

My gratitude goes to my family (for thinking along about family history), and particularly to Lucy J. Gaynor, Ph.D. researcher at the University of Amsterdam (UvA) and at the NIOD Institute for War, Holocaust and Genocide Studies, for their conversations, comments, critique, edits and input, which greatly improved this essay.

References

Adler, N. (2018). *Understanding the Age of Transitional Justice. Crimes, Courts, Commissions, and Chronicling*. New Brunswick: Rutger's University Press.

Bouwknegt, T. B., Nauta, B. (2023). A Cage Went in Search of a Bird: On the Politics of Condemnation, Compensation and Convalescence. *Journal of International Criminal Justice*, 21(1), pp. 185–209.

Bouwknegt, T. B. (2020). Investigating International Crimes: Pitfalls, Problems and Promises. In: X. Agirre Aranburu, M. Bergsmo, S. De Smet, C. Stahn (Eds.). *Quality Control in Criminal Investigation*, Brussels: Torkel Opsahl Academic EPublisher, pp. 67–113.

Cole, T. (2015). Unmournable Bodies, *The New Yorker*, retrieved 23 June 2025 from https://www.newyorker.com/culture/cultural-comment/unmournable-bodies

De Swaan, A. (2015). *The Killing Compartments. The Mentality of Mass Murder*. Yale University Press.

Groen, P., van Dissel, A., Loderichs, M. Limpach, R. Brocades Zaalberg, T. (2021) *Krijgsgeweld en kolonie. Opkomst en ondergang van Nederland als koloniale mogendheid (1816-2010)*. Amsterdam: Boom.

Huyse, L. (2009). *All Things Pass Except the Past*. Van Halewyck: Kessel-Lo.

Limpach, R. (2016). *De brandende kampongs van Generaal Spoor*. Amsterdam: Uitgeverij Boom.

Moyn, S. (2010). *The Last Utopia. Human Rights in History*. Cambridge: Harvard University Press.

Overy, R. (2014). "Ordinary men," extraordinary circumstances: Historians, social psychology, and the Holocaust. *Journal of Social Issues*, 70(3), pp. 515–530.

Schabas, W. (2023). *The International Legal Order's Colour Line. Racism, Racial Discrimination, and the Making of International Law*. Oxford: Oxford University Press.

Sontag, S. (2003). *Regarding the Pain of Others*. New York: Picador.

Scarface (1994). 'I Have Seen a Man Die', On *The Diary*, Rap-A-Lot; Noo Trybe.

Üngör, U. Ü. (2012). Studying Mass Violence: Pitfalls, Problems, and Promises, *Genocide Studies and Prevention: An International Journal*, 7(1), pp. 68–80.

Wintour, P. (2024). Gaza at risk of becoming 'graveyard of international law' – Palestinian lawyer, *The Guardian*, retrieved 23 June 2025 from https://www.theguardian.com/world/2024/oct/15/gaza-at-risk-of-becoming-graveyard-of-international-law-palestinian-lawyer.

CHAPTER 5

Emotions and Ethics in Teaching Mass Atrocities Using Archives

Andy Aydın-Aitchison and Annalisa Battista

1 Introduction

In this chapter, we reflect on the ethical and emotional aspects of teaching a course on atrocity crimes, making heavy use of, and requiring students to research using, the online archives of the International Criminal Tribunal for the former Yugoslavia (ICTY). Using these archives in teaching raises the same ethical issues encountered in research, particularly duties to those whose lives, experiences and trauma are represented in the archives. Due to potential emotional responses to sensitive material, the course also generates an ethical responsibility towards students as audience members and co-participants in researching violence. The course aims to encourage independent ethical reflection and practice on the part of the students and to compare this with current institutional frameworks for research ethics.[1]

After discussing scholarship on teaching sensitive material, we introduce the course, *Criminologies of Atrocity*, outline our data and methods, and present an analysis of the course in terms of its emotional and ethical dimensions. Ultimately, through an account of students' emotional and ethical journeys, we argue for the importance of delivering courses which do not shy away from dealing with difficult and sensitive material, as these are precisely the parts of a law degree that offer students some of the most meaningful spaces to reflect on and develop their ethics as researchers and as potential future lawyers.

Both authors conduct research using ICTY archives (e.g., as Aitchison, 2014; Battista, 2023), and the course is informed by this. Aydın-Aitchison designed the course, piloted it, and was the lead instructor for five of six iterations. Battista was the lead instructor for the fifth iteration of the course, having previously worked on the course as a Teaching Assistant.

1 Researchers at the University of Edinburgh School of Law require ethical approval for research involving human data-subjects, regardless of whether those are active participants or subjects of data in archives.

© 2026 THE AUTHOR(S) | HTTPS://DOI.ORG/10.1163/9789004754720-007

2 Scholarship on Teaching and Learning Sensitive Topics

Lowe and Jones (2010, p. 2) argue that "any topic can become sensitive if emotional responses are raised, if there are competing explanations about events, if there are political differences…" Political violence and atrocity crimes fall within this territory and are both emotionally demanding (Biddolph, 2021) and ethically charged (Subotić, 2020), resulting in a higher degree of sensitivity. Lowe and Jones (2010, p. 1) note a wealth of material on researching sensitive topics but less on teaching. The former is still useful to instructors reflecting on parallels between ethical and emotional issues in research and pedagogy. Here, our primary focus is on the scholarship of teaching and learning. This literature is most strongly developed in relation to sexual violence (Bedera, 2021; Heath, 2005; Nenadović & Somun, 2021); racism and hate crime (Gibbs, 2021; Heath, 2005, p. 130); violence, interpersonal violence, and trauma (Dalton, 2015; Gladden et al., 2023; Jenney et al., 2021); and genocide education (Kearney et al., 2012; Sadique & Tangen, 2022). In many instances, the focus of this body of work relates to the likelihood of teaching students with lived-experience of the phenomenon. This is less prominent in genocide education but remains relevant as we teach students from atrocity-affected communities. The primary focus of the literature is on student experience, but Nikischer (2019) provides an exception to this. While work on the emotional impact of research (e.g., Biddolph, 2021) has much to offer to instructors reflecting on their own experience of teaching atrocity-related material, there are important differences: instead of working alone or in close research teams, instructors work with a broad group of students, often with potentially limited prior study of atrocity, and have the responsibility for leading the class. Finally, Gladden et al. (2023) found a lack of 'effectiveness research' in their systematic review of teaching methods designed to reduce the potential for secondary forms of stress or trauma, or traumatization, when delivering trauma content. Rather, many texts offer instructors' own reflections and observations, although these can be thorough and systematic (e.g., the fully auto-ethnographic approach by Nikischer, 2019). While our study includes some basic quantitative evidence, we offer no measures of effect. Rather, by combining an account of course delivery with survey data, focus groups, and our own reflections as instructors, we aim to provide a robust interrogation of the place of ethics and emotion in teaching on atrocity, in particular in teaching through the ICTY archives. In the remainder of this review of literature, we identify prominent issues in teaching sensitive topics and some of the practical strategies instructors employ.

2.1 *Sensitive Material, Emotions and Harm*

Negative emotions experienced by students or staff in relation to sensitive materials in a pedagogical setting dominate accounts: hopelessness, anger, sadness (Gladden et al., 2023, p. 85; Kearney et al., 2012, p. 349); fear, pain, stigma (Heath, 2005, p. 134); guilt, feeling overwhelmed (Nikischer 2019; Kearney et al., 2012, p. 350); pessimism, defeatism, and powerlessness (Nenadović & Somun, 2021, p. 71); disgust (Sadique & Tangen, 2022, p. 552). These emotional states or experiences have both ethical and pedagogical implications. Dalton (2015, p. 6) observes that while instructors have a moral duty to "minimize the potentially deleterious impact of exposing students to sensitive materials," this is not a guarantee that materials will neither upset nor disturb students. Indeed, he notes that it is the 'troubling' nature of these topics that drives many students to learn. Recognizing that students may already carry past wounds, Jenney et al. (2021, p. 798) focus on not inflicting *further* harm. Negative effects and mitigating strategies are largely discussed under two headings: 'triggers' and vicarious trauma or other secondary stress reactions. Triggers, which can reactivate past trauma, are specific to individuals (Bedera, 2021, p. 268) and, therefore, unpredictable (Dalton, 2020, pp. 91–92). Vicarious trauma (McCann & Pearlman, 1990), secondary traumatic stress, and the related phenomenon of compassion fatigue (Figley 1995; Figley, 2002) are more general and are not specific to prior personal experience of trauma. The origin of these concepts relates to professionals working in the medical sector, social work, and counseling, where exposure to others' trauma is prevalent. Secondary trauma relates to long-term exposure and short-term reactions to particular interactions (McCann & Pearlman, 1990, p. 132), so it is a relevant consideration for instructors. Effects include intrusive images, sleeplessness and anxiety (McCann & Pearlman, 1990, pp. 131–132) and longer-term negative changes in five areas of practitioners' cognition: "safety, trust, esteem, intimacy, and control" (Baird & Kracen, 2006, p. 182). While these reactions lack the individual specificity of a link to prior trauma, they still vary across individuals. Even if exposure to sensitive material is limited in terms of occurring as one feature of a varied workload, and potentially for a limited period (e.g., in the context of a semester-long elective), instructors should be aware of the potential for negative reactions and harm in and *beyond* the class-room. This final point is not always explicitly recognized. Writing specifically on remote learning in the context of a global pandemic, Parrotta et al. (2021, p. 327) call for mindfulness that students are digesting the material independently. Students on regular on-campus courses also spend most of their time studying away from instructor supervision. In both online and on-campus versions of our own course, 90 per cent of allocated study time is *outside* face-to-face seminars, so students work independently the majority of the time.

2.2 *The Ethics of Representing Political Violence in the Classroom*

Aside from negative emotions, stress, and trauma, further issues arise from using material relating to atrocity. They mirror many of those in the literature on research ethics (see, e.g., Campbell, 2017; Houge, 2023; Subotić, 2020) and victims (e.g., Golubović, 2019; Houge, 2023, p. 1252; Schwöbel-Patel, 2018). Reflecting on how researchers represent political violence, Houge (2023, pp. 1245, 1251–53) unpacks the challenge of navigating tensions between respecting the agency of victims who have decided to share their story, concerns around sensationalism and instrumentalizing suffering, and the effect that the sensational can have in obscuring enduring social and political barriers that shape life after peace agreements are signed. At the same time, the distancing effect, stepping back to give more generic accounts stripped of horrific detail, can block certain types of understanding. In trying to comprehend the actions of Nazi *Ordnungspolizei*, shooting naked Jewish men, women, and children, it matters to know that the killers were confronted immediately and viscerally with the results of their violence (see Matthäus, 1996, p. 139). Representations of violence in writing interface with pedagogical imperatives when we teach about that violence.

Although much of the material on teaching and researching extreme violence carries a suitably cautionary tone, one strand is oriented toward hope. As Dalton, above, noted, some students decide to study these issues precisely because they are troubled by them. They learn in order to work towards a less violent world. Others may not have the same motive, but for both sets of students, working through difficult material has the potential for growth (Parrotta et al., 2021, p. 329). Drawing on the work of Ahmed, Seear et al. (2019, p. 490) note that our emotions have a political dimension and can lead us to action. The aspiration for students to go through a transformative process of reflection and to act in line with this is a common theme in genocide education (e.g., Sadique & Tangen, 2022, p. 523). Neglecting the emotional aspect of this does not make it go away; it simply obscures it (Sutton, 2024).

2.3 *Ethical Obligations and Good Practice in the Classroom*

Several authors share examples of the practices they have developed in response to the implications of bringing sensitive material into a pedagogical setting. 'Trigger warnings' are common (Bedera, 2021, p. 267; Dalton, 2015, p. 7; Gladden et al., 2023, p. 3391; Parrotta et al., 2021, p. 325), although some are reluctant to use this terminology. Bedera (2021, p. 267) notes that such warnings tend to put the onus on individual students, rather than on the instructor, to ensure a safe classroom. Contrasting the specific psychiatric and psychological roots of the term with its looser use in popular discourse, Dalton (2020) avoids applying the term to his practice. Nonetheless, he seeks to prepare the students with advance notification of the nature of the material to be covered. Accepting Bedera's point about a duty to ensure safety, this kind of upfront transparency also respects students' autonomy as decision-makers. Again, mirroring the research literature, the scholarship on teaching and learning suggests the importance of recognizing that emotional responses are normal (Dalton, 2015, p. 9; Gladden et al., 2023, p. 3391; compare to Stanko, 1997, p. 79). Talking about emotions upfront has several benefits. Students will have valuable information for making decisions. Heath (2005, p. 136) compares this to informed consent practices in research; their own emotional reactions are normalized; and it creates an opportunity to discuss the ways in which we handle and work with emotions, including accessing support and what formal support services are there for students (Bedera, 2021, p. 267). It also helps to frame a discussion around what Dalton (2015, p. 7) calls the "terms of exposure." This includes allowing students to absent themselves from class without needing to give an explanation (Bedera, 2021, p. 267; Gladden et al., 2023, p. 3391; Dalton, 2020, p. 97), but also includes setting boundaries and practices around the discussion of sensitive material (e.g., Gladden et al., 2023, p. 3391; Dalton, 2015, p. 7; Dalton, 2020, p. 97). As well as explicitly setting out guidelines for good practice, instructors can act as models of compassion and integrity in how they handle material and interact with others (Heath, 2005, p. 133). Dalton (2015, p. 9) suggests looking out for signs of emotional exhaustion, but as we note above, it is likely that students will be spending a large proportion of their time engaging with difficult material out of sight of instructors. As such, conversations about emotions, how to recognize them, and how to respond to them become important structures to support students during periods of independent study. Because of a duty of care towards students, most of the guidance on good practice focuses on mitigating the negative effects of dealing with difficult material. Heath (2005, p. 143) provides something of a balance by stressing the value of creating space for optimism when dealing with material that tends more to despair. Many of these elements of good practice are built into the delivery of *Criminologies of Atrocity*, and we were able to explore how students experience them in discussion with our focus groups.

3 The *Criminologies of Atrocity* Course and Its Use of ICTY Archives

We offer *Criminologies of Atrocity* to senior undergraduates, most of whom are taking a degree in Law, or Law with International Relations. After ten contact weeks, each with a 2-hour seminar or workshop, students have further time to work on their assessment. We assume approximately 200 hours of study time in total. The course begins with four weeks on the study of atrocity in criminology and other disciplines, with particular attention to perpetrators and victims. The last of these four weeks (Victims and Atrocity) introduces students to ICTY testimony for the first time, through the examination and cross-examination of Dr. Youssef Hajir, a medic in an emergency hospital in Sarajevo during the siege, in the *Karadžić* case. The fifth week introduces students to *The Yugoslav Wars of the 1990s* using Catherine Baker's (2015) book of the same title. Week six covers the work of the ICTY. Students are given court documents[2] to consider their potential use in criminological research. The final weeks focus on methodology and methods. The seventh week considers general issues in using court testimony as criminological data. Groups are assigned witness testimony from the ICTY archives and discussion prompts supporting an assessment of the value of the source for research purposes. Three computer laboratory-based weeks give students basic skills in the computer-assisted qualitative data analysis software package NVivo and let them start exploring the ICTY archives and analyzing transcripts of witness testimony for their assessment. The assessment requires students to write a research report in which they use the ICTY archives, including testimony from a minimum of four witnesses, to answer their own research question concerning either perpetrators or victims. Where the data allows, they are invited to come to a preliminary conclusion on substantive issues. Regardless of such conclusions, they are expected to give an assessment of the benefits and limitations of ICTY testimony as criminological data. This general description of the course shows that students encounter witness testimony from the ICTY archives both in and beyond the classroom, in pre-seminar reading, in class discussions, and in working towards their assignments (for a further discussion of the course, see Aydın-Aitchison, 2024).

Ethics are explicitly covered in the course at several points. In the initial seminar, we identify our own responsibility as instructors to the students, our collective responsibility to act ethically when researching in an archive of political violence, and the importance of self-care when dealing with emotionally demanding material. Students are introduced to Caitlin Biddolph's (2021) account of the emotional experience of researching in the ICTY archives. We

2 Case information sheet; indictment; trial judgment; transcripts of two complete examinations and cross-examinations of witnesses; and court exhibit.

talk through our experiences and ways of handling these, and identify support available to students. In the third week, dealing with different approaches to studying perpetrators, we discuss an extract from Jessica Stern's book *My War Criminal* (Stern, 2020a, 2020b) along with a response to the book (Zakaria, 2020). Combined with a cautionary reading on perpetrator research (Jessee, 2015), this always prompts a discussion of good and bad ethical practices in researching and representing atrocity perpetrators. The fourth week (on victims) draws on Campbell's (2017) work on researching war crimes, and on critical socio-legal and anthropological work problematizing hierarchies of victimhood (Golubović, 2019; Schwöbel-Patel, 2018). By looking at representations of victims in the media and on the stand at the tribunal, students are encouraged to think about the choices that are being made, and the choices that they will make as researchers. In week 7, students work closely on transcripts in groups. Supported by a reading from Subotić (2020), we ask students to reflect on our institutional research integrity framework and the extent to which it encourages good ethical reflection and practice for archival research on atrocity violence. Students are not required to go through this institutional process, but the course assignment does require them to explicitly address ethical issues in their own research.

Box 5.1 Extract from Course Handbook 2023–2024

Genocide, Crimes against Humanity, and War Crimes include some of the worst aspects of human behavior and inflict extreme suffering on large numbers of people based on their identity. While every effort has been made to develop an approach to the topic that is both analytic and sensitive, we will inevitably encounter accounts of brutality, suffering, and loss. With this in mind, please bear in mind the following:

- Please be self-aware and manage your time working on the course to avoid being overwhelmed by any such material
- It is OK to take time out from discussions or live seminars if you are having difficulties arising from any material we cover
- Please bear in mind the sensitivity of the material we are handling and treat it respectfully – behind the documents we are looking at, there are real lives, real communities
- Similarly, please treat each other sensitively and respectfully
- If you are having difficulties, please approach the Course Organizer. She has direct, personal experience of research using these materials
- Remember, there are university services such as the Listening Service run by the Chaplaincy and Counseling Service [URLs provided]

The course handbook, available to students assigned to the course before teaching commences, includes a section explaining that the course inevitably involves accounts of brutality, suffering, and loss (see Box 5.1). Up to the end of the fifth iteration of the course, we had not routinely included warnings about the nature of the course content at the point of course selection, assuming that the course title, *Criminologies of Atrocity*, would signal this clearly. Following the data collection for this chapter, further text has been added to the course summary to expand on this. In the next section, we outline the data before we analyze students' experiences of emotions during and after the course, as well as the ethical dimensions in terms of how they perceive our fulfillment of a duty of care and their own development as ethical scholars.

4 Data

There are three main sources of data for this study. In 2023, a survey was sent to all available students from the first four cohorts of the course. The survey covered several topics, including a final section on ethics. Of 115 students contacted, 49 per cent ($n = 56$) submitted responses. In 2024, we ran focus groups with students from the fourth and fifth cohorts. Three students (Caroline, Faris and Maddy) participated in the first group in February 2024 (FG1), just over a year after they completed the course. Four students (ACS, Balo, Chloe and Nina) joined a discussion in March 2024 (FG2.1), during the teaching phase of the course but before the final assignment. Both these groups met face-to-face. Students from FG2.1 reconvened for a hybrid meeting in May 2024 (FG2.2) after submitting assignments. These focus groups were transcribed and analyzed to explore specific emotions and related symptoms, triggers, responses, and ethics. The transcripts cover around 4 hours of conversation and just under 40,000 words. Finally, we engaged in reflective conversations on the data and our own experiences. The focus groups are not exhaustive but represent a range of students of different genders and backgrounds, including their connection to atrocity through intergenerational links and membership in communities impacted by contemporary atrocities, and on programs of study in Law and Social and Political Sciences. All research with students was undertaken after institutional ethical approval was secured.[3] For the survey, information was not collected on individual identity. For the focus groups, students provided their own preferred pseudonyms, which are used in the reporting of data here.

3 March 2023 and November 2023 respectively for the survey and focus groups.

5 Initial Survey Findings

The survey (see Aydın-Aitchison 2024, 542) asked questions concerning the extent to which students felt prepared for the kinds of sensitive material they would cover in the course, the way in which that material was handled, and the extent to which the course promoted wider thinking regarding ethical issues. The results (see Table 5.1) were largely, but not universally, positive. The survey invited free-text comments to elaborate on scores. Among seven comments, some reinforced the scoring, noting that they were well-prepared or were supported through the class in dealing with difficult material and in reflecting on ethical issues. Of these, two went further. One noted the upsetting experience of courses where graphic accounts of sexual violence came up without any advance warning or preparatory groundwork. The other noted that the kinds of things that could shock were not always the most graphic representations of violence, but other forms of cruelty, giving the example of Muslim prisoners being forced to eat pork. While one student indicated that they found the research ethics texts somewhat difficult, another took the opportunity to identify how they had learned to be more sensitive about language used in representations of perpetrators and victims. The quantitative findings point in a positive direction, and the comments indicate the value of messaging in the early stages of the course. The issues still merit further exploration, and for this, we used focus groups. In the following discussion, we draw primarily on a combination of our reflections on our own practice and the students' reflections on the course.

TABLE 5.1 Ethical issues, frequencies (%) and mean, "assess the extent to which…" (7-point scale, low to high, n = 56)

	1	2	3	4	5	6	7	Mean
…course guidance and instructor input prepared you for the nature of the material	0.0	1.8	5.4	3.6	19.6	26.8	42.9	5.93
…sensitive material was handled appropriately	0.0	0.0	1.8	1.8	5.4	17.9	73.2	6.59
…the course has helped you to identify and deal with ethical issues in other work or study contexts	1.8	1.8	5.4	17.9	23.2	25.0	25.0	5.34

6 Emotions and Atrocity Education: So I Let Myself Feel All of the Heavy Things

This section focuses on the emotional dimensions of the course, looking at the emotions experienced by students, the contexts in which these were experienced, the role that emotion played in some of their choices, how they responded to emotions, and, finally, some specific emotions in relation to their triggers. At the very beginning of FG1 and FG2.1, students were asked to write down the emotions they had felt in association with the course. This served as data collection, reflected in the word cloud in Figure 5.1 below, and provided prompts for subsequent discussions. These emotions are in line with those reported in the existing scholarship. In the word cloud, size reflects the frequency of words, ranging from 1 for the smallest (e.g., horror, detached, faith) through to 5 for the largest (e.g., sad). The focus groups spent more time exploring the most commonly reported emotional states. Several emotions may be grouped as variations on a theme (e.g., rage, anger, hatred; detached, numb; intrigued, fascinated, curious). Emotions were associated with physical symptoms, as articulated by Caroline (FG1), who described a sense of nausea, physical pain, and tearfulness. While the bulk of emotions associated with the course tend to be negative, a number of more positive emotional reactions were reported (e.g., relief, thankfulness, hope).

Most emotions were reported in the context of independent study, particularly in relation to working on the assessment. This reflects the ratio of time in and out of class (1:9), but also the features of those contexts, expectations, and the focus on working together to analyze material in the classroom. Chloe (FG2.1) reflects:

> it's designed, I guess, in the uni[versity] environment to be also a professional environment and I suppose it's typical to not mix emotions with the professional… it's been very expressly clear that there is room for emotion in this course, but I think a lot of the material we've been doing is highly analytical and that makes it difficult to allow emotion to be in the driver's seat.

In as much as emotional states can be inferred from outside when looking at a group of around 30 students, Chloe's observation and reflection largely align with our observations. There have been no obvious signs of emotional distress in class. At the same time, when asked for their own observations on the emotions of those around them, Maddy (FG1) gave a hint of internal emotional processing that goes on without obvious signals:

FIGURE 5.1 Word cloud: emotions identified in the opening exercise, focus groups 1 and 2.1

> I think I was just so in my head about my own emotions that I was kind of oblivious to everyone else's.

Reflecting on the analytical nature of the material handled in class, when transcripts are used, they are indeed always framed with specific questions that give a particular focus to the exercise. Nonetheless, in terms of visible emotions or emotional drivers, the classroom is not a sterile space. On the one hand, Nina (FG2.1) says she did not detect specific emotions from people, yet observed that you could tell when people are more 'passionate.' We can square this with students' own reports of anger and our observation of this in the class. Furthermore, our own emotional entanglements with the material came across in different ways, as evident in this exchange with Faris and Caroline (FG1):

> Faris: ... We're all observing you for whatever, 10 weeks, so you can always tell... It was very clear that you were weaving your own emotions into the course. It comes across in the delivery. It comes across in the

> material that we're reading, just the general feedback, the kinds of conversations we were encouraged to have...
>
> Caroline: ... the fact that you create this privileged space to talk about all this pain and all these experiences, just shows how much you care and your position on that.

Aside from this, most emotions were reported in relation to individual study, and especially in the period after seminar delivery had ended and students were working on their research assessments (Caroline, Maddy, and Faris, FG1; Chloe, FG2.1; ACS, FG2.2). This was a period that could be overwhelming as students spent more focused time finding their own way through the archival material:

> For me it was overwhelming. Reading everything again and again... Reading what happened, like what the witness is saying with specific details. So, it's kind of like, 'oh, this again and again and again'. So it was overwhelming.
>
> ACS FG2.2

To some extent, students had been primed for this by instructors (see below). It was also something they could factor into their choices in terms of how they directed their research:

> I came to you and I said I wanted to study sexual violence, but I'm not sure if I'm going to be able to cope with it... in the end I did decide to study it, because it was something that... really interested me. And I don't know, I felt like I could go through it or should go through it. Maybe there's even like a sense of indebtedness. Like these people have gone through these things like the fact that I can't read that. What does that say about me? I'm sure that's not how you're supposed to feel, but...
>
> Maddy FG1

A sense of obligation provides a link between the feelings students encounter and the ethical commitments they form in relation to the material in the archives, discussed under ethics below.

Although the assessment period could be overwhelming and represented a concentrated space of emotions for students in the course, the emotions were not always negative and were rooted in the course as a meaningful exploration of atrocity or a space to work through challenging issues. Faris reported a feeling of 'relief', explaining:

> I still felt more like I was doing something purposeful in this course… It felt like it was the most realistic thing I could have done in university, realistic to my experience as someone who comes from a very marginalized victim group myself.
>
> Faris FG1

It is evident in the focus groups that emotions are sometimes difficult to pin down, but in the following, Balo (FG2.2) works toward a sense of the assessment as a space to process emotions generated by the course:

> Balo: I no longer felt as hopeless when I was writing… the whole thing had come to some sort of culmination… I felt like… my opinions were finally coming out in some sort of… Where you were actually getting across… So, it was there… There was a means.
>
> Andy: So it's some sort of realization…?
>
> Balo: More like an opportunity to just get those feelings out in a way, through that medium.

One challenge in pinning down emotions comes from the fact that they shift over time and even in the short term. Emotional voyages connect to students' strategies for dealing with negative emotions, particularly in taking time away from difficult material on atrocity violence. Maddy described sadness transitioning into a kind of numbness, and a process whereby time mediates any initial shock:

> …When you go away for a bit and come back to it, your brain has the time to accept it. Obviously you don't want to accept that you live in this kind of world, but you do accept that it is a reality. And when you go back to it, you're like this is horrible, but I've kind of almost come to terms with it.
>
> Maddy FG1

Balo also gives an account of an emotional voyage, ending in temporary disengagement.

> I was reading the case summaries on the ICTY database and it was harrowing stuff and it built up… at first… well you know, at this point in the course I'm used to seeing facts like this and then it went a bit further. I

> started getting a bit upset thinking this is really harrowing stuff and then ultimately it got to the point of anger and disengagement where I thought like... I'm not... I don't want to read this anymore, so I started doing something else.
>
> Balo FG2.1

For Balo, turning to less emotionally demanding coursework was a possibility – in this case, Roman Law. Similarly, ACS (FG2.2) would take a walk if things got to be too much, leaving the difficult material behind. However, as emotions have a strong personal dimension, in how they are experienced and handled, there is variation across our respondents. For example, Chloe (FG2.1) felt that there was value in stopping, not to get away, but rather to use time to 'feel' the emotions:

> ...when those emotions come up, or when I start feeling overwhelmed, to me, that's part of my process of understanding the material, feeling the material, and feeling the weight of it... so I let myself feel all of the heavy things...

We asked students what triggered specific emotions. What emerged from discussions is that emotional reactions extend beyond atrocities to legal and academic responses to the atrocities. First, in relation to disgust, revulsion, and shock, students focused on atrocities in terms of specific events and the level of detail:

> I watched the video of the Scorpions[4]...You said disgust and [it was the] first thing that came [to me].
>
> ACS FG2.1

> [responding to prompt, 'what triggers that kind of feeling of disgust for you?]... the details of the atrocities, and I think it goes with shock... I don't think that in school we really go in[to] the details of all of this.
>
> Caroline FG1

> For me it was reading about what humans had done to each other and just being revolted with the species.
>
> Maddy FG1

4 ACS refers to footage shown during the *Milošević* trial in which members of a Serbian paramilitary unit murder captive Bosniaks. For an account of this, see Vukušić (2018).

Thinking about research and legal practice, students were moved to anger when they perceived unethical practices, and in turn, this helped them reflect on their own practice. In the exchange below, we are discussing a point in a session on perpetrators where we discuss Jessica Stern's book, based on interviews with Radovan Karadžić.[5]

> Faris: I remember something specific that made me really angry… I really remember that one class where we looked at a publication *My War Criminal*.
>
> Andy: Yeah, that's quite early in the course…
>
> Faris: Yeah, that really made me angry. Just the way someone could be really senseless… just the way someone could approach these things with so much… like a lack of tact, lack of understanding, it made me really angry.
>
> Faris FG1

Similarly, students felt anger when they read exchanges in the transcripts and drew the conclusion that counsel were not treating victim-witnesses with due care:

> The lawyer was questioning… the victim, and they were being so rude and so… just like had zero emotional awareness for the victim and that made me really angry.
>
> Maddy FG1

> …that made me angry. Like how defendants' [counsel] will try to twist what the victims were saying.
>
> ACS FG2.1

Conscious of the possible symptoms of trauma from secondary exposure to the trauma of others, we asked students about any enduring effects they had experienced arising from the course and the material they dealt with. Our aim as instructors is to offer students adequate preparation for dealing with this difficult material and tools to recognize and respond to emotional impact. It is also our expectation that the context in which students work on this material reduces the intensity of their exposure, in that they are dividing their time

5 This also came up in FG2.1 and Chloe's response is discussed below, under ethics.

across multiple courses. The physical symptoms reported by Caroline, above, were passing. Nina (FG2.2) was the only one who reported a nightmare directly related to material linked to the course, in particular, images. She explained that she tended to experience vivid dreams more generally and would expect it to stay with her for a while. In this instance, it was some images relating to a killing, and Nina had earlier expressed a preference for visual media, including video (FG2.1). The other lasting effect was not directly linked to the course but rather related to films recommended to students, in this case *Quo Vadis, Aida?* by Jasmila Žbanić, and a particularly emotional scene:

> ...watching that, probably for 3 days afterwards... do you know that scene where she's walking through and she's identifying the skulls and bones of her husband and two sons. She breaks down crying, and that just stayed with me.
>
> Balo FG2.2

Taken together, students' accounts of emotional experiences related to *Criminologies of Atrocity* show a range of negative and positive emotions, in keeping with observations in the scholarship of teaching and learning sensitive material; that they have been able to engage with negative emotions without indications of harm; and that the emotional aspects of the course are important in relation to their own ethical reflections and commitments. In the following section, we expand on our ethical commitments in the course and how we seek to support students, and on outcomes in terms of students' own engagement with ethical questions relating to atrocity research and legal practice.

7 Ethics and Atrocity Education

This section focuses on the ethical dimensions of the course, including how students perceive our fulfillment of an ethical obligation to prepare them for dealing with sensitive material, and then looking at the students' engagement with ethics during and after class, the role played by ethics in their research choices, and finally how it shapes their critical evaluation of the work of lawyers.

7.1 *You Can Never Fully Prepare Someone: Ethics in Class*

Criminologies of Atrocity places emphasis on the ethics of conducting research on atrocity crimes, as indicated in the course outline above. In the first meeting, students are informed about the three ethical dimensions of the course, which are their responsibility towards the material analyzed, their responsibility towards themselves (self-care) and our responsibility towards them. This refers our obligation to prepare students for handling the task of researching and writing atrocity crimes. When asked if they had felt prepared enough to complete their summative assessment, the students' responses were positive.

> In the first seminar you [Annalisa] and MJ [Teaching Assistant] ... were very assertive..., saying "this is very intense material. This is serious. You might experience very harsh emotions." That was one of the first things that you guys talked about... making it very, very clear what we were getting into. And likewise creating a very safe space for when you have issues, when you're struggling, you can come to me, you can come to MJ, you can come to anyone on this course and you can leave whenever you want to. That was the first thing that you said and it was very, very clear and explicit, and that came across very strongly...
>
> Chloe FG2.1

> We knew that we were going to encounter this kind of violence and these kinds of descriptions... So I'm not really sure how you could have done more.
>
> Caroline FG1

On the issue of sensitive material, students recognized that the nature of the topics studied, the variety and volume of the material, and the diverse ways of reacting make it impossible to disclose all possible issues right at the outset. Students acknowledged the difficulty of providing an exact list of all the different materials held in the ICTY digital archive and reflected on whether it was necessary. Indeed, students suggested that everybody has an expectation of the type of material they will encounter in a course on atrocity crimes.

> ...you can never fully prepare someone, like you are going to see this, this and this... what can you expect if you are looking into war crimes and specifically crimes against humanity, which is like the worst of the worst.
>
> ACS FG2.1

> I think the title from *Criminologies of Atrocity* is specific enough [...] It's also built up from the first week... it was clear that at some point the

> readings were going to turn into pretty harrowing stuff, but, but it wasn't immediate.... [Nina interjects, "Oh yeah"].
>
> Balo FG2.1

These opinions are shared by Nina (FG2.1) as well, who says, "I think I knew what I was getting myself into."

Research ethics are addressed again in week 3 of the course when talking about perpetrators of atrocities. Students are presented with a series of readings in preparation for the class, and among the two focus groups, there is agreement on the importance of looking at good and *bad* research practices. Students appreciated being offered podcasts in which the ethics of atrocity research are discussed. Balo (FG2.1) mentions *Asymmetrical Haircuts* (not dated) and *Terribly and Terrifyingly Normal* (not dated). Jessica Stern's (2020) *My War Criminal*, discussed above in relation to student anger, is also highlighted as "the most egregious and the one that probably stands out the most" (Chloe, FG2.1) among examples of how not to approach research.

The week centered on the study of victims of atrocities explores researchers' ethical obligations. What emerged from the focus group is the students' feelings of closeness and indebtedness toward victims, which came from reading their testimonies and the very traumatic experiences they have been through. This perceived affinity to the victims influenced the students' approach to the final assessment, making the students feel that their work has meaning.

> you feel close to the victims on some level I would say, because you read about their stories, you read about their testimonies and so it feels like an obligation to represent their voices and their experiences as well. And also, it feels meaningful to work on this because this is so important, right, to study?
>
> Caroline FG1

Talking about the choice behind the topic for their summative assessment, Maddy, already quoted above in the emotions section, pointed to a relationship between researcher and researched, how that influences the way research is conducted, and why a particular type of research is carried out.

The students' reflections on the importance of being aware of what the study of atrocity criminology entails, the comparison between examples of good and bad practice, as well as the researchers' positionality in relation to the material and the people studied, whether victims or perpetrators, all constituted meaningful steps towards their own research. The following section moves on to findings regarding ethical considerations in the post-class phase of the course, when students worked independently and were personally involved with, and confronted by, the archival material.

7.2 *Wanting It to Be as Ethical as Possible: Ethics after Class*

In relation to how students' understanding of what ethical research looks like developed over the course, Faris recounts the influence of the course on his summative assessment and on his own identity as a researcher.

> I think to answer the first question about being aware of ethics outwardly while you're doing the work, I think it was very clear... for me when I was doing the writing up and the research, that there was sometimes a clear distinction between wanting to write something that is a good piece of work and then wanting it to be as ethical as possible and as productive as possible. So, one thing I struggled with is where I was reading a testimony and you were feeling like, 'yes, I found a very good thing that's good for my argument' because it's not the same as... Maybe that's why it's easier sometimes to deal with legislation, because then you're like, it's good for my argument, but it's not someone's personal experience. But where you don't want to have a moment where you're like, yes, I found a very good piece of information... but it's [objectively someone's recollection of a harrowing personal trauma]."
>
> Faris FG1

In an exchange after the meeting, Faris expanded on how the course had moved their work away from direct accounts of trauma to uncovering the systems and processes behind victimization (private correspondence, May 9, 2024). Faris expresses the necessity that researchers have to balance academic fascination[6] with ethical considerations underlying any piece of research and knowing how to report sensitive material. This shows a transformative effect through which the student understands how ethics and research are deeply interconnected in every single aspect of the research process.

> I think one of the things that I came out of the course with that I didn't really think about as actively before... is just how much the practice of researching, the practice of being an academic in this field shapes the field in itself. That's just as important to the field as the actual material

6 Captured in the word cloud under 'curious' and 'intrigued'.

> that you're studying. So I think to match that, the ethics needs to be as profound and as woven into the course as any other component of it.
>
> Faris FG1

This is a particularly insightful remark as it introduces us to comparisons the students made about the role of ethics in *Criminologies of Atrocity* and other courses. Ethical considerations are evident in courses focused on clinical legal practice and, for students outside the Law School, in social science research methods training (Chloe, Nina, FG2.1). Other law courses tend to briefly mention the need for ethical awareness in relation to specific topics but leave the analysis of such ethical considerations at a less in-depth level. Students were critical of how ethics were handled in some other courses. They not only mentioned different approaches to the issue of ethical considerations but also recognized the limitations arising from leaving ethics in a marginalized role. Caroline (FG.1) reflected on the difference in dealing with the Bosnian genocide between our course and one with a legal approach. She acknowledges how criminology gives much more space and recognition to victims of atrocities and genocide in general compared to more legal courses. Reflecting on a legal article where the author argued the absence of genocidal intent in the Yugoslav wars of the 1990s, Caroline expressed her emotional reactions and ethical concerns.

> And the international lawyer was saying that for him, the judgement is not right, that it's not genocide, and it created a lot of anger because obviously we went through all the facts. So he was, you know, completely disregarding some things. And I think it's more indignation, maybe than anger. But it just feels like taking away that recognition from the victim.
>
> Caroline FG1

Contrasting criminological and legal courses allowed students to develop and express concerns about the ethics of examination and cross-examination in criminal trials, as well as the interactions between lawyers and witnesses, which leads us to the analysis of the ethics of law.

7.3 *Ethics of Law: Oh, I Can Critique the Lawyers*

Since the majority of students enrolled in the course were working towards a Law degree, the course was often a rare element of social science studies in their program. The interdisciplinary approach of the course gave students new tools to look at legal sources critically, questioning how the work of the court is carried out. According to Faris, this was a novelty and an unexpected outcome:

> Even like to ask that question… It was inconceivable before. Not to say that, you know we don't analyze the law, but it was a conscious effort to actually be like, 'oh, I can critique how the lawyers are asking questions,' because that, that is so different. Always, it's just you take the law, you take the facts, you take it for what it is you can critique, like how this precedent interacts with another precedent, but you never sit down and look at the institutional factors that shape the law. So, I think just having to ask that question for the first time was, like, 'oh I, you know, I can, I can do this!'
>
> Faris FG1

Students identified questions asked in court that were problematic and noted that the examination process conducted in court has limitations as a source of criminological data due to its structure and focus on criminal justice outcomes, meaning that all witnesses do not get the same chance to talk about their experiences in the same way. This is expressed by Balo, who, in both focus group sessions, pointed out the limitations of International Criminal Law, from the way victims are not allowed agency and how their experiences are shaped by the interests of the court. He recognizes the obligation to prove someone is guilty beyond a reasonable doubt as the job of the lawyer, which determines why lawyers may decide to follow different lines of questioning with witnesses sharing similar experiences. This, in turn, shows why researchers who are not guided by such constraints may be allowed to adopt a more ethically sensitive approach.

> …lawyers fail for seemingly not many obvious reasons to reproduce language which would help victims and witnesses have greater agency. And some who have maybe suffered exactly the same thing or very similar things don't have that agency simply because that lawyer on that day has decided to take it elsewhere. And it seems like a flawed way of getting that testimony from the victim.
>
> Balo FG2.2

The students' engagement with ethics, from the work carried out in the classroom to that of conducting criminological research, passing through a critical evaluation of the ethics of law, unveils a journey of ethical self-discovery as students, researchers and future lawyers. Knowing what is good practice and what is not has played a significant role for the students, whose wariness of these matters shows how much care, interest, and involvement they have developed toward the topic researched, as well as the practice of researching.

8 Conclusion: The Most Realistic Thing I Could Have Done in University

Emotions constitute a normal response to the study of atrocity crimes. Our course aspires to provide students with the emotional support and ethical awareness necessary to shield them from harm, but not from the challenge of researching and writing about atrocity crimes. Honesty about the challenges we, as instructors, face in researching and teaching particular topics helps establish what Stanko (1997, p. 84) defines as a "collective sensibility about violence." It is fundamental to establish emotionally and ethically responsible ways of teaching mass atrocities through archives rather than avoiding the coverage of sensitive, traumatic topics, since this type of study offers opportunities to grow both in and out of the class-room (Parrotta et al., 2021, p. 329). *Criminologies of Atrocity* offers a place where students have the opportunity to develop ethically. Ethical development takes the form of students' reflections on how to conduct research approaching the material used and the people researched respectfully, in part by drawing on their emotional reactions. As the focus groups showed, feelings of indebtedness towards victims of atrocities as well as anger towards examples of bad practice in research and in court, have acted as prompts for the students when working on their own research, thus motivating them to be as ethical as possible. Consciousness of the sensitive nature of the object of study further motivates students to engage with the study of atrocity crimes (Dalton, 2015, p. 6). This demonstrates the importance of providing a place for a course grounded in ethics and open to emotions in a criminological or legal curriculum. Indeed, the emotional and ethical journeys made by students demonstrate the effectiveness of creating a supportive place for ethical and emotional growth and evaluation of research and legal practice.

References

Aitchison, A. (2014). Police and Persecution in the Bosnian Krajina: Democratisation, Deprofessionalisation and Militarisation. *Criminal Justice Issues/Kriminalističke Teme*, 14(5–6), pp. 1–19.

Asymmetrical Haircuts (not dated), retrieved, 30 June 2025 from https://www.asymmetricalhaircuts.com/

Aydın-Aitchison, A. (2024). Teaching Atrocity Criminology with ICTY Archives: Disciplinarity, Research, Ethics. *Journal of Criminal Justice Education*, 35(3), pp. 528–546. https://doi-org.eux.idm.oclc.org/10.1080/10511253.2023.2205472.

Baird, K., Kracen, A. C. (2006). Vicarious Traumatization and Secondary Traumatic Stress: A Research Synthesis. *Counselling Psychology Quarterly*, 19(2), pp. 181–188. https://doi.org/10.1080/09515070600811899.

Baker, C. (2015). *The Yugoslav Wars of the 1990s*. London: Palgrave.

Battista, A. (2023, September 6–9). *Feminist State Crime Theory: Studying Atrocities by Learning from the Yugoslav Wars of the 1990s* [Conference Session]. Eurocrim 2023, Florence, Italy, retrieved, 28 July 2025 from https://esc-eurocrim.org/v2/wp-content/uploads/2024/02/Programme-with-abstracts.pdf

Bedera, N. (2021). Beyond Trigger Warnings: A Survivor-centred Approach to Teaching on Sexual Violence and Avoiding Institutional Betrayal. *Teaching Sociology*, 49(3), pp. 267–277. https://doi.org/10.1177/0092055X211022471

Biddolph C. (2021). Emotions, De/Attachment, and the Digital Archive: Reading Violence at the International Criminal Tribunal for the Former Yugoslavia (ICTY). *Millennium*, 49(3), pp. 530–555. https://doi.org/10.1177/03058298211033027

Campbell, K. (2017). Ethical Challenges: Researching War Crimes. In: M. Cowburn, L. Gelsthorpe, A. Wahidin (Eds.)., *Research Ethics in Criminology: Dilemmas, Issues and Solutions*. London: Routledge, pp. 150–165

Dalton, D. (2015). Crime, Law and Trauma: A Personal Reflection on the Challenges and Rewards of Teaching Sensitive Topics to Criminology Students. *Enhancing Learning in the Social Sciences*, 2(3), pp. 1–18. https://doi.org/10.11120/elss.2010.02030008

Dalton, D. (2020). Trigger Warnings in Criminology Teaching Contexts: Some Reflections Based on Ten Years of Teaching a Sensitive Topic. In: Palmer, D. (ed.). *Scholarship of Teaching and Learning in Criminology*. London: Palgrave Macmillan, pp. 87–108, https://doi.org/10.1007/978-3-030-35158-8_5

Figley, C. R. (Ed.) (1995) *Compassion Fatigue: Coping with Secondary Traumatic Stress Disorder in those who Treat the Traumatised*. New York: Brunner-Mazel.

Figley, C. R. (Ed.) (2002). *Treating Compassion Fatigue*. New York: Brunner-Routledge.

Gladden, J., Waller, B. E., Hernandez, A., Hopkins, A. (2023). Teaching Trauma Content in Higher Education: A Systematic Literature Review. *Trauma, Violence and Abuse*, 24(5), pp. 3384–3397. https://doi.org/10.1177/15248380221129575

Gibbs, B. (2021). “Strange Fruit”: Teaching and the Present and Past of Racial Violence in the Rural South. *Equity and Excellence in Education*, 54(2), pp. 165–81. https://doi.org/10.1080/10665684.2021.1951632

Golubović, J. (2019). ‘One Day I Will Tell This to My Daughter’: Serb Women, Silence, and the Politics of Victimhood in Sarajevo. *Anthropological Quarterly*, 92(4), pp. 1173–99. https://doi.org/10.1353/anq.2019.0065

Heath, M. (2005). Encounters with the Volcano: Strategies for Emotional Management in Teaching the Law of Rape. *The Law Teacher*, 39(2), pp. 129–149. https://doi.org/10.1080/03069400.2005.9993178

Houge, A. B. (2023). Violent Re-presentations: Reflections on the Ethics of Representation in Violence Research. *Qualitative Research*, 23(5), pp. 1244–1260. https://doi.org/10.1177/14687941221079532

Jenney, A., Straka, S., Walsh, C. A. (2021). Responsible Pedagogy During a Pandemic: Teaching Social Work Courses on Interpersonal Violence during COVID-19. *Journal of Social Work Education*, 57(4), pp. 769–808. https://doi.org/10.1080/10437797.2021.1957739

Jessee, E. (2015). Approaching Perpetrators. *Conflict and Society*, 1(1), pp. 4–8. https://doi.org/10.3167/arcs.2015.010102.

Kearney, K. S., Krumm, B., Hughes, R. L., Satterfield, J. W. (2012). Organized for Genocide: Student Reactions and Learning from Use of Emotive Documentaries on the Holocaust. *Journal of Management Education*, 37(3), pp. 342–366. https://doi.org/10.1177/1052562912438764.

Lowe, P., Jones, H. (2010). Teaching and Learning Sensitive Topics. *Enhancing Learning in the Social Sciences*, 2(3), pp. 1–7. https://doi.org/10.11120/elss.2010.02030001

Matthäus, J. (1996). What about the Ordinary Men: The German Order Police and the Holocaust in the Occupied Soviet-Union. *Holocaust and Genocide Studies*, 10(2), pp. 134–150. https://doi.org/10.1093/hgs/10.2.134

McCann, I. L., Pearlman, A. L. (1990). Vicarious Traumatization: A Framework for Understanding the Psychological Effects of Working with Victims. *Journal of Traumatic Stress*, 3(1), pp. 131–149. https://doi.org/10.1007/BF00975140.

Nenadović, M., Somun, K. (2021). Teaching about Sexual Violence as Part of Mass Atrocity Crimes: Model International Criminal Court Non-Formal Educational Program. *Review of Education, Pedagogy and Cultural Studies*, 43(2), pp. 69–84. https://doi.org/10.1080/10714413.2021.1911614

Nikischer, A. (2019). Vicarious Trauma inside the Academe: Understanding the Impact of Teaching, Researching and Writing Violence. *Higher Education*, 77, pp. 905–916. https://doi.org/10.1007/s10734-018-0308-4

Parrotta, K., Bergquist, A. C., Hans, K. R. (2021). Student Perspectives on Trauma Informed Education Practices in Criminal Justice and Forensic Science. *Journal of Criminal Justice Education*, 32(3), pp. 323–343. https://doi.org/10.1080/1057123.2021.1958885

Sadique, K., Tangen, J. (2022). 'I Feel Like I Can't Do a Lot': Affectivity, Reflection and Action in 'Transformative' Genocide Education. *Journal of Adult and Continuing Education*, 28(2), pp. 522–539. https://doi.org/10.1177/14779714211061590.

Schwöbel-Patel, C. (2018). The 'Ideal' Victim of International Criminal Law. *European Journal of International Law*, 29(3), pp. 703–724. https://doi.org/10.1093/ejil/chy056

Seear, K., Bliss, L., Galowitz, P., Klein, C. F. (2019). Exploring the Role of Emotions in Clinical Legal Education: Inquiry and Results from an International Workshop for

Legal Educators. *The Law Teacher*, 53(4), pp. 487–499. https://10.1080/03069400.2019.1667087

Stanko, E. A. (1997). I Second that Emotion: Reflections on Feminism, Emotionality, and Research on Sexual Violence. In: Schwartz, M. D. (ed.). *Researching Sexual Violence against Women: Methodological and Personal Perspectives*, Thousand Oaks: Sage, pp. 74–85. https://doi.org/10.4135/9781483327907.

Stern, J. (2020a). *My War Criminal: Personal Encounters with an Architect of Genocide.* New York: Ecco.

Stern, J. (2020b, January 16). Why Did I Let a Convicted War Criminal Practice Energy Healing on Me? My 48 hours Alone with Radovan Karadžić. *New York Times*, retrieved 21 June 2024 from https://www.nytimes.com/2020/01/16/opinion/sunday/radovan-karadzic.html

Subotić, J. (2020). Ethics of Archival Research on Political Violence. *Journal of Peace Research*, 58(3), pp. 342–354. https://doi.org/10.1177/0022343319898735

Sutton, R. (2024). Reflections on Teaching 'Emotion Bites' in an Llm Course on Human Rights and Conflict Resolution. In: Gauci, J. and Sander, B. (eds.) *Teaching International Law: Reflections on Pedagogical Practice in Context.* London: Routledge, pp. 94–108.

Terribly and Terrifyingly Normal (not dated), retrieved, 30 June 2025 from https://open.spotify.com/show/2Bt5Wg5nbekeSo8UBDI5MY?si=48a82419b6a64779

Vukušić, I. (2018). Nineteen Minutes of Horror: Insights from the Scorpions Execution Video. *Genocide Studies and Prevention*, 12(2), pp. 35–53. https://doi.org/10.5038/1911-9933.12.2.1527

Zakaria, R. (2020, February 21). Empathy for the Devil: a Terrorism Scholar Gets Up Close and Personal with a War Criminal. *Alienated*, retrieved 21 June 2024 from https://thebaffler.com/alienated/empathy-for-the-devil-zakaria

CHAPTER 6

Emotional Dimensions of Complex Learning Environments

Adopting a Trauma and Resilience-Informed Approach within a Global Justice Investigations Lab

Brianne McGonigle Leyh and Koko Christiaanse

1 Introduction

Globalization and the advancement of digital technology have facilitated the unprecedented dissemination of knowledge and information. Consequently, misinformation, disinformation and fake news are on the rise, posing a societal challenge to cultivate and teach critical inquiry skills that transcend traditional disciplinary boundaries. To address this need, more universities worldwide are establishing digital open-source investigation courses or labs. Often, these programs educate students from various disciplines on investigating global justice issues such as serious human rights violations and environmental damages. Specifically, students learn to identify, collect, verify, critically analyze, evaluate and securely store digital open-source materials such as news reports, social media posts and satellite images. Students could be involved in tracking illegal shipping containers or geolocating images shared across social media and verifying their authenticity. They could be learning how to piece together a timeline of events around an attack or protest, similar to journalists working at major news outlets such as The New York Times or BBC. Due to the real-world significance of this work, increasingly, students acquire these skills by collaborating with societal partners on real-world projects.

Students and teachers working on open-source investigations, especially those working on global justice issues, may be exposed to traumatic material. It is, therefore, important that they receive information and training on trauma and resilience. This information and training are relevant not only for the work carried out while at university but, more importantly, for any future exposure to similar types of material. This chapter begins by explaining the growth of digital open-source investigation labs at universities around the world, the types of collaborative and experiential learning that take place, and their relationship to emotion and ethics in the classroom. Next, it delves into the litera-

© 2026 THE AUTHOR(S) | HTTPS://DOI.ORG/10.1163/9789004754720-008

ture on trauma and resilience before detailing the design of Utrecht University's Global Justice Investigations Lab and the choices we made in relation to adopting a trauma and resilience-approach. Among other things, this included incorporating the advice of our societal partners, learning from the experiences of other labs around their design and set-up and underpinning our work with five core values associated with a trauma and resilience-informed approach. Afterwards, through baseline and endline survey results, as well as student reflection logs, the chapter examines in more detail the trauma and resilience-informed approach taken, focusing on how students experienced the training and reflection moments. The results are analyzed against the literature and examined critically to gauge which elements of the approach were successful and which could be improved.

Finally, the chapter ends with a reflection on what lessons can be drawn from the lab's approach for other complex learning environments dealing with sensitive, potentially traumatic material. We stress the importance of (i) starting early to think about what a trauma and resilience-approach could mean in a particular classroom environment; (ii) adopting an approach that aligns with scholarship and that best fits the specific contexts of the relevant learning environment; and (iii) regularly reviewing and adapting the approach based on student and teacher experiences.

2 Universities and the Rise of Digital Open-Source Investigation Labs

Universities around the world have a long history of working together with societal partners on issues that affect both local and global communities (Bringle & Hatcher, 2011; Latta et al., 2018). University collaboration with societal partners is commonly referred to as 'community service learning,' 'community-engaged learning,' 'international community-engaged learning,' 'community-based research,' or other similar labels such as transdisciplinarity (Bringle & Hatcher, 1995; Kenny & Gallagher, 2002; Meijs et al., 2019). These types of complex learning environments enable students to bridge theory and practice while providing a space for reflection on their experiences (Bringle, Hatcher, & McIntosh, 2006). They are founded on reciprocity and respect among students, teachers and societal partners, necessitating careful attention to learning objectives, activities, assessments and outcomes, and with a specific focus on experiential learning, also known as 'learning by doing.' One specific type of collaborative and experiential learning space that is on the rise in the last decade, in response to the growth of open-source information, is the digital open-source investigations lab.

The rise of open-source information, particularly in the human rights and environmental harm context, has been described as 'ad hoc' (Dubberley et al., 2018a, p. 5). At first, it was journalists who realized the potential of the wealth of freely available information online. Later, human rights and environmental activists and lawyers recognized the value of being able to document and verify information, especially for accountability purposes. In 2012, the Human Rights Centre at the University of California, Berkeley hosted a workshop where scholars, journalists, lawyers and human rights organizations met to discuss the potential of open-source investigations and the role of technology in human rights-related work, leading to a rapid development in interest in this field (Berkeley Human Rights Center, 2012). According to Dubberley et al. (2018a, p. 8), it has been essential to adopt an approach that fills the interdisciplinary gap between 'lawyers, journalists, sociologists, data scientists, activists, and researchers with the cutting-edge skills and insights needed to work in an increasingly digitized and information-saturated environment.'

It is unsurprising that a range of actors from various fields has linked up with universities to work with students and teachers in advancing open-source investigation skills, which are so necessary for the future of global justice work focusing on human rights and environmental protection. University-supported open-source investigation labs have been established on six continents and are growing in number. For instance, Amnesty International's Digital Verification Corps works together with no fewer than seven universities around the world (McGonigle Leyh, 2021), winning the Times Higher Education award for best international collaboration in 2019 (Dubberley, 2019).

These types of labs or courses acknowledge the need to foster critical thinking *and* digital literacy, while simultaneously responding to new global challenges like the rise of disinformation and fake news. They are increasingly being integrated within university curricula because students learn to identify, collect, verify and evaluate freely available information – skills relevant across disciplinary contexts that can be practically implemented by students for the benefit of addressing real-world challenges. Because the labs provide theoretical context together with a focus on the real-life application of practical skills, they are geared to help prepare students for jobs in a wide-variety of sectors. Importantly, as part of this preparation, many of the labs have begun to focus not only on the specific knowledge and skills necessary for this work but also on the emotional and ethical aspects of the work. This is because open-source investigations have inherent risks related to trauma.

Digital open-source investigations can be conducted anytime and anywhere, allowing student investigators to carry out their work safely, free from perilous situations. These lifted restrictions have clear benefits, opening the world of human rights and environmental harm investigations to a new level of accessibility. However, as noted by Dubberley et al. (2018b), inherent risks remain in any investigation focused on serious harms. Student investigators may have to work with a high volume of violent, potentially traumatizing visuals and sounds. They may need to sift through hours of graphic and triggering footage, which may result in what is referred to as 'vicarious traumatization,' the emotional impact of being regularly exposed to stories or footage of traumatic events (Canfield, 2008; Shapiro, 2015). Real mental distress or psychological harm can be inflicted if investigators are not resilient to the material or lack coping mechanisms. Psychological studies have shown that viewing and listening to potentially traumatizing content on the internet can contribute to symptoms associated with post-traumatic stress disorder (PTSD) and other mental health issues (Flannery, 2022; McHugh et al., 2018). Active coping mechanisms are required to bolster resilience in individuals doing this work to avoid long-term harms (McHugh et al., 2018), with trauma education being a significant predictor of trauma literacy, which refers to the ability of individuals to adopt such coping mechanisms to protect themselves from trauma impacts (Seely, 2019). As a result, many university labs have begun to adopt trauma and resilience-informed approaches in their teaching, recognizing that the emotional and ethical demands placed on students (as well as on teachers and practitioners) in this space are high. But what exactly is a trauma and resilience-informed approach?

3 Trauma and Resilience-Informed Approaches within University Curricula

Research has shown how the impact of trauma and serious stress impacts individual development, emotional regulation and social behavior. Individuals may struggle with "concentration, memory, executive functioning, information processing, language acquisition," and more (Henshaw, 2022, p. 2). For students at university, this can influence their classroom engagement, academic performance and overall well-being. Given the pivotal role universities play in student development, the adoption of trauma-informed practices in higher education has increasingly received attention (Davidson, 2017). This increasing attention is warranted for several reasons. First, the rise in global conflicts, natural disasters and other crises, such as the COVID-19 pandemic, has increased the number of students who have experienced trauma (Forbes-Mewett & Sawyer, 2016; Henshaw, 2022; McBride, 2018). Second, students may also be more frequently indirectly exposed to traumatic material through curricula, field work, while carrying out research, or through their everyday online activities (Carello & Butler, 2015; Goodwin & Tiderington, 2022). In particular, "technology has made viewing traumatic events readily accessible for students, contributing to individual exposures" (Hollman et al., 2020, as cited in Henshaw, 2022, p. 2). Third, there is growing recognition of the prevalence of mental health issues, including trauma, among students (Kleber, 2019). Universities are more aware of the need to support students' mental health to ensure their overall well-being and academic success (Davidson, 2017).

While most trauma-informed practices are focused around courses dealing with social work, nursing, education and medicine, attention has been given more recently to other types of university environments. Various studies have laid bare the glaring gap in teaching trauma literacy in journalism education, despite high risks of vicarious traumatization (Hill et al., 2020; Izzeldin Malik et al., 2023; Ogunyemi, 2023; Specht & Tsilman, 2018). Similar discrepancies have been noted in research about human rights advocates and investigators (Dubberley et al., 2018b; Nah, 2019; Knuckey et al., 2018). In her work, Kelly A. McBride (2018) emphasizes the need for trauma-informed practices, particularly in courses dealing with sensitive subject matter like human rights. When studying sensitive material like human rights or environmental abuses, students may often encounter negative emotions due to the distressing content, impacting their learning environment and overall well-being. McBride (2018) argues that a trauma-sensitive approach, which adopts trauma-informed strategies, is essential for effective learning in these environments. Unfortunately, unlike in other fields like social work or medicine, educational staffs are generally not trained to manage students' emotional challenges. In law, for example, educators are not used to acknowledging and discussing emotions and trauma (Kaur, 2021). This can lead to frustrations and unease if and when students seek emotional support. Accordingly, McBride posits that having a better understanding of trauma's impact on students and integrating trauma-sensitive practices into human rights classrooms will enhance learning outcomes and student well-being. The ultimate goal should be to create educational spaces that support both students and educators, fostering resilience and better educational experiences for all involved (Kaur, 2021; McBride, 2018). 'Resilience' is a key concept referring to the ability to adapt to potentially traumatic or stressful situations (Wu et al., 2013), which can be fostered through specific strategies such as trauma-informed care and educational practices.

Already in the early 2000s, Maxine Harris and Roger Fallot outlined five core values of trauma-informed care, which emphasized how to respond to the trauma of an individual from within an organizational structure (Harris & Fallot, 2001), including, for instance, educational structures and organizations.

The five core values include safety, trustworthiness, choice, collaboration and empowerment, which also translate to the classroom context. They argue it is important to instill a "sense of control and autonomy" in individuals (Harris and Fallot, 2001, p. 14), working off the strengths of the individual (the student) and fostering "genuine collaboration" (2001, p. 17), which involves giving an "active voice" to the individual (p. 19). They suggest that "trust and safety, rather than being assumed from the beginning, must be earned and demonstrated over time," for example, by "eliminating ambiguity and vagueness." In a classroom context, this requires transparency, structure, and, where possible, certainty. Balancing the risks of the service provider (in this case, the educator or educational institution), which could involve the emotional or financial costs involved in ensuring the care, and that of the individual (the student) is also important. In the end, the goal is to equip individuals with the resources to handle situations without assistance (p. 15) and to foster strategies to build resilience. Later research on trauma-informed approaches also emphasized the intersectional identity aspects integral to this approach, including considering one's age, cultural background and gender (Henshaw, 2022). Taking note of where individuals come from and practicing positionality, reflexivity and "self-assessment" (Kaur, 2021, p. 116) allow awareness to be built around potential trauma in international, interdisciplinary classrooms where prior experiences may differ greatly (Weerdesteijn, 2024).

A number of important practical steps for educators linked to the five core values have been noted in the literature and through online resource tools (Berkeley Human Rights Center). These include, for instance, maintaining a predictable classroom structure, trigger warnings (safety), creating an inclusive environment that acknowledges and addresses trauma and resilience (trustworthiness), and allowing students to discuss their emotions and take breaks when needed (choice) (McBride, 2018). Other steps involve decisions around course set up (collaboration), course content, trigger warnings and learning about and sharing coping strategies (empowerment). Learning about coping strategies is especially important as it helps students learn how to manage their stress and trauma but also builds their resilience by teaching them how to process and handle distressing experiences effectively. Coping mechanisms can be built through strong student-staff connections, but also by fostering a supportive atmosphere with fellow peers (Weerdesteijn, 2024). Fostering community is thus also part of designing a trauma-informed classroom.

By acknowledging and addressing trauma, educators can help students develop the resilience needed to succeed academically and personally. In this sense, emphasizing resilience in conjunction with trauma is beneficial in adopting a trauma-informed approach. Here, educators have an important role to play by normalizing discussions about difficult emotions and helping students find meaning and a sense of purpose in what they do. They should not act as replacement therapists (Weerdesteijn, 2024), but they can adopt thoughtful strategies to support students' well-being and resilience.

4 Global Justice Investigations Lab at Utrecht University and a Trauma and Resilience-Informed Approach

The idea for starting the Global Justice Investigations Lab at Utrecht University began in 2020 when one of the authors was working on an article related to the role of universities in documenting international crimes and other serious human rights violations, including environmental damage (McGonigle Leyh, 2021). During research for that article, she carried out interviews with supervisors involved with other open-source investigation labs around the world, such as those at UC Berkeley, Hong Kong, Essex and more. It was after her talks with these educators when she realized that digital open-source investigation skills, combined with relevant ethical considerations and other competencies such as critical thinking and reflection, were essential for students interested in working in the field of global justice. She was able to secure university and national funding to set up an interdisciplinary open-source investigations lab.

Our teaching team, comprised of six teachers from four different faculties across the university, met regularly during the 2022–2023 academic year to create the Lab. The teaching team included teachers from cultural anthropology, criminology, information and computer sciences specializing in artificial intelligence, law and media and communications. This team also included an expert in open-source investigations working for the pioneering open-source journalism group Bellingcat. We also worked closely with three educational specialists from Utrecht University's Education and Training Department, providing input on aspects of constructive alignment around learning objectives, activities and assessment. During this preparatory stage, we first identified the key principles underlying the Lab: human rights and global justice (substantive knowledge); digital open-source investigation skills (skill focus); interdisciplinarity (didactic context); international community-engaged learning (didactic context); and trauma and resilience (didactic context).

It is this last key principle of the Lab which forms the focus of this chapter. In our early conversations with the societal partners that would be working with our students, and with supervisors from similar labs operating around the world, we learned about the importance of thinking about trauma and resilience from an early stage. Our contacts shared their experiences and provided us with literature and tools on the topic of trauma and open-source investigations (Berkeley Human Rights Center; Canfield, 2008; Dubberley et al., 2018a, 2018b) as well as on managing stress and trauma in investigative projects more generally (Shapiro, 2015). Thankfully, a member of our teaching team from Bellingcat had also previously published on how best to maintain mental health through trauma literacy as an open-source researcher (Fiorella, 2022). Once we collected relevant literature and practical tools, we followed up on the suggestion of one of our societal partners, Airwars, and reached out to the DART Center for Journalism and Trauma in New York, USA.

The DART Center for Journalism and Trauma is a global resource and training center for journalists who cover violence, conflict and tragedy. It is affiliated with the Columbia University Graduate School of Journalism and aims to improve reporting on traumatic events while supporting the emotional well-being of journalists and other actors involved in investigations. The DART Center offers training programs, workshops and seminars on trauma-informed practices. These are designed to help journalists, as well as others, handle sensitive stories responsibly and ethically. As part of our trauma and resilience-informed approach, we decided that all teachers and students in the Lab would receive training from the DART Center. The three-hour training for teachers took place in-person before the start of the Lab.

In the teacher training, we learned about coping techniques to maintain resilience, including tips such as distancing oneself from the material by "incorporating rituals into a research routine that help you 'park' the work or mentally distance yourself from it" (Rees, 2017). Other techniques included regulating oneself by taking regular breaks from the material, sleeping well and avoiding isolation. The DART Center stressed that, although distress is not per se a sign of an underlying emotional injury, investigators should be concerned if certain reactions and behaviors become a routine part of life outside of the work. Warning signs of vicarious trauma include changes in character, unusual isolation, increasingly self-medicating, and persistently feeling apathetic, empty or numb. We learned that self-care is a way to restore resilience and better deal with the materials (Rees, 2017). Bellingcat, a leading non-profit organization doing open-source investigation work and our key societal partner for training our students in open-source investigation techniques, provided further tips for resilience that are tailored to open-source investigations. These included learning to carefully curate what one must watch for the investigation, muting videos and fast-forwarding them, installing apps that blur images on social media, and creating boundaries between work and life (Fiorella, 2022).

These early preparatory steps certainly provided us with a better understanding of the impact that trauma (or serious stressors) can have on students and teachers. It was during this time that we decided to adopt the phrase 'trauma and resilience-approach to education' rather than just a 'trauma-approach' or 'trauma-sensitive approach' during teaching. We felt it was important to stress the connection between both 'trauma' and 'resilience' to emphasize the role of student empowerment in our approach. As Weerdesteijn (2024, p. 172) notes, it is essential to avoid portraying students as unwell; coping and resilience should be treated as a skill instead.

Overall, the literature on trauma and resilience, together with the practical tips we learned, helped to ensure that the teaching team would be ready for the first cohort of students in the 2023–2024 academic years. For the first iteration of the Lab, we had 25 students from different faculties and programs, consisting of 11 Masters students (4M/7F) and 14 BA (5M/9F) students in their second or third year of study. The Lab is a 7.5 EC elective course running over two periods from early November to mid-April – approximately 20 weeks. The students are expected to spend 10 hours/week on the course, which allows them to combine it with their mandatory courses. The Lab has three components: (i) team-taught lectures covering topics such as global justice, human rights (including a right to a healthy environment), positionality, critical thinking and framing; (ii) skills training and workshops covering different types of digital open-source investigation skills such as geolocation, chrono-location, internet scraping and flight and vessel tracking; and (iii) the opportunity to apply their open-source investigation skills within interdisciplinary teams working with a societal partner on real-life global justice projects. Partner organizations that students worked together with on specific open-source investigation projects were Airwars, Amnesty's Digital Verification Corp, Free Press Unlimited, and Friends of the Earth Netherlands (*Mileudefensie*).

As noted above, our decision to adopt a trauma and resilience-informed approach to the Lab developed out of an awareness of the need for such support among professionals. Our approach included: (i) an emphasis on understanding trauma and resilience through literature and training for all teachers and students; (ii) options for students to make choices concerning the course; (iii) regular group check-in moments to foster a sense of community and support; and (iv) individual reflection reports with specific prompts related to trauma and resilience in order to practice and reflect on their habits. As the later sections will show, we strove to incorporate the five core values: safety, trustworthiness, choice, collaboration and empowerment.

As a teaching team, we aimed to research how our students would experience this trauma and resilience-informed approach within the Lab. To measure experiences, we carried out a baseline student survey before the start of the first lecture and an endline student survey at the conclusion of the Lab. The survey questions used both a Likert scale (1–5) paired with open-ended questions to allow students to provide explanations for their responses. We also asked for regular written reflection reports (nine in total) using guiding prompts and questions, and collected information from teachers in the form of a teacher log. We received ethical approval from our Faculty's ethical board to carry out and use the student surveys as well as their reflection reports. Students also signed consent forms to use this material for educational and research purposes and were informed they could revoke this consent at any time.

5 Results from Students on Their Expectations and Experiences around Our Trauma and Resilience-Informed Approach

5.1 *Baseline Survey Results*

The baseline survey, which was conducted after the introduction to the lab, comprised both Likert-scale questions and open-ended questions. Students were asked, 'What expectations do you have about learning which steps to take in response to graphic and potentially triggering material?' Four of the 25 students noted that they had no expectations in relation to learning how to respond to potentially triggering material, with one student noting, "None, I've spent most of my life connected to the internet; I'm jaded as hell." The remaining 21 students, however, identified various expectations regarding what they would learn, such as learning to manage emotions. Here, students specifically noted the expectation of learning how to manage vicarious trauma, distancing oneself, and 'not let the images overwhelm' them. A vast majority of the students wanted to learn ways to deal with emotions, with one student expecting 'to have some guidelines to deal with emotional reactions [that] the materials may trigger.' Many students expected to learn 'practical strategies', 'coping strategies' or 'psychological tips' for dealing with the material.

The students had already noted the importance of protecting themselves, mentioning aspects related to mental hygiene, which are measures taken to promote and preserve mental health (Tremblay et al., 2021), and self-regulation. One student wrote that they 'should be careful not to overload' themselves with the material, while another wrote that 'knowing where to draw the line and end the investigation in order to prevent any harm' would be important. There was a strong understanding of 'boundary setting,' 'self-protection' and 'listening to [their] own needs.' One student specifically commented that they expected to learn how to 'leave it [the material] behind afterwards.'

Finally, the students expected to learn whom to turn to for assistance in case they needed help. This is important because it made us, as teachers, aware that we could be the first individuals approached by students encountering problems and should know how to point them towards trained professionals both inside and outside the university environment. Some students specifically noted the expectation of having a 'supportive and understanding environment where things/feelings/experiences can be addressed.' At least one student noted, "I have a strong stomach and think I am capable of seeing graphic content," while at the same time appreciating the opportunity to talk with others about it afterwards if needed.

5.2 *Reflection Logs*

In the third week of the course, and prior to working with their societal partners, the students had a two-hour online DART Center training, which they were asked to reflect on both immediately after as well as periodically throughout the Lab. We also held check-in moments with the full class and within their project groups. Most of the students were positive about this training and its value as their work progressed. One student wrote in a reflection log:

> I have come to realize how after the trauma and resilience training, I feel calmer and more confident about the project. I know that I am quite sensitive to sensory input and can quite easily be triggered by traumatic material. Yet addressing this and sharing concerns with the other students really helped me feel more connected, especially in our breakout group conversation about guilt and how it works in different ways in this context of indirectly witnessing human rights abuses – be it in potentially feeling like not doing enough, guilt about feeling emotions or the lack thereof. I think that only from this small glimpse into working in groups with fellow students, I realized that working together also means working together through perhaps challenging effects of the project and the investigations on us. In any case, being sensitized to the effect of traumatic material on those who are exposed to it really helped me personally to feel calmer about starting the projects, perhaps because I feel like my fear of being triggered by material was acknowledged to be valid, and I realized how different people in different ways share their own fears about being exposed to material. So feeling like we are all in it together, sharing our concerns, while at the same time learning about strategies gave me a great degree of calmness.

Another student wrote about the training in their reflection log:

> The trauma and resilience training was both familiar and completely new for me. Being honest, I did not think about these topics when starting this course and maybe did not expect them to play such a large role; I realize the naivety of that now. I do not have experience with trauma, but I do have experience with cognitive behavioral therapy, which I received after being diagnosed with a panic disorder. I recognized a lot that was being said in the trauma and resilience training from the therapy I received for my panic disorder. I think there are positive and negative sides to this. On the one side, I am more used than most people to recognizing my own triggers and protecting my mental wellbeing, but on the other side I recognize that my mental health issues might make me more vulnerable to issues in the future.

One student, who started off in the Airwars project group, which tackled the most sensitive and potentially triggering material, chose to switch groups after a number of weeks. He valued the space given to trauma awareness in the course, writing in his reflection log:

> I found the trauma and resilience training to be very helpful. I learned how to protect myself better from content that was potentially traumatic or reducing its effects through a series of steps. For instance, as a student and night owl, I would have done the research I did on the Airwars project, which involved graphic imagery, around 9–12 pm. Instead, per advice, I used the morning hours when I was fit, most awake, and resilient to look at this content, which helped me deal with it a lot better. Other tips, like turning off the volume on videos, have also translated into my everyday media consumption, for instance, when watching news on current conflicts. Furthermore, I felt that the recurring emphasis on the importance of protecting one's mental health allowed me to (relatively comfortably) talk to my supervisors and eventually switching projects. Thus, I think it was important that there was a lot of room for mental health concerns in this lab, given the nature of some of the content. Moreover, in this context I have, for the first time, explicitly prioritized my health over academic pursuit, which had its up and downsides, but was an important learning and precedent for me. This would not have happened in a less tolerant setting. My personal goal for the future is, to better integrate health concerns and academia, and use the strategies I learned in all aspects of my life.

Even students more experienced in the human rights field found the approach and training useful:

> Given the nature of the images we worked with, I really appreciated the emphasis that has been put on mental health and trauma training throughout the whole Lab. From the introductory lecture held by Manisha Ganguly in November 2023 to the impact event of Wednesday 17 April 2024, the risks for mental health were addressed constantly. My awareness of the risks involved in conducting open-source investigations, and how to prevent them, has been significantly raised thanks to this experience. […] In particular, the training provided by [the DART Center] was extremely useful. I have already specified that my past experience as a human rights lawyer dealing with refugees exposed me to stories, images and experiences which I often found overwhelming. In this regard, I still consider the suggestion of having compassion for myself of utmost importance. It must be noted that mental health is often overlooked in daily life; people usually do not fully realize the severity of the consequences. I am extremely grateful for the training that has been provided during the Lab. My only regret is that I had not been able to learn about this before: perhaps some things in my life would have been gone differently.

While the vast majority of students were positive about the trauma trainings, a handful had clear suggestions around the trauma trainings and how they can improve. One student, for instance, noted the emphasis on human rights issues rather than complex sustainability concerns, making a suggestion for change in their final reflection report:

> The trauma and resilience training provided a valuable preparation for our project, however with some limitations. While emphasizing the importance of avoiding evening research and incorporating pleasant activities afterward, I believe the training lacked depth in addressing nuanced challenges. Personally, I find dealing with violence and graphic imagery somewhat less intricate and I have experienced this through my exposure to war content coming from my country (Ukraine). For me, grappling with issues of sustainability proved to be more complex. There is a sense of helplessness inherent to addressing sustainability concerns, particularly when confronting large companies without adequate legal frameworks. Seeing instances of greenwashing intensified feelings of hopelessness and powerlessness. While my academic studies in global

> sustainability science exposed me to these issues theoretically, engaging in real-life investigations made them feel much more real. [...] Trying to process the scale and impact of environmental degradation that we saw through satellite imagery was challenging. Although the trauma and resilience training covered essential aspects, it seemed to focus predominantly on more obvious challenges. I believe discussions on environmental pessimism and the feelings of doom in tackling large corporations could have been better addressed by the training as this was relevant part of the lab.

Overall, the reflection logs and final reflection reports demonstrate that students highly valued the trauma trainings and raised their trauma awareness. Students noted that the trainings helped them protect themselves from traumatic effects and prioritizing their mental health. It is also notable that students specifically stated the trainings taught them to adopt practices outside of their usual routine. The trainings, furthermore, helped foster a classroom environment in which students felt connected to other students, comfortable talking to supervisors, and more confident in doing the projects. In addition, the reflections revealed that trauma and resilience trainings may have to be tailored to specific projects. While the trainings we provided were useful to students working on human-rights-associated projects, students also noted their limited utility in addressing 'sustainability concerns.'

5.3 *Endline Survey Results*

At the end of the course, all 25 students were asked to fill in an endline survey, which consisted of both Likert-scale and open-ended questions. Students were asked about how they experienced the reflections incorporated throughout the course. In this regard, using a Likert scale of 1–5, they were asked to rate how helpful the reflection assignments were for deepening their understanding of their own work and to provide an explanation for their rating. We viewed scores of 1–2 as falling within a negative response, 3 as neutral and 4–5 as falling within a positive response. They were also asked: "What are your three most important take away messages from the online trauma training at the beginning of the course and check-in moments during the course?" in an open-ended question. Their responses to the open-ended questions helped us better understand their overall experiences.

In asking what made the course an overall success for students, two students mentioned the check-in moments, where students reflected together, as a specific success factor. One student wrote, "Working on these heavy and sometimes graphic issues really emphasized the importance of teamwork," and another saying check-in moments, where the teams reflected together, were a 'great way to feel where the others were at and share our struggles.' On the other hand, one student noted this as a less successful aspect of the course because they found it difficult to share their personal experiences with others.

In regard to the reflection logs, 11 out of 21 students who provided qualitative feedback expressed that they found the reflections helpful, important, or beneficial. Five of these students specifically noted the value of the reflections in monitoring their emotions. One student said, "They allowed me to think about my emotions around the course more often than I probably would have without them." Two other students noted that the reflections were beneficial for the project but not for themselves individually, for example, by helping them 'become more aware of group dynamics.'

Five students (three positive, two neutral) noted that they initially had difficulty with the reflection assignments. One student wrote, "At first, I found it difficult to do them, but then I felt they were like safe spaces for me to reflect on myself." Another student wrote, "It was very challenging, but it made me realize how important it is to reflect on my actions and actually see what I do and feel when doing my work." Students said that the reflections were helpful for going back and looking at how they were feeling or how they developed over time.

There was also negative feedback in relation to the individual reflection reports. One student said, "Sometimes, certain things felt very personal, and I felt uncomfortable writing them down for the supervisors to read." Eight students said that they thought there was too much reflection during the course, which some felt resulted in repetitive submissions and 'diminishing returns' in terms of the quality of reflections. Three students also lamented that it was unclear why they were reflecting due to a lack of feedback. One student said, "It was good to reflect but it was too much in proportion to the work for the project. It did not really help the project work as the reflections have been sent and not spoken about a lot."

Prompting self-awareness through reflection is significant in taking a trauma-informed approach to open-source investigation labs. When asked what their greatest takeaways were from the trauma check-ins, eight students mentioned that they learned the importance of being in touch with their own feelings and looking out for signs of potential harm. For example, one student wrote, "Pay attention to your mental health," and another "it's not necessary to be insensitive, just to be aware." Overall, a comparison of the baseline and endline survey data reveals that students demonstrated a significant increase in awareness around trauma and resilience, as well as their overall emotional health. Fifteen students were able to identify various 'digital hygiene' strategies (e.g., taking breaks from mentally taxing work), and 12 students noted the importance of sharing feelings and working together as a major takeaway from the workshop.

Incorporating reflection throughout the course, while frustrating for some students, is valuable for others. The *practice* of reflecting is valuable due to the relationship between the reflecting and a student's ability to interpret signals of their own well-being, which is the foundation of maintaining mental hygiene. As noted by Rees (2017), and as raised in our trainings, by simply itemizing one's own physical and emotional reactions and giving a name to them can help bolster a sense of control. The workshops were highly effective in teaching students how to maintain mental hygiene, with 15 students listing methods learned in the course, such as 'taking breaks frequently,' 'take measures to limit exposure,' 'watch videos without sound' and 'doing emotionally straining work in the best hours in the morning when you feel focused and fresh' and 'not to mix work and daily life.' All these responses strongly reflect the DART Center's trainings as well as Bellingcat's guide on how to avoid vicarious trauma and maintain mental hygiene.

Students also mentioned the importance of talking to others, checking in with their team and having a support network. Three students mentioned the importance of letting go of shame, fear of sharing feelings, or 'feeling guilty about your emotions (or the lack thereof).' This broadly shared takeaway points to the significance of building a strong group dynamic and providing students with opportunities to give and receive support when working with high-risk materials. Although students were shown to have learned to maintain mental hygiene in completing their own tasks, fostering an environment in which students feel comfortable sharing also remains crucial in adopting a responsible trauma and resilience-informed approach to teaching, especially within open-source investigation environments.

6 The Necessity and Value for Students and Teaching in Adopting a Trauma and Resilience-Informed Approach in Open-Source Investigation Classrooms

For years, scholars have emphasized the need for educators to start thinking about and adopting trauma and resilience-informed practices in their classrooms (Kaur, 2021; McBride, 2018). This is particularly important in courses dealing with sensitive subject matter like human rights, a field where emotions play a significant role (Weerdesteijn, 2024). Even when students do not themselves suffer from PTSD or other serious stressors, studying certain subject matter, such as human rights or environmental damage, may cause them to experience negative emotions from engaging with distressing content. This has the potential to negatively impact their learning experience and overall well-being.

As a teaching team, we benefited from early conversations with societal partners and other labs introducing us to the need for trauma and resilience considerations from the outset. This allowed us to spend a good deal of time thinking about what a trauma and resilience- approach to teaching would mean for our students, who would come from different disciplinary backgrounds and stages in their education. Inspired by scholars and practitioners writing in this area, our lab took concrete steps to work out its approach.

As a teaching team, we sought to create an educational space as outlined by McBride (2018) and to incorporate Harris and Fallot's (2001) five core values: safety, trustworthiness, choice, collaboration and empowerment. With our ultimate goal being the creation of an educational space that supported both students and educators and which fostered resilience and better educational experiences for all involved. First and foremost, teachers within the Lab needed to become familiar with scholarship on trauma, emotions and education. Next, we needed to be trained by professionals working in this space. All of us needed to be aware of how to identify and support students and colleagues experiencing emotional distress. Third, we needed to design a useful approach for the Lab, with check-in moments and reflection. To this end, we focused on creating an inclusive environment that acknowledged and addressed emotions, feelings of distress, trauma and resilience. Much of our approach seemed to resonate with students. In fostering a safe environment, we issued trigger warnings and worked to create a space where feelings could be shared freely among students, stressing this from the beginning of the course.

Although McBride emphasizes the importance of maintaining a predictable classroom structure, which is linked with notions of safety and trustworthiness, this step proved more difficult as it conflicted with other course goals and, in many respects, would not be possible since it was the first iteration of the Lab. In this respect, we knew that there would be many unknowns, both for the students as well as for the teachers. Much of the uncertainty is also part and parcel of work associated with community-engaged learning, since students are working with societal partners on real-world projects, and that is something we sought to explicitly bring into the course (Lamnina & Chase, 2019). This meant that we, as educators, could not control all aspects of the Lab environment, but we could provide a general structure (team-taught lectures; skills workshops; project or lab work). To mitigate stress and ensure safety in this uncertain environment, we appointed a supervisor for each of the projects from the teaching team. The supervisor's role was to regularly meet with their students and mediate between students and partners. Nevertheless, the work with societal partners would, in particular, prove to be very unpredictable, and students definitely struggled with the unpredictability, such as slow replies from societal partners or having to come up with their own meeting schedule and deadlines. Based on their reflections, we learned that the teamwork environment and overall collaborative process that we fostered allowed students to navigate the irregularities in the course by trusting and coordinating closely with team members and supervisors.

Other steps adopted by the Lab as part of our trauma and resilience-informed approach involved decisions around course content, the use of trigger warnings and learning about and sharing coping strategies. In terms of course content, we thought carefully about what materials we would cover and what images and text we would use as examples or in assignments. We aimed to provide trigger warnings, giving students a choice to attend particular sessions or read specific material prior to the materials being shown or given, thus fostering a safe environment. However, it is difficult to know what type of material may trigger an emotional response in students. You may not always be able to control what images guest lecturers decide to show at the last minute, which may affect the perceived trustworthiness of educators. What we therefore found important in our experience is to create a space in class for discussions about the material and any emotional responses to that material. Other ways in which we incorporated choice into the curriculum included allowing students to choose which societal partner they wanted to work with. By having an array of societal partners and different projects with different subject matters (e.g., verification of airstrikes, verification of human rights abuses, verification of environmental degradation), we gave students a choice to work with the topic they felt most comfortable with and also allowed students who signaled their needs to change groups.

In terms of collaboration, there were at least two types of cooperation the students valued. First, the students highly appreciated the teamwork aspects of the course, including the group check-in moments to check on their well-being and team dynamics. Many were better able to understand how their own feelings and contributions were contributing to a greater whole. Second, and related to their peer teamwork, they found the collaborations with societal partners extremely valuable. At times, it was messy and unpredictable, but they felt a sense of purpose in contributing to real-world work. In this sense, they felt empowered by the course because they were able to participate in larger global justice processes.

We also aimed to empower students by equipping them with the building blocks for resilience, placing a good amount of attention on learning about coping strategies and the value of collaboration. This is where the DART Center training and other material, such as material prepared by Bellingcat or UC Berkeley's Investigation Lab, played a large role. Our hope was that these tools would help students learn how to manage their stress and potential trauma, but also learn how to build their resilience by teaching them how to process and handle distressing experiences effectively, both individually and within their groups. As the survey results and reflection logs indicate, students responded positively to these trainings and tools, as well as to the collaborative components. However, some felt that the trainings could go even further and cover information or material largely left out, such as distress over environmental damage.

Before the next iteration of the Lab, our teaching team will come together to evaluate and discuss our approach to trauma and resilience. This regular reflection and review moment is important (Harris & Fallot, 2001). We will go through the recommendations made by the students in the endline survey and in their final reflection reports. It is already clear that, as teachers, we need to provide them with more feedback on their reflection logs, as this was something desired by students. We may also want to think about bringing in a professional from the university, such as a student psychologist or counselor, for at least one of our check-in moments. This would flag to the students that, even though their teachers are available to them, we are not professionals who are equipped for dealing with serious distress. Rather, they should turn to professionals, which would also prevent "role strain" on the part of educators (Weerdesteijn, 2024, pp. 171–172).

By acknowledging and addressing (potentially) traumatic experiences, we have learned that educators can help students develop the resilience needed to succeed academically and personally. Our work in the Lab has made us conclude that educators do, in fact, have an important role to play in normalizing discussions around student emotions; we can and *should* help students better understand their emotional responses to sensitive materials and experiences. It is the responsibility of educators to adopt a trauma and resilience-sensitive approach because we care about the well-being of our students. Moreover, we are responsible for helping to prepare our students for future careers in fields that are likely to grapple with distressing material. Linking this approach to the future work field was very important within our Lab. Even though many of the fields related to open-source investigations traditionally treat trauma as "part of the job" (Markovikj, 2023) and foster cultures of "suffering in silence" (Buchanan & Keats, 2011 in Seely, 2019), we wanted to move away from that stance. Instead, we want our students to learn how to acknowledge and deal with their emotions in a safe but challenging environment.

The findings from the data we collected have made it clear to us the necessity and value of adopting a trauma and resilience-informed approach for students enrolled in open-source investigations classrooms. First, given the substantive subject matter of the Lab, which focused on global justice and human rights, there was always going to be an inherently distressing or sensitive aspect to the material covered. There is no way around that fact. Students looking to gain experience in open-source investigation techniques in this subject area will be exposed to both text and visual images that may be disturbing. A trauma-informed approach in this context means incorporating the five core values to build resilience to such materials, not to avoid such materials altogether. Second, the set-up of the Lab, as a community-engaged learning course, meant that there would be inherent uncertainty and unpredictability to the work due to the involvement of third-parties, who brought with them different ways of working and different ways of communicating. The students needed to deal with the real-world challenges of working with societal partners, which can be messy and complex at times. As teachers, we were not able to provide all the structure they may have desired. And, indeed, this would be contrary to our learning objectives. Instead, we sought to create an environment of collaboration which would help navigate the unpredictability.

Despite these two specific qualities of the Lab, the findings around the value of the trauma and resilience-informed approach are relevant to other complex university learning contexts. Any course that deals with sensitive or distressing materials, such as courses on human rights and mass atrocity, but also on environmental damage and sustainability, would benefit from thinking about such an approach and making room for the emotional reactions of students. In addition, any type of community-engaged learning project, which centers on reflection and emotion, could also think about adopting a specific trauma and resilience-sensitive approach where students learn specific coping skills as well as reflexivity. As educators, we have a responsibility towards our students, both in the present and in preparing them for their future work. From our findings and experiences, we recommend that educators working with open-source investigation labs or in classrooms dealing with sensitive material take a number of steps. First, they should start early when thinking about what a trauma and resilience-approach could mean in a particular classroom environment. Become informed through literature and tools about what trauma and resilience mean for students. Second, educators should adopt an approach that aligns with scholarship and that best fits the specific contexts of their learning environment. For some, this may mean controlling for uncertainty. For others, particularly in a community-engaged learning context, this may not be possible. Third, educators should regularly review and adapt their approach based on student and teacher experiences. Student populations change over time, and our approaches to their learning experiences need to change as well.

7 Conclusion

A growing number of universities globally are establishing digital open-source investigation courses or labs. These programs educate students from various disciplines on investigating and documenting serious human rights violations and environmental damages, teaching them the necessary skills in how to manage and analyze open-source materials. Since students may encounter potentially traumatic material, it is crucial that they receive training on emotional well-being by adopting a trauma and resilience-informed approach. This chapter used literature, survey results and student reflection logs to examine a complex learning environment, namely a digital open-source investigations lab established at Utrecht University in 2023. It explored how five core values around a trauma and resilience-informed approach, focusing on safety, trustworthiness, choice, collaboration and empowerment, can be successfully implemented. It further explored what lessons can be relevant for other courses tackling sensitive subject matter. In particular, the chapter stressed the importance of (i) starting early to think about what a trauma and resilience-approach could mean in a particular classroom environment; (ii) adopting an approach that aligns with scholarship and best fits the specific contexts of that learning environment; and (iii) regularly reviewing and adapting the approach based on student and teacher experiences.

References

Berkeley Human Rights Center (2012, October 23–24). Beyond Reasonable Doubt: Using Scientific Evidence to Advance Prosecutions at the International Criminal Court. Workshop Report, retrieved 20 June 2024 from https://www.law.berkeley.edu/wp-content/uploads/2015/04/Beyond-Reasonable-Doubt-October-2012.pdf.

Berkeley Human Rights Center. Resilience: Trauma-Informed Practice, retrieved 13 September 2024 from https://humanrights.berkeley.edu/projects/resilience/.

Bringle, R. G., Hatcher, J. A. (2011). International service-learning. In: R. Bringle, J. Hatcher, S. Jones (Eds.). *International service-learning: Conceptual frameworks and research*. Sterling: Stylus Publishing, pp. 3–28.

Bringle, R., Hatcher, J., McIntosh, R. (2006). Analyzing Morton's Typology of Service Paradigms and Integrity. *Michigan Journal of Community Service Learning*, 13(1), pp. 5–15.

Bringle, R. G., Hatcher, J. A. (1995). A service-learning curriculum for faculty. *Michigan Journal of Community Service Learning*, 2(1), pp. 112–122.

Buchanan M., Keats P. (2011). Coping with traumatic stress in journalism: A critical ethnographic study. *International Journal of Psychology*, 46, pp. 127–135.

Canfield, J. (2008). Secondary Traumatization, Burnout, and Vicarious Traumatization: A Review of the Literature as It Relates to Therapists Who Treat Trauma. *Smith College Studies in Social Work*, 75(2), pp. 81–101.

Carello, J., Butler, L. D. (2015). Practicing what we teach: Trauma-informed educational practice. *Journal of Teaching Social Work*, 35(3), pp. 262–27.

Davidson, S. (2017). Trauma-informed practices for postsecondary education: A guide. *Education Digest*, 82(8), pp. 44–48.

Dubberley, S., Koenig, A., Murray, D., (2018a). Introduction: The Emergence of Digital Witnesses. In: S. Dubberley, A. Koenig, D. Murray (Eds.)., *Digital Witness*. Oxford: Oxford University Press, pp. 3–11.

Dubberley, S., Satterhwaite, M., Knuckey, S., Brown, A., (2018b). Digital Human Rights Investigations: Vicarious Trauma, PTSD, and Tactics for Resilience. In: S. Dubberley, A. Koenig, D. Murray (Eds.)., *Digital Witness*. Oxford: Oxford University Press, pp. 271–291.

Dubberley, S. (2019, December 6). The Digital Verification Corps: Amnesty International's Volunteers for the Age of Social Media. *Amnesty International website*, retrieved 20 June 2024 from https://citizenevidence.org/2019/12/06/the-digital-verification-corps-amnesty-internationals-volunteers-for-the-age-of-social-media/

Fiorella, G., (2022, November 23). How to Maintain Mental Hygiene as an Open Source Researcher. *Bellingcat*, retrieved 20 June 2024 from https://www.bellingcat.com/resources/2022/11/23/how-to-maintain-mental-hygiene-as-an-open-source-researcher.

Flannery, R. B. (2022). News Journalists and Posttraumatic Stress Disorder: A Review of Literature, 2011–2020. *Psychiatric Quarterly*, 93(1), pp. 151–159.

Forbes-Mewett, H., Sawyer, A-M. (2016). International Students and Mental Health. *Journal of International Students*, 6(3), pp. 661–677.

Goodwin, J., Tiderington, E. (2022). Building trauma-informed research competencies in social work education. *Social Work Education*, 41, pp. 143–156.

Harris, M., Fallot, R. D. (2001). Envisioning a trauma-informed service system: A vital paradigm shift. *New Directions for Mental Health Services*, 2001(89), pp. 3–22.

Henshaw, L. A. (2022). Building Trauma-Informed Approaches in Higher Education. *Behavioral Sciences*, 12(368), pp. 1–13.

Holman, E. A., Garfin, D. R., Lubens, P., Silver, R. C. (2020). Media exposure to collective trauma, mental health, and functioning: Does it matter what you see? *Clinical Psychology Science*, 8(1), pp. 111–124

Hill, D., Luther, C. A., Slocum, P. (2020). Preparing Future Journalists for Trauma on the Job. *Journalism & Mass Communication Educator*, 75(1), pp. 64–68

Kaur, M. (2021). Negotiating Trauma & Teaching Law. *Journal of Law and Social Policy*, 35, pp. 113–119.

Kenny, M., Gallagher, L. (2002). Service-Learning: a History of Systems. In: M. Kenny, L. Simon, K. Kiley-Brabeck, R. Lerner (Eds.). *Learning to serve. Promoting Civil Society Through Service Learning*. Boston: Kluwer Academic Publishers, pp. 15–30.

Kleber, R.J. (2019). Trauma and Public Mental Health: A Focused Review. *Frontiers in Psychiatry*. 10(541), pp. 1–6.

Koenig, A. (2018). Open Source Evidence and Human Rights Cases: a Modern Social History. In: S. Dubberley, A. Koenig, D. Murray, (Eds.). *Digital Witness*. Oxford: Oxford University Press, pp. 32–48.

Koettl, C., Murray, D., Dubberley, S. (2018). Open Source Investigations for Human Rights Reporting: a Brief History. In: S. Dubberley, A. Koenig, D. Murray, (Eds.). *Digital Witness*. Oxford: Oxford University Press, pp. 12–32.

Lamnina, M., Chase, C. C. (2019). Developing a thirst for knowledge: How uncertainty in the classroom influences curiosity, affect, learning, and transfer. *Contemporary Educational Psychology*, 59(101785), pp. 1–13.

Latta, M., Kruger, T. M., Payne, L.., Weaver, L.., Van Sickle, J. L. (2018). Approaching Critical Service-Learning: A Model for Reflection on Positionality and Possibility. *Journal of Higher Education Outreach and Engagement*, 22(2), pp. 31–59.

Malik, S.I., Boudhane, Y., Alafranji, M., Makki, A. (2024). Awareness of Trauma-Focused Education and Attitudes Toward Incorporating Trauma-Focused Education in Curricula Among MENA Journalism Educators. *Journalism & Mass Communication Educator*, 79(1), pp. 38–58.

Markovikj, M., Serafimovska, E. (2023). Mental Health Resilience in the Journalism Curriculum. *Journalism & Mass Communication Educator*, 78(2), pp. 233–250.

McBride, K. A. (2018). Creating a trauma-sensitive environment for teaching human rights. In: L. N. Kingston (Ed.)., *Human Rights in Higher Education*. Palgrave Macmillan, pp. 129–144.

McGonigle Leyh, B. (2021). The Role of Universities and Law Schools in Documenting Serious International Crimes and Advancing the Rule of Law. *Utrecht Law Review*, 17, pp. 87–101.

McHugh, B. C., Wisniewski, P., Rosson, M. B., Carroll, J. M. (2018). When social media traumatizes teens: The roles of online risk exposure, coping, and post-traumatic stress. *Internet Research*, 28(5), pp. 1169–1188.

McMahon, C. (2008). Journalist reporting for duty: Resilience, trauma, and growth. In: K. Gow, D. Paton (Eds.). *The Phoenix of Natural Disasters: Community Resilience*. New York: Nova Science Publishers, pp. 101–121

Meijs, L., Koolen-Maas, S. A., Aramburuzabala, P. (2019). Institutonalisation of service learning in European higher education. In: P. Aramburuzabala, L. McIlrath, and H. Opazo (Eds). *Embedding Service Learning in European Higher Education: Developing a Culture of Civic Engagement*. New York: Routledge, pp. 213–230.

Nah, A. (2019). Navigating mental and emotional wellbeing in risky forms of human rights activism. *Social Movement Studies*, 20(1), pp. 20–35.

Ogunyemi, O. and Price, L. T. (2023). Introduction: Trauma Literacy in Global Journalism: Toward an Education Agenda. *Journalism & Mass Communication Educator*, 78(2), pp. 107–111.

Rees, G. (2017). 'Handling Traumatic Imagery: Developing a Standard Operating Procedure.' *Dart Center website*, retrieved 20 February 2025 from https://dartcenter.org/resources/handling-traumatic-imagery-developing-standard-operating-procedure

Seely N. (2019). Fostering trauma literacy: From the classroom to the newsroom. *Journalism & Mass Communication Educator*, 75(1), pp. 116–130.

Shapiro, B. (2015, August 5). Managing Stress & Trauma on Investigative Projects. *DART Center*, retrieved 20 June 2024 from https://dartcenter.org/content/staying-sane-managing-stress-and-trauma-on-investigative-projects.

Specht D., Tsilman J. (2018). Teaching vicarious trauma in the journalism classroom: An examination of educational provision in UK universities. *Journal of Applied Journalism and Media Studies*, 7(2), pp. 407–427.

Seely N. (2019). Fostering trauma literacy: From the classroom to the newsroom. *Journalism & Mass Communication Educator*, 75(1), pp. 116–130.

Tremblay, G., Rodrigues, N. C., Gulati, S. (2021). Mental Hygiene: What It Is, Implications, and Future Directions. *Journal of Prevention and Health Promotion*, 2(1), pp. 3–31.

Quigley, F. (1995). Seizing the Disorienting Moment: Adult Learning Theory and the Teaching of Social Justice in Law School Clinics. *Clinical Law Review* 2, pp. 37–72.

Weerdesteijn, M. (2024). Coping as an Academic Skill. In: L. Harris, M. Kaur (Eds.). *How to Account for Trauma and Emotions in Law Teaching*. Cheltenham: Edward Elgar, pp. 171–185.

Wu, G., Feder, A., Cohen, H., Kim, J. J., Calderon, S., Charney, D. S., Mathé, A. A. (2013). Understanding resilience. *Frontiers in Behavioral Neuroscience*, 7(10), pp. 1–15.

PART 3

Reflections from Practitioners

CHAPTER 7

Emotions in International Criminal Justice: Where Do They Take Us?

Martin Witteveen

1 Introduction

I am speaking with a colleague who works in our international crimes team. He announces his farewell. I congratulate him on his next move and commend him for the work he has done. For the past 10 years, he has greatly contributed to our cases as a historian and country specialist, drafting lengthy analyses that were indispensable for successful prosecutions. His knowledge and professionalism are widely recognized among us, and his strong views are appreciated in discussions.

We reminisce on some of the older cases he and I worked on together. I tell him he has so much to look back on and be proud of. He responds immediately: Yes, but there are many frustrations too. For a moment, I am taken aback. Then I realize what he is referring to: cases that have not been resolved, court rulings he could not understand, perspectives of others he fundamentally disagreed with and ultimately the injustices he witnessed.

Frustration may be a prevalent emotion among international criminal justice practitioners. It can be a tremendously intense emotion that overshadows other, more positive emotions also felt in our line of work. Frustration is particularly felt when we are deeply involved in our work, when we are highly motivated and driven by the injustices we see. Oftentimes, we are convinced that we can do something about it, and then it does not happen. Frustration is a tricky and treacherous emotion. Frustrations, certainly when felt consistently, can lead to hopelessness. Hopelessness can then lead to anger, and anger to feelings of exhaustion. This exhaustion can finally turn into indifference, which I consider the greatest sin of all.

Most of my career, I have worked as a prosecutor in my national jurisdiction in the Netherlands. I have done most of what we call the ordinary criminal cases and organized crime, including cases in which we had to deal with victims from those crimes. Over the years, I have seen emotions of all kinds gradually but irrevocably slip into courtrooms. Victims were given the right to speak during trials, and they massively exercised that right. In court, they passionately spoke how the crime had affected them. Many times, they could not hold back their emotions, which led to outbursts, sometimes directed towards the defendant and yelling at them. Defendants are also very emotional at times. They show anger towards people who have accused them or filed complaints. Many times, they feel repentant about what they have done and show remorse. The tremendous number of male defendants who cry before a court amazes me.

When I started as a prosecutor, I do not remember the public generally showing much interest in criminal justice. Now the media is all over it. The number of television shows on crime has exploded, and there is hardly any evening news anymore without an item on crime. Newspapers even specialized reporters flooding the courtrooms. All this is to say that emotions certainly occur in ordinary crime cases too and are not unique for international criminal justice. These emotions might be what triggers or spurs on media interest.

I have been fortunate to find my place as a practitioner in international criminal justice, first as a team lead in the Office of the Prosecutor of the International Criminal Court (ICC) for the situation in Northern Uganda. I spent three and a half years there, and a good part of it was spent doing fieldwork in an area I was totally unfamiliar with. Then, I worked for five years as an investigation magistrate for international crimes in the Dutch District Court in The Hague, where I conducted pre-trial investigations in our cases, mainly by hearing witnesses abroad. I spent two years in Palestine on a European Union Rule of Law mission and one full year in Rwanda as an advisor to the Prosecution Service on their genocide cases. More recently, I worked for two years as a coach and mentor to local defense lawyers in Myanmar as part of a free legal aid project. Finally, I spent a year in Ethiopia advising the Ethiopian Human Rights Commission, which investigated the war in Tigray.

Looking back, all these experiences came with many emotions. Emotions I felt myself and emotions I observed in other people. Somehow, they were more intense, deeply felt and impacted me more. I may have forgotten most of them, but some will never leave my system.

In my contribution here, I will try to unearth some of the emotions I have experienced myself and some I have witnessed in others. All these emotions have inevitably affected me in many ways, and not only me as a person but also the criminal justice system I have worked in as well. I will explore how. Ultimately, I have always rejected the idea of remaining in despair, hopelessness or exhaustion, let alone indifference. Is there a remedy for these feelings? As a person, maybe as a man, I am not accustomed to writing about emotions. Could it be a healing experience? This will certainly not be an academic piece, nor do I claim it to be. I will write from personal experiences and views.

2 Examples of Emotions

2.1 *Trauma*

I have never spoken so much about trauma, nor have I read more about trauma than when I worked as a practitioner in international criminal justice. When we deal with witnesses, and we deal with them all the time, we wonder: is this witness traumatized? Can I see it and, more importantly, can I do something about it? What does it mean for the case? Are traumatized witnesses credible and reliable? Maybe I am traumatized myself? How could I know for sure? Can I be my own psychologist? Does my superior know, and does he or she care at all? Do I need to start doing different work?

Trauma is everywhere. In my first years as a prosecutor, I cannot recall much about trauma or the parties in a criminal case being traumatized. That quickly changed when I started to work in international criminal justice, especially when I got to do fieldwork. To be clear: trauma does exist. I have seen it with my own eyes and felt it. It is scary.

It is 2008. It is my first year as investigation magistrate for international crimes. The case before me is against a defendant charged with his role in the Rwandan genocide. In this case, there was an attack by a group of perpetrators on thousands of Tutsi victims who, at the time, thought they had found shelter at a religious complex in a remote part of Western Rwanda with a church, hospital and schools. I have done a number of hearings before this one but am still learning to cope with the negative effects of hearing witnesses. Then comes this female witness. She is a victim of the attack in that complex. I am trying to meticulously go over the events of that horrible day. To ensure her testimony can be assessed as reliable, I need to know where she was positioned when she witnessed the events twenty-four years earlier. Rwandan witnesses tend to have difficulty estimating distances and numeral measurements. To assist her, I ask her to go to a window in the room where the hearing is taking place. I point at an object outside and ask her to estimate the distance. I see her staring, and after a while, her body starts to shake uncontrollably. She does not know how to stop it. She is unresponsive to everything we say. It is clear that, in her mind, she is back at the scene where the horror took place. We bring her back to her seat to help her calm down. I realize that we need to stop this hearing. This scene has haunted me for years. I realize she completely lost herself because of what I asked her to do. I re-traumatized her.

A few years later, still in office, I receive a request from the war crimes court in Bosnia to hear a witness. He is a former soldier who served in a UN-battalion at Srebrenica, named Dutchbat. I have my staff send him the summons to appear. Then I receive a call from the Ministry of Defense asking me whether I know this man and what is the matter with him. I say I don't know. The man from the ministry explains to me that the witness no longer serves in the army because of trauma incurred while serving in Dutchbat. At this point in time, I had hired a psychologist who was experienced in assessing war-related trauma to assist me. I invite him to assess the man before the hearing. On the day of the hearing, I am notified the man has arrived. I meet him in the waiting room, where he is with his girlfriend. I introduce myself, and he immediately starts to shout at me, demanding an explanation why he was summoned. He yells if I know what had happened and how unfairly the ministry handled his situation. He completely loses it right there in the waiting room until his girlfriend calms him down. I can still feel the anger and rage of the man in my mind. I have him assessed by the psychologist, who deems him unfit to be heard. I cancel the hearing and notify the Bosnian authorities.

In the Uganda investigation, a substantial portion of the witnesses were young men and women, all former Lord's Resistance Army (LRA) abductees. The boys were used as child soldiers and the girls as sex slaves for the commanders. We selected some of them as witnesses from rehabilitation centers with whom we have excellent collaboration. The team is assisted by a professional psychologist who examines the boys and girls first. The interviews with them are painful. I have seen these boys and girls. I remember their faces as numb and without expression, unable to even talk. The staff of these rehab centers did wonders in bringing most of the boys and girls back to life.

2.2 *Fear and Stress*

Most of us have suffered from levels of stress in our work. It is nothing out of the ordinary. We all need a bit of adrenaline to function well. Yet, some people cannot cope with high levels of stress and suffer from burnout. The prevalence of burnouts is high, unfortunately. I have had my share of stress at work, but nothing compared to the situations of extreme stress and even fear I experienced as a practitioner during fieldwork.

It is 2006, and the Uganda investigation at the ICC is progressing well. The Chamber has issued arrest warrants against the five top commanders of the LRA. We, as a team, are digesting tons of information, processing some as evidence, doing additional investigations, and trying to develop strategies for arrest. The stress levels in the Office of the Prosecutor have been high, in part due to the work climate. We have a great team that can deal with it, but nothing prepared me for the personal stress from conducting field work. The office is notified that Dominic Ongwen, one of the five commanders, is killed in a battle with the government army. If that is true, his arrest warrant must be nullified, but his death first needs to be investigated and proven. Eric, our forensic expert, and I will take on that job. We travel to Uganda, where we identify and meet family members. We sample their DNA and begin preparations for exhuming the body. His alleged grave is at a dumpsite just outside of an IDP camp near Soroti. The exact location is pointed out to us, and I hire a few local workers to do the actual digging. I also ensure that there will be cooperation from local authorities and the army. A few weeks later, we go back to the site. The day of the actual exhumation is nearing. I start to panic. I can't sleep anymore. My mind is haunted by images of a half-decomposed body that will appear from the grave. Then the day of exhumation and identification arrives. We are there at the dumpsite. I see various makeshift graves; many are of babies and young children. I shiver. I position myself behind a camera to film the scene. The men start digging but back off when they spot a piece of cloth. Eric asks me to assist, and together we pull the cloth out, along with the body. We see the body has partially decomposed. My blood runs cold. We put the remains in a body bag and bring it to a hospital morgue that I had arranged beforehand. Eric and I are the only ones in the room. He zips open the bag and cleans the inside with a hose. He needs to find four pieces of bone and starts cutting with a small handsaw. He fumes at the office for not providing him with sufficient equipment and then asks me to hold the bones so he can saw them. I cannot refuse, but I silently wish I could disappear into the ground. He manages to get the four pieces he needs. We put the rest of the remains back in the body bag. It's finally over. Eric, who has now fallen sick, immediately leaves for Kampala. This leaves me with the body bag, and I wonder what to do with it. I call the office and am told not to rebury it where it came from. I am panicking again. What am I supposed to do? There is no cemetery. I go to the local churches where people are buried, but, knowing who is supposed to be in the body bag, nobody gives permission. Finally, the solution is to bring the bag to Kampala, where it will be buried. The next morning, I have police officers and two pick-up trucks set for the trip. We put the bag in the back of a pick-up and are ready to leave. However, there is no fuel in the tank, so we first stop at a petrol station. While we refuel, many schoolboys pass by and start yelling and showing an interest in the body bag. My blood begins racing, and my head pounds from the nerves, but we manage to leave without interference. Close to Kampala, the pick-up truck breaks down. An hour later, we find ourselves in a back alley of Jinja in what is supposed to look like a garage. The bag is still in the back of the truck. Eventually, we arrive in Kampala. Later that night, Eric and I return home together. When

I start to relax, a feeling of guilt kicks in. I have just 'kidnapped' a body from a grave and had it moved to an anonymous grave. The results later revealed that it was not the body of Ongwen. Whoever the person was, their relatives will never know what happened to their beloved family member. What have I done?

I have also seen fear among witnesses. Fear to testify and fear of any repercussions. Potential witnesses are often fearful, and so was this lady, who lived in the United States. As an examining magistrate, I had to hear her as a witness in a Rwanda case tried in the Dutch court. She was identified and located, but she refused to communicate out of fear. I requested to meet her informally, and she consented to meet, provided it was not in a governmental building. So, I met her at a McDonald's far away from her town. I will never forget the intensity of her anxiety when we spoke and the expressions on her face. I thought it was a hopeless situation, but in the end, she consented to be heard.

2.3 *Shame*

Not only do witnesses sometimes feel afraid when approached or summoned to appear, but they often also feel shame. Moreover, the prevalence of shame can have very different dimensions.

The story of the Lord's Resistance Army in Uganda is well known. They abducted children, brought them to their camps in the bush, and used the boys as child soldiers and the girls as sex slaves for their commanders. Over the years, the strength of the rebel movement crumbled, and many of the children could be freed or were able to escape. By this time, the girls often had babies from these commanders. Rehabilitation centers received the former child soldiers and the girls, and cared for them so they could reintegrate in their societies. For the investigation, they were a rich source of potential witness evidence. However, the collection of information from these centers and the selection of witnesses was a tedious job. The interviews with the girls, in particular, posed challenges. The protocol in the office prescribed that they needed to be interviewed in the presence of a parent or guardian. During an interview, they would be asked about their experiences in the bush and their abuse. At first, many denied being raped and sexually abused. It appeared that they had never spoken about it with their parents, many of whom were often ignorant about the issue. Their level of shame was immense. The girls simply fell silent. The interviews were extremely painful to conduct, and to see these girls like that, was heartbreaking.

As an investigation magistrate conducting hearings with witnesses in Rwanda, shame among witnesses was everywhere. Witnesses often did not want to speak about the events during the genocide; some even blamed themselves. During one hearing with a female witness, after doing the introduction and explanation, I routinely asked whether she had any concerns about being heard and what I could do to accommodate her. She responded by saying she did not want to be heard as she was ashamed. Although authorities had brought her to the location where I heard her, her family and her church had told her not to cooperate. They said she should refuse to come because she is supposed to forgive her wrongdoers, the perpetrators of the crimes. With a grim expression on her face, eyes looking downwards, she requested to be excused. In the end, she stayed, but I wondered how voluntary that was.

2.4 *Humor and Laughter*

Working in the field of [international] criminal justice is not something you do for fun. If you want to laugh, you need to change jobs and do something else. Yet, sometimes there is room for a joke or a laugh. Maybe cynicism or dark humor keeps us alive. Sometimes, the burden of our work and the heaviness from the substance in cases require us to compensate and have a laugh.

I do not recall a lot of fun or laughter in all the years of work as a practitioner in international criminal justice, apart from the inappropriate jokes some people made. I do, however, remember a strange event when someone broke out in laughter for no real reason. A witness hearing conducted by an examining magistrate, as I have performed many times, is a formal occasion that is informally performed. I do not wear a robe; the prosecutor and defense lawyer attend, there is a clerk who registers the witness statements, and we use an interpreter as needed. The setting is informal, usually around a table in a meeting room. Part of our procedure, as prescribed by law, is reading back the statement to the witness and providing an opportunity to make amendments or comments. It is the most unexciting part of the hearing and when boredom looms. One day, when we performed this part of the hearing, the interpreter broke out in uncontrollable laughter after remarks from the clerk. He could not compose himself, and looking at us only led to more extensive giggles. I am not a psychologist, but it seemed to be an outlet for him, as there was nothing funny to laugh about in the middle of a hearing where a witness recounts the horrors of a genocide.

2.5 *Disillusionment*

We tend to think of perpetrators of international crimes, such as genocide, crimes against humanity and war crimes, as monsters. I am sure many are. I have been overwhelmed by the stories of atrocity crimes when I heard dozens of witnesses who recounted these crimes in every painstaking detail, therewith detailing all the cruelties. Hearing the stories directly from those who suffered them is, at times, a horrifying experience. Immediately, you picture a perpetrator as the worst of humankind. However, when I see the perpetrators in my cases and even sit with one or two, I feel disillusioned. They look like normal people, although they could not be. Were these seemingly regular people the monsters that had committed the crimes the witnesses testified about?

I had to think of Oliver Hirschbiegel's 2004 movie '*Der Untergang*' about the last months of Hitler's life in his bunker in Berlin. Yes, the scenes where he was outraged, shouted and completely out of his mind were played so realistically that even on a film screen, it frightened me. On the other hand, there were scenes where he acted completely human by being kind to children and caring for the people around him. Was this the same monster?

When investigating the Lord's Resistance Army during fieldwork and encountering numerous victims – with children especially impacting me – I could only think of the five commanders against whom arrest warrants were issued as monsters. The pictures of them in the bush did not help change that impression; on the contrary. I remember I felt totally disillusioned when I saw Dominic Ongwen for the first time, albeit on a screen. He dressed in a civil suit and maintained a calm demeanor as he sat there quietly on a bench, listening. He came across as a normal person, childlike even. He was a victim himself; he was originally recruited as a child soldier and then turned into a perpetrator. How could he have committed all these cruelties? It triggered a surge of questions in me about guilt and punishment.

The second Rwanda case was another sobering experience in this regard. The defendant was a woman charged with, and ultimately convicted for, incitement to genocide. Interestingly, the defendant requested to be heard by me, an unusual move in Dutch criminal procedure. The sessions lasted several days and came after most of the witness testimonies. She was quite responsive to questions, although evasive where it really mattered. Nevertheless, my feelings were certainly not those of repulsiveness. I grew curious and wanted to understand why she became the person she was during the genocide. I did my best not to feel pity.

A few years ago, I was prosecuting a member of the military junta, the Dergue, in Ethiopia during the 70's. He was charged, among other things, with ordering the execution of 72 political opponents who were murdered in a prison compound. The Dergue was the military, totalitarian power at the time in Ethiopia and extremely cruel in their oppression of political opponents. Their torture methods were particularly heinous. Hearing witnesses recount the horrors of those times and reading their statements was very painful. Yet, when he appeared in court and was willing to defend himself, I still felt a sense of sympathy for him because he had terminal cancer. He died shortly after being convicted to life imprisonment. Even in this situation, he was able to give his side of the story and explain his views on historical events in Ethiopia at the time.

I started reading Hannah Arendt's *Eichmann in Jerusalem – A Report on the Banality of Evil*, which she wrote after reporting on Adolf Eichmann's trial in Jerusalem. She was equally disillusioned about Eichmann and his role in the Holocaust, describing him as neither perverted nor sadistic; in fact, terrifyingly normal (Arendt, 1964).

2.6 *Frustration, Anger, Disgust, Revulsion, Exhaustion and All of That*

After all these years of work and, to be honest, after taking in all the books I have read, movies and videos I have seen, and after consuming all the news and television – not to forget the massive stream of information from the omnipresent internet that never seems to stop – the feelings that have mostly stuck with me are anger, disgust, revulsion and sometimes near exhaustion. The massive violence in the world, the incomprehensible amount of suffering of victims of atrocity crimes, and the arrogance with which the powerful actors of this world feel completely free to do whatever they like, disregarding any sense of humanity, is shocking and overwhelms me. It strikes me more and more that this evil in the world is not primarily conducted by armed groups, bad individuals, or even by rebel groups and what we call terrorists – it's done by states and the powers within states, such as state militaries. Often by governments which have been democratically elected.

I often think back to times when I was first exposed to the atrocities, albeit not in person but through investigations. My gut reaction was: "I do not believe this happened." My brain blocked the truth. After three years of conducting investigations in Uganda, I thought there was nothing worse than what I heard and seen there, but it turned out there was so much more to come. As an investigation magistrate, the very first hearing I conducted was with a victim of the Rwandan genocide who lived in Switzerland. I spent two days with him, and he recounted what happened to him as best as he could. During the genocide, he lived in Western Rwanda. First, he, like so many of the Tutsi population, sought refuge in buildings such as churches. After he survived the attacks on these churches, he went to open places such as stadiums. Again, he survived attacks there and fled to the hills of Bisesero. Week after week, he told me, the attackers came every day. They came to those hills with their guns and machetes, chased the people who had fled, and killed them by hand. Again, he survived. He said the attackers, often ordinary citizens of the villages, even neighbors, considered the attacks to be regular work. They were bussed to the hills every morning and would stop hacking with their machetes for lunch. Then they continued during the afternoon and would return to the village at the end of the day to have a beer and dinner, sleep and continue killing the next morning. I was stunned humans could do this. I was in disbelief.

I remember another female witness who was a victim of an attack in the religious compound in Western Rwanda, where approximately two thousand Tutsis were killed in one day. She told me that she saw the attackers arrive in the morning and that she went from building to building to survive the ordeal. In the afternoon, she ended up in the hospital and tried to hide in the toilets with a group of women, but they were discovered. One by one, an attacker killed the women with his spear. She was the last one alive from the group. When the attacker killed the last woman before her, the spear broke and the attacker said he would get another one and come back. He, however, didn't come back and she survived. I have never cried during a hearing, but I was utterly shocked by this story and fell silent for a while, trying to swallow my emotions.

One day in Rwanda, after finishing weeks of similar hearings and concluding a case, before leaving for home, I had breakfast at this posh hotel in Kigali we were staying at before I left for home. It was busy, and I joined other people at a table. They told me they were businesspeople from Singapore and other parts of the world exploring business opportunities in Rwanda. The woman was a salesperson for Gucci and told me there was a great market for her products with female customers in Rwanda. She was excited. I felt despaired. What on earth was I doing there, trying to bring some justice for victims of a genocide, while some people in the population were apparently keen on buying Gucci bags.

I have always advised people who are in this field of work to change jobs after five years to avoid exhaustion. I changed jobs but still returned to similar jobs in which I had to deal with international crimes because I could not let go. Feelings of exhaustion are familiar for colleagues and others I have spoken to. Recently, I was in a job interview. The person had worked with non-governmental organizations, trying to push for justice in many cases but often failed. He was clearly overqualified for the job he applied for now, and I asked him what led him to this step. He said that after all his work and seeing the horrors in the wars in Syria, Ukraine and Gaza, he felt exhausted and wanted a simpler life. We all feel like that sometimes.

And, of course, there is a fair share of frustration, as my colleagues felt as well. Frustration about the loss of life and the suffering, frustration about impunity, which seems to reign when the powerful believe accountability is not for them, frustration about cases we cannot conduct, failed investigations, and even some acquittals, which are not necessarily unfair but still feel like a loss.

3 How Have Emotions Influenced Our Work or Decisions?

3.1 *Our Decision-Making*

There is no doubt that every practitioner who is either directly or remotely involved in international criminal justice work is subjected to emotions. However, how they affect us as practitioners is a different matter and may depend on what our role is. I believe the closer you have been to the crimes committed, the more you will have incurred emotions and be affected by them. First responders to the crimes, and, for instance, crime scene investigators, will be impacted by what they experience and will experience subsequent emotions that are multifold compared to anyone else working behind a desk. But even when practitioners are confronted with the crimes in a much more indirect way, for example, by reading victim witnesses' statements, these statements can still trigger intense emotions.

And then there are many practitioners in between: forensic scientists, such as Eric, with whom I was sawing the bones from the remains of an LRA-fighter; police officers; the many intermediaries we use, who oftentimes work for non-governmental organizations, aid organizations, rehab centers and others like interpreters, analysts, psychologists and prosecutors. All of us have emotions that are tied to a role we had in a situation or something we saw, but everyone will experience their emotions in a unique way. In all of this, we must remember that we are not only professionals who work in international criminal justice, but that we are also individual human beings, each with our own personality and character. Who we are and what we become in life depends mainly on our genetics, upbringing and social environment. What we choose to be is just a small part, as I used to tell my children.

The big question, of course, is how these emotions influence our work, and particularly our decision-making. That question is especially relevant for trial judges, whose responsibility it is to rule on guilt and punishment. As far as I am concerned, I do not know the answer, simply because I have no clue how to measure such influences and connect them to decision-making, such as court verdicts. I spend a lot of my time on reading, but it is mostly legal, historical or political material. As far as I know, there is very little academic research done and academic writings on this topic (Liden, 2020).

But what I have done is observe. I try to understand my emotions, verbalize them, and analyze them. I do the same with emotions I have witnessed in others – the witnesses themselves, but also equally with the emotions of professionals I have worked with, including my colleagues, investigators, staff of non-governmental organizations and others as indicated above. I am acutely aware of how the facts of the field have made it to the court rooms and the judges' chambers, and how they have led to verdicts. It doesn't mean I understand everything, but I can try to piece it together.

First of all, I know I cannot separate emotions from cognitive behavior or reason. They are intertwined and originate in my brain in areas that are connected to each other and influence each other. I am also, as a human and a professional, part of a social group, each with a mission and goals to fulfill, as well as expectations to live up to. I have been fortunate to have worked in different places: in an investigation team, in a court as a judge and as a member of the prosecution service. That helps. From these experiences, I am expected to uphold a standard to be objective and independent. As a judge, I also must be impartial. The Rome Statute, the founding document for the ICC, says the Prosecutor seeks incriminating as well as exculpatory evidence. Various rulings by the ICC Chambers have reminded us that, as a legal actor, I must not only appear to be impartial and objective, I must actually be so internally. Supposedly, this means that, as a legal actor, I should try to prevent emotions from influencing my ability to reason impartially and objectively, regardless of whether these influences are conscious (explicit) or subconscious (implicit).

This is all great, but the issue is that I cannot prevent having a certain implicit bias, the same way everyone else cannot. I am biased towards people, particularly witnesses and the defendant, and I am preoccupied towards a certain outcome in the case. Over the years, in the field of international criminal justice, I have developed a sense of skepticism towards myself and most other justice actors regarding the claim that we are professional, independent and objective. I am also convinced that my experiences and the emotions they have triggered are the cause of this skepticism. We simply develop too many preconceived notions, and these are mainly based on what we see rather than what we hear or read. I believe that our bias is visually based. Our eyes, in particular, deceive us and bring about emotions we cannot control sufficiently.

Sometimes I provide trainings or give workshops on witness evidence. On these occasions, I, for instance, show a video clip of the first Presidential debate in United States history between Richard Nixon and John Kennedy. Viewers overwhelmingly felt that Kennedy was the winner, while radio listeners favored Nixon, the reason probably being that he looked pale, suspicious and sweated on camera. There are endless examples.

There is an ongoing debate about whether it is better for trial judges to see and hear the witnesses themselves or to only have the hearing transcripts. It is an important question, in my view, because it highlights the heart of the bias-issue. Do the judges who both hear and see the witnesses show more favor towards convicting the defendant than judges who do not see the witnesses? I don't think this is always the case because the visual appearance of a witness may also lead a judge to dislike them, depending on their impression of the witness.

I have found reason to think that the visual aspect might have led to a biased witness assessment in some of my cases. During the hearings of witnesses in one of our Rwanda cases, I heard an insider witness, a person who was involved in the crime the defendant was charged with and is convicted and serving a prison sentence for it. Admittedly, the man was erratic in his behavior but ultimately was heard over several sessions. In the middle of those sessions, a new prosecutor joined the team and was catching up on all the material by reading the statements. Interestingly, he had quite a different view about the credibility and reliability of this witness and his statements than his colleague who sat in the hearings and had seen the witness testify. Clearly, the visual component made the difference. Ultimately, the court threw out his statements and deemed him unreliable. Although I could see the court's point, I was much more in favor of the witness than the court. I saw the witness multiple times and spoke with him, so I guess that made a difference.

International criminal justice has often been criticized as being biased towards Africa. There is certainly some validity in that. There are prejudices causing people to more easily believe that things are horrific in Africa and that there are permanent wars there where people kill each other. A stark example is the case against Charles Taylor in the Special Court of Sierra Leone. The Prosecution brought a witness before the court with the ominous name Charles 'Zigzag' Marsah, who claimed he was in Mr. Taylor's security service and was ordered, among others, to engage in cannibalism on the victims. He gave unbelievable examples of ripping children out of their mother's wombs, cooking and eating human flesh. Although the tribunal did not use his testimony as evidence, the Prosecution was heavily criticized for presenting this witness to play into the judges' emotions and into the idea of 'savage peoples' in Africa. Watching the video of his testimony is proof of visual power.

This all begs the question of whether emotions are a source of bias and error in international criminal justice. Observers and writers have pointed out the risks of certain emotions among crime scene investigators or first responders to a crime. This is dubbed the 'fear and panic' emotions, which can impede the ability to apply professional standards. This was the case in the Special Tribunal for Lebanon [STL] investigating the killing in 2005 of Rafik Hariri, the prime minister at the time. A report by the Inspector General of Police revealed that first responders to the scene of the blast that killed Hariri, including police and military, failed to meet the required standards for the investigation and errors were made. Police officers did not wear gloves, crime scene tape was not used, there was chaos and unauthorized vehicles contaminated the crime scene (Liden, 2020). Emotions lead to bad quality evidence.

The emotion of sheer shock when confronted with atrocities that are committed, in combination with empathy for the victims, can lead to confirmation bias. Usually, during an investigation, witnesses are heard first; then the defendant is arrested later and provided an opportunity to respond. In that order, the tone is set by the witnesses, and we tend to believe them. Investigators who interview the witnesses, and I myself when I hear the witnesses pre-trial, are prone to believe the witnesses because of our emotions when hearing the horrors they suffered. It obstructs our objectivity, and we consciously or subconsciously forget to be critical of what witnesses say. I have seen examples of it in interviews and am convinced I have fallen short too.

In relation to this is the dilemma of how trial judges assess the witnesses and their statements as credible and reliable or not. This has become a bigger issue, both in court practice and rulings, as well as in academia and other writings. It has two sides. First and foremost, I see courts, at least in the Dutch jurisdiction of international crimes cases, as being much more critical towards the witnesses and their testimony than in domestic cases. A few years ago, in a case against an Ethiopian Dergue member, the trial judges outlined nine pages of criteria they would use to assess credibility and reliability. This was followed by twenty pages of scrutinizing every individual testimony, ultimately disqualifying about half of the testimonies. I hardly see anything that meticulous in domestic cases. It seems that courts in international cases are hyper-skeptical towards evidence presented by the prosecution, inspecting each individual item in isolation and disqualifying it for reasons of disbelief or downplaying it. Conversely, in the ICC, judges have heavily criticized the Prosecutor for zealously and blindly pursuing their case theories based on shaky narratives. I have also seen examples, both in national courts and international tribunals, where judges accepted testimonies from witnesses who clearly contradicted themselves multiple times and whose testimonies were inconsistent. Judges invoked the argument that the witnesses may be traumatized, even after a long time has passed since the crimes, without explaining how this applies to credibility.

Another interesting question arising from this is whether justice actors in international cases are more emotional than those in national cases. One could think this is true, but some observers have argued the other way around, basing themselves on empirical studies showing that prolonged exposure to multiple victims and their harrowing testimonies leads to a deficit in empathetic capacities, known as the *compassion fade effect* (Liden, 2020, p. 6). It is simply impossible to absorb a huge amount of suffering from unspeakable atrocities and approach each new situation afresh, rather than creating hierarchies of suffering where only the worst of the worst suffering incites empathy.

I also see a risk that justice actors or other decision makers may find the content presented by witnesses to be so horrific that they are prone to reject the evidence as unimaginable or, at a minimum, implausible. Acquittal based on disbelief. Although this psychological effect is understandable, and I have felt it personally during some witness hearings, it impedes objectivity and impartiality. It emphasizes the need for specialized justice actors for these types of cases – professionals who have been to these sites and have accrued an understanding of the cruelties in this world.

3.2 *Organizational Change*

Another issue is whether the emotions I have described above, along with the challenges and opportunities I have pointed out, have led to institutional reforms and changed practices. The good news is that significant progress has been made.

First, we have learned to value the position of a victim in criminal trials and throughout criminal proceedings. A few decades ago, victims filed a complaint with the police, and when proceedings were initiated against a defendant, the victims would be called to testify and were often grilled by defense lawyers, feeling the skepticism of judges. This has completely changed, albeit gradually and still imperfectly. Today, victims are seen as full and equal parties in criminal proceedings. They are often represented by skilled lawyers and have rights such as the right to participate in the trial proceedings, speak about how the crime has affected them and share what they believe the judges should rule based on the evidence, including which punishment they think is fit. Also, just as importantly, witnesses can join the criminal case, file a civil suit and claim financial compensation.

We also care for the well-being of witnesses in criminal cases involving international crimes. Before they are called to testify, they are examined by a psychologist to assess whether they can stand for a hearing and to minimize risks of re-traumatization. When I became investigation magistrate, I introduced it in the proceedings. As I had seen in the Rwandan cases, where I heard the witnesses in situ to avoid taking them out of their own environment, I had to find a psychologist specialized in post-genocide trauma. At the time, it seemed that there were very few, and those qualified worked for the International Criminal Tribunal for Rwanda (ICTR) in Arusha, which didn't want to share them with me. After much effort, I found one psychologist who could perform this task. He confirmed that, at the time, there were only three psychologists in all of Rwanda specialized in this work. This was about twenty years after the genocide occurred. He assessed all the witnesses before I started the hearings. This led to a few cancellations of hearings. I also commenced hearings and then stopped because the witnesses couldn't endure the hearing. In other cases, he gave valuable advice on how to minimize the risk of psychological damage. His suggestions included having shorter hearings, more breaks and supplying sufficient food, drinks or other necessities.

One of the biggest achievements in international criminal justice is the fact that we have learned from our experiences. When I joined the Office of the Prosecutor (OTP) in the ICC, I was a seasoned prosecutor but had to learn international criminal justice work anew, as if I had to learn to walk again. The learning curve was extremely steep, and doing such intense fieldwork accelerated that. Above, I have talked extensively about emotions and how they can negatively impact work in international criminal justice cases, even leading to undesirable outcomes. I have become absolutely convinced that there is only one way to minimize those risks: applying accepted rules and techniques. In the early days of the OTP in the ICC, it was acknowledged that our work needed to be embedded in standards and rules reflecting accepted techniques. The Office developed Manuals and Guidelines and subsequently trained investigators and lawyers. What I have learned, I brought to the court when I became an Investigation Magistrate. Certainly, when hearing witnesses with all the abundant emotions, it is absolutely paramount to exercise discipline in the accepted standard of witness hearings. It has prevented me from making huge mistakes and witnesses being assessed as unreliable. Applying strict rules reflecting accepted standards is also necessary when working with others. The role of an interpreter is often overlooked. I have seen an interpreter during a hearing with a Rwandan witness unable to control her emotions because her family members had been victims in the genocide as well. Emotions can run so high that it impede the quality of the translation.

What definitely needs to be mentioned is our own well-being. The above shows that emotions have a huge impact on us as practitioners in international criminal justice. Everyone who operates in a working environment can experience stress that can lead to burnout. For international criminal justice actors, this is even more so. Working in the OTP of the ICC was a challenge, not only because of the fieldwork and the examples I have described above, but because the internal dynamics were hard to cope with and led to stress. Yet, the OTP did not provide any counseling of any kind. The five years as an Investigation Magistrate were demanding because of the nature of the work, which was further exacerbated by the many travels and time away from home and family. Yet, any support was absent apart from the encouragement from colleagues. When I returned to the Prosecution Service after various foreign adventures and temporary assignments abroad, my superior advised me to speak to a psychologist, which I did, and I chose someone from a specialized institution who was familiar with trauma from international work. I was relieved to hear I was not the only one dealing with heavy emotions. Lately, my office has us monitored by a psychologist from the same institution due to risks in domestic cases.

This is all in stark contrast with the practices from the past. Several years ago, our International Crimes Team was contacted by a former colleague who had retired. It appeared he was recruited by the Ministry of Foreign Affairs in 1994, right after the genocide, to assist in the investigations which had just started. It was the time thousands of corpses were still in the streets, and the smell of death was everywhere. He spent six months there with a number of Dutch police officers. When he came back, he gradually started to experience the effects of the traumatic exposure to the genocide. He told us he remembered when he and the police officers returned to Schiphol Airport. The police officers were warmly welcomed by the police force colleagues and brought to a place where they were debriefed. For my colleague, there was nobody. He took the train home by himself. It left huge scars on his soul. He had requested to return to Rwanda after all these years and revisit the places he had worked at. It turned out to be a very healing experience, but his story also reminded us of the risks of emotional damage we can incur from our work, damage that manifests itself even many years later.

4 How Emotions Affected Me While Working in International Criminal Justice?

I was asked to reflect on my own personality and elaborate on how all the emotions incurred during the years of this work have impacted me. I find it challenging to describe that. After all, I am not my own psychologist, and what I think I feel could be caused by experiences in my private life as well.

The first thing that comes to my mind, however, is, as I get older, a feeling of deep gratitude. Gratitude for having been, and still being able to be, part of this great adventure. It gives my life meaning to contribute, even a little, to justice in this big and evil world. I remind myself of this constantly, although not to downplay other forms of violence or criminality. I suffer from the *compassion fade effect*. Every time, it seems there are even more serious crimes and atrocities being committed. It makes common crimes, committed every day, almost meaningless or futile. But for those who suffer from those, it is not meaningless. To compensate for this, I have insisted in my office that I also represent the prosecution in court trials where petty crimes are adjudicated, such as shoplifting, minor violent crimes and the like.

But for the rest, I must admit I have to battle against the negative feelings briefly mentioned above because of the work: feelings of frustration, anger, meaninglessness, revulsion, disillusionment, disgust and maybe some light exhaustion. Is it my age? Am I getting too cynical, or is it really this awful world with all its wars, extreme violence and dictators or other totalitarian, powerful leaders that increasingly seem to rule and unleash terror unrestricted? Why is humanitarian law, with all the humanity it embodies, sacrificed for the purpose of politics? What are the lives of victims worth? Is accountability really built for our enemies, not for us and our friends? Is impunity increasing? Why are bullies ruling this world?

The fieldwork I have done in various places, and certainly the years I have spent hearing witnesses in these extremely complex but interesting cases, have satisfied my intellectual desires and were a professional joy. As long as I was occupied with those responsibilities, I was hardly bothered by emotions and negative feelings. Those came later, after the work was completed. Yet, the longer I heard witnesses and the more I saw adverse effects on them, the more guilty I felt. Guilty because I had a role in witnesses being re-traumatized. I tried to ameliorate the adverse effects, but it was not enough. In the verdict of the Appeals Court in the first Rwanda case, the court hammered me over the fact that I had heard witnesses for extremely long periods of time and exhausted them further, which could have had a negative effect on the veracity of their witness testimony. First, I was appalled. Who were they to reprimand me? They had never been in Rwanda. But over time, as I have reflected on this, they may have been right.

I feel more strongly for the victims and witnesses. I know some of them are quite keen to be heard. They feel someone is interested in their story, and that helps them cope with the situation. I also know they cooperate because they hope someone, somewhere, will take action, arrest perpetrators and throw them in jail. It rarely happens. I have worked in Ethiopia, where this has happened, and the seriousness of the crimes there certainly warrants accountability, but the international community does not provide it. I worked a lot on the situation in Myanmar. The plight of the Rohingya deserves action. It is insufficiently provided. Yet, the camps in Bangladesh keep being flooded with investigators and staff from NGO s that, again and again, give them a space to tell their stories. When the investigators and researchers have left, it becomes silent again in the camps. Usually, the victims don't hear anything back. Do the NGO s fulfill the needs of the witnesses, or just their own needs and those of their donors?

I have become addicted to this work. I cannot let it go. Or maybe the subject does not let me go. I have read endless books and reports related to the situations I was in. The internet is not helpful in trying to create more distance from work. It is always there, the same way your phone, tablet, or computer is always near you, with information just a fingertip away. The internet is treacherous, though, as it prevents you from reading books. Gradually, I lost my appetite for anything fictional, be it books or movies. Even books and movies need to be work-related to be interesting. Consuming fiction seems like a waste of time.

I have sensed another effect of doing this work – more doubt about whether criminal law is effective. Criminal law is such a blunt instrument. It punishes defendants, if that is the result at all, but does it really help victims? Victims' desires may be different. They may want recognition about their fate, peace and security, a house and income to send their children to school. Restorative justice must replace retributive justice.

5 Disbelief and Faith

My experiences, displayed here in this chapter, may leave the impression that working in this field is all bad and dark. Admittedly, working in international criminal justice can make you depressed and gloomy. Feelings of despair, frustration, anger, revulsion, disgust and exhaustion are not what you want to dominate your life. Rather, our minds are much more receptive to what commercials present to us: live happy! So, is there a remedy for these negative feelings other than the seduction of consumption?

I was born and raised in a quite conservative and Christian environment in a rural area of the Netherlands. My parents were strict about attending church and about which information we were allowed to consume. They reluctantly accepted a television in their house, but we were not allowed to watch it on Sundays. The Christian faith, as taught to me, was about dogmas, tenets and rules. I have never resented or rejected my upbringing. To the contrary, I am deeply convinced it has led me to study law and pursue a working life as it has unfolded.

Unfortunately, it took me decades to discover that the Christian faith, in fact, is very much about pursuing justice. That God is a God of justice. We need to care for the weak, the widow and orphan, the refugees and everyone that fall victim to corruption, the horrors of war and abuse by the powerful. God is a socialist, and Jesus is very woke. Increasingly, I have difficulty discerning people who call themselves Christians, who adhere to this faith. Thank God I see many non-believers who do. I cannot change the evil that brings darkness, but I can dig into my deepest emotions of faith to bring a spark of light.

In 1966, shortly before he was killed, Robert Kennedy gave what is called the 'Day of Affirmation Address' to the National Union of South African Students at the University of Cape Town, South Africa. In the address, Kennedy talked about individual liberty, apartheid and the need for justice in the United States at a time when the American civil rights movement was ongoing. He spoke about the 'ripples of hope' that could build a current that can sweep down the mightiest wall of oppression and resistance (Kennedy, 1966). And then he quoted Archimedes in what is my favorite expression which would be the most appropriate quote to end my contribution: "Give me a place to stand, and I will move this world."

References

Arendt, H. (1964). *Eichmann in Jerusalem: A report on the banality of evil.* New York: Penguin Books.

Liden, M. (2020). Emotions and Cognition in International Criminal Justice: An Exploration from Cognitive Biases to Emotional Intelligence. *Forensic Science International: Mind and Law*, 1, pp. 1–10.

Kennedy, R. F. (1966). *Day of Affirmation Address*, retrieved 21 November 2024 from https://www.jfklibrary.org/learn/about-jfk/the-kennedy-family/robert-f-kennedy/robert-f-kennedy-speeches/day-of-affirmation-address-university-of-capetown-capetown-south-africa-june-6-1966

CHAPTER 8

The Toll it Takes: Working with and for Survivors and Eye-Witnesses of Atrocity Crimes

An Michels

1 Introduction

Victims of atrocity crimes frequently experience trauma and other mental health impacts as a result of the acts of extreme violence they suffered from. They furthermore may face significant difficulties to regain control over their lives and to re-establish a connection with their communities. Eye-witnesses and perpetrators of atrocity crimes are also not spared from the negative mental health impacts of the severe crimes they witnessed or were involved in. The expanding and "contagious" effect of trauma takes its toll on professionals and practitioners working closely with victims and witnesses.

Listening to harrowing stories and engaging closely with victims and witnesses can lead to secondary and vicarious trauma, can contribute to burnout or otherwise harm the well-being of professionals. In addition, it may impact their capacity to fulfil their duty of care[1] toward victims and witnesses.

This chapter focuses on the work of psychologists and other mental health professionals who engage with victims and witnesses of atrocity crimes. The topic will be addressed starting from the personal experiences of the author, who works since almost twenty-five years as a psychologist with victims and witnesses of atrocity crimes in the context of justice mechanisms. It will further offer a theoretical framework to understand vicarious and secondary trauma and burnout. The chapter then focuses on ways in which mental health professionals manage the risk for secondary and vicarious trauma in their work with victims and witnesses of atrocity crimes. Finally, the chapter will demonstrate

1 "Duty of care" refers to the ethical and legal obligation to ensure safety and well-being of those who health and legal professionals support. In the Rome Statute, for instance, the obligation can be found under Art 68.1 ("The Court shall take appropriate measures to protect the safety, well-being, dignity and privacy of victims and witnesses."...) and Art 43.6 ("This Unit (Victims and Witnesses Section) shall provide (...) protective measures, and security arrangements, counselling and other appropriate assistance for witnesses, victims who appear before the Court (...)".

HTTPS://DOI.ORG/10.1163/9789004754720-010

how the work of psychologists can offer a roadmap for other professionals to handle risks and protect their well-being in their work around atrocity crimes.

2 Looking Back

On a rainy day, somewhere end of July 2004, I was sitting in the Courtroom of the Special Court for Sierra Leone in Freetown. The heavy rain was pouring down on the thin roof of the Courtroom, creating an uneasy soundscape, sometimes making it difficult to hear what the man in the witness box had to say. He was telling the Court about how he lost his entire family in an attempt to escape Freetown during the siege. He referred to one of the many very violent episodes of the Sierra Leonean civil war, which had ended just a few years earlier. The witness explained how they passed a child soldier at a checkpoint. The witness was hoping that they would be able to drive by safely, as he had hidden his family under blankets on the backseat of the car. But the small boy with a gun at the checkpoint spotted them through the low car window. They were all killed, except for the father.

I do not remember many more details of his story, but I can vividly recall the feeling of exhaustion I felt listening to this harrowing account. It felt in that moment as if I had to use all the energy I had left in me to listen and support the man emotionally during the breaks of his very moving testimony. I remember the heavy, humid air, so typical for the peak of the rainy season, pushing me down and leaving me with a strange sense of loneliness. The witness was one of the last ones to take the stand before the court would go in summer recess, and like many colleagues I was longing to take some vacation. At the same time I felt a deep respect for this man who was able to tell his story with great serenity, and I was bothered by my own fatigue and loneliness, which felt so futile next to his.

I remember more moments of such "internal dissonance" throughout the many years I have worked as a psychologist with victims and witnesses of atrocity crimes. One day in 2000, I was driving through the hills of Rwanda, on my way back from a visit to one of the women's groups we were supporting at the time.[2] The women were all survivors of the worst imaginable violence during the genocide in 1994. They shared stories of their daily struggle with trauma and poverty in one of the regular group meetings with the counsellor. On my way back with my Rwandan colleague, I was suddenly taken aback by the unique beauty of the landscape of misty and endless hills, while at the same time my brain was trying to process the tales of horror I had just heard.

2 In a psychosocial project for Médcins Sans Frontières. For background, see Michels (2002).

Also this experience left me briefly with a sense of being disconnected and lost in contradictory and confusing emotions.

I had learnt years before to be attentive to my own thoughts and emotions while listening to clients. As a clinical psychologist and family therapist I had gone through years of training to be observant and self-observant; to learn to notice, explore, and analyze every detail of interaction with the person sharing a story or seeking help. I had studied the dynamics of transference and counter-transference. I had learned to look carefully at sources of trauma in my own history and was told endless times by my supervisors that all the contradictory and sometimes confusing emotions and thoughts one experiences in our work had their reason and are a normal part of the process of helping. As such, they therefore deserved "a seat at the table" of our experiences. I thought I had learnt to observe them without judgment. And I thought I had learnt that they would pass as long as I take care of myself.

And yet, I must admit that all the skills that made me so confident in my work, sometimes failed me in the messy reality of the line of work I had chosen. Listening to the experiences of survivors or witnesses of atrocity crimes is oftentimes overwhelming. Also to me, as a listener, their trauma and losses feel from time to time as unimaginable and unexplainable and create a sense of alienation. At other times, the stories are so compelling that they pushed me to work harder, do more, even disregard my own emotional and physical boundaries. However, I always recognize that while witnessing only a glimpse of their suffering is difficult, it is even far more challenging to support witnesses and survivors with empathy while trying to contain their intense emotions or, in some cases, the complete absence of emotion. Or, as Judith Herman wrote: "The dialectic of trauma constantly challenges the therapist's emotional balance, who may, like the patient, defend against overwhelming feelings by withdrawal or by impulsive, intrusive actions" (Herman, as cited in Canefield, 2005, p. 82).

The scale of mass atrocities in itself is a factor that is utterly disturbing. The widespread nature of crimes is a component that amplifies individual suffering in the aftermath of violence (Michels et al., 2024) and it contributes to the sense of alienation and disbelief for anyone who witnesses this suffering. For instance, one of the things that struck me most when I was working in Rwanda were the numbers: the number of dead and wounded, the number of orphans, the number of *rescapés* and internally displaced persons (IDPs) in the camps, even the number of machetes used. As if the statistics in itself, illustrating the massive scale of violence, became an abstract source of alienation.[3]

3 For background, see Human Rights Watch (1999).

When I reflect on how working with survivors affected me throughout the years, three additional factors come to mind. Firstly, the cumulative effect of years in this field of work certainly deepened its impact. While I became used to hearing tales of horror and more skilled at interacting with witnesses and survivors, I sometimes felt as if the contagious effect of trauma slowly crawled under my skin. Brief moments of despair or fatigue at times turned into a more deeply rooted feelings of negativity and, luckily only rarely, a darker world view. At the same time my growing experience and the sense of being a "pioneer" in a partly still uncharted field, gave me energy to continue my work. The expanding, tightly knit circle of colleagues, many of whom became friends, provided me the warm connection and support I so desperately needed to do this work and showed me that I was not alone in my dedication to find justice for survivors of atrocity crimes. Above all, the joy I witnessed in witnesses and victims who successfully testified, offered me a lasting feeling of satisfaction and a sense of purpose. These positive impacts levelled out any moments of anguish, at least most of the time.

Secondly, working for witnesses and survivors of atrocity crimes often required me to be present, often for an extended time, in the areas where the conflict had occurred or was still ongoing. While the closeness to the communities tremendously helped me in understanding suffering in the cultural context at hand, the stress from working in a humanitarian environment with regular security incidents, or situations of active conflict, also made me more vulnerable. My experiences in conflict or post-conflict zones were also often not easy to explain to those at home, although I learned through the years to find my voice to speak about them, through publications and presentations about my work.

The third factor is one which I found more difficult to handle. The more my work took place in the context of a judicial institution, the more I too, experienced the poisonous impact of harassment, abuse of power and other expressions of a toxic workplace culture. These are unfortunately features which are not uncommon in the field of legal institutions.[4] The work climate became a burden which, bizarrely enough, was at times much harder to carry for me than the load of working with survivors. Toxicity combined with a high workload and a lack of boundaries damaged at one point my trust in some of my colleagues, who were supposed to be an important source of support and energy for me. The experiences also undermined, at least for a while, my trust in an institution which was built to pursue the purpose I so eagerly wanted to be part

4 See International Bar Association (2018 and 2021).

of. The confrontation with poor leadership and injustice eventually made me doubt myself and my choices.

However, I regained energy and found my path again because of the strong personal and professional bounds I had built throughout the years, and guided by the professional support I sought. I was also able to fall back on my training and knowledge about how trauma affects survivors and impacts professionals working closely with them. Importantly, I found again agency, by advocating for policies and other measures to improve the mental health of survivors and create well-being and a healthy work climate for professionals.

Eventually, looking back at almost twenty-five years of working in this field, it is hard to disentangle how this work shaped me, but the balance seems overall positive, at least most of the time. Ultimately, like many professionals in this field, I am driven by a strong sense of purpose and my motivation is fueled by the many meaningful interactions and by a great level of academic curiosity – wanting to understand how survivors can find justice. What prevails for me is a deep sense of hopefulness about the capacity of human beings to overcome and transform their traumatic experiences. While this work takes a toll, it has also enriched my life in a very significant way.

3 Trauma, Secondary Traumatic Stress, Vicarious Trauma, Compassion Fatigue, and Burnout

Secondary traumatic stress, vicarious trauma, compassion fatigue, and burnout are common work-related outcomes attributed to mental health workers (Leung et al., 2023). These occupational hazards are not unique to psychologists, anyone who engages empathetically with survivors, witnesses, and perpetrators of atrocity crimes may experience similar effects. Mental health professionals are particularly vulnerable due to their prolonged, empathetic engagement with traumatized clients. However, their professional training offers some protection against these impacts.

To comprehend the individual experiences of mental health experts working with victims of atrocity crimes, it is essential to apply a clear theoretical framework that elucidates the relationships and distinctions between various psychological impacts. This conceptual clarification is essential, as these terms are often used interchangeably and the initial presentation of issues often appears similar, despite referring to distinct psychological processes (Canefield, 2005). Employing precise and consistent terminology can provide valuable guidance for preventing negative mental health outcomes. Furthermore, understanding the nuanced differences between these experiences enables the identification of diverse sources of stress while highlighting the protective coping mechanisms employed by psychologists. These "tools for resilience" can serve as a roadmap for other professional groups at risk of similar challenges.

3.1 *Trauma*

The impact of atrocity crimes is multifaceted and survivors often struggle to recover from acts of extreme violence. In addition to individual harm, communities and societies may also suffer, as widespread violence leads to the rupture of the social fabric and loss of connection, leaving communities fragmented (Michels et al., 2024, p. 30). Individual and collective suffering are also interlinked and interdependent, which makes the experience of direct and indirect victims and future generations multi-dimensional (Smith, 2020, p. 128; Michels et al., 2024, p. 30). Trauma is considered to be one of the critical psychosocial impacts of direct exposure to atrocity crimes for survivors, eye-witnesses, and also perpetrators. It is often defined as "an event, series of events, or set of circumstances that is experienced by an individual as physically or emotionally harmful or life-threatening and that has lasting adverse effects on the individual's functioning and mental, physical, social, emotional, or spiritual well-being" (SAMHSA 2014, p. 7).

The concept of trauma is frequently reduced to the psychiatric diagnosis of post-traumatic stress disorder (PTSD), which involves a specific set of symptoms – such as intrusion, avoidance, and hyper-arousal – arising from exposure to traumatic events (APA 2013). However, this diagnosis only captures a subset of the psychological consequences of atrocities and broader mental health challenges often emerge.[5] Given the complexity and multi-dimensional nature of trauma, a multidisciplinary framework is necessary to adequately describe its effects (Danieli, 2009; Hamber, 2009).

3.2 *Secondary Traumatic Stress*

Secondary traumatic stress can be described as the behavioral and emotional consequences of exposure to traumatic events experienced by others (Figley, 1995; Leung et al., 2023), such as survivors or witnesses who tell their story, in a courtroom, an investigative setting or in a counselling session. The concept refers to symptoms that may appear after listening to trauma stories and which are similar to symptoms trauma survivors experience. The signs of stress typically also repeat the intrusion-avoidance dynamic that is characteristic for

5 Especially anxiety disorders, depression, substance abuse, anti-social, and suicidal behavior increase in post-conflict settings; see Krug et al. (2002, p. 222) and De Jong et al. (2003) as cited in Michels et al. (2024, p. 30).

trauma symptoms, namely an oscillation between trying to forget and being forced to remember, as observed in trauma survivors (Michels et al., 2024). Symptoms of secondary traumatic stress can include dreams, re-experiencing traumatic events as described by the survivors, or intrusive thoughts; as well as efforts to avoid reminders of the survivors' traumatic stories, numbing, avoiding certain activities or situations and feelings of alienation or estrangement from others; or signs of persistent emotional arousal, such as sleeping problems, irritability, hypervigilance or concentration difficulties. As the symptoms mirror the symptoms of trauma survivors, secondary traumatic stress may develop into PTSD, if left unaddressed (UNITAD 2022).

3.3 *Vicarious Trauma*

Whereas secondary traumatic stress can occur suddenly (Figley, 1995; Leung et al., 2023), vicarious trauma refers to the slow cumulative and transformative process that occurs over the course of being directly or indirectly exposed to a significant number of personal stories. Symptoms of vicarious trauma can include: anger, anxiety, depression, emotional exhaustion, low self-esteem, numbness, withdrawal, indifference, difficulties to make decisions, fatigue, changes in eating or sleeping patterns, and addiction, among others (Michels et al., 2024; UNITAD 2022). Studies indicate that through prolonged (vicarious) exposure and interactions with clients suffering from trauma, therapists inevitably undergo a similar transformative process that affects their cognitive schemata, meaning, beliefs as well as their identity. While secondary traumatic stress focuses on the emotional and behavioral symptoms resulting from work with trauma victims, vicarious trauma leads to deep, enduring changes in the therapist's inner experience, altering psychological needs and core beliefs about safety, intimacy, and control (Leung et al., 2023, p. 214).

3.4 *Compassion Fatigue*

Compassion fatigue is a process closely related to secondary traumatic stress and refers to the physical, emotional, and psychological impact of helping others. Traditionally the concept is used to describe a process of disengagement of caregivers to their patients (UNITAD 2021; UNITAD 2022), but it can also express a sense of disconnection to colleagues, friends and family (Coetzee & Laschinger, 2018; UNITAD, 2022). Compassion fatigue is the declining ability to be empathic with clients due to an overexposure to suffering, stressful work conditions, and inadequate organizational resources (Coetzee & Laschinger, 2018). It is often associated with intense emotional exhaustion that occurs when the emotional demand exceed a person's capacity to assist. The progressive and cumulative process of disconnection leads to an inability to provide the appropriate level of support to clients or patients.

3.5 *Burnout*

Burnout is also a psychological syndrome that occurs gradually. Burnout is sometimes described as "a dislocation between what people are and what they have to do" (Canefield, 2005, p. 84). The term refers to the feeling of depletion and exhaustion, cynicism and detachment, associated with a sense of ineffectiveness or failure, caused by prolonged response to chronic, often interpersonal, stressors in a work environment (Leung et al., 2023; UNITAD 2022). The key difference between burnout and secondary traumatic stress or vicarious trauma lies in their distinct causes. Both type of conditions share symptoms such as depression, insomnia, and diminished intimacy with friends and family, and both develop cumulatively. However, secondary traumatic stress and vicarious trauma arise directly from listening to emotionally distressing material from clients, while burnout can occur in every occupation (Canefield, 2005; Leung et al.; 2023; McCann & Pearlman, 1990; UNITAD 2022).

4 A Cumulation of Risk Factors

Aside from the risks for secondary and vicarious trauma stemming directly from the prolonged interaction with survivors and witnesses of atrocity crimes or from exposure to their stories, a number of additional risks can be identified. These are mostly linked to the context in which the work takes place and can amplify the negative impact of secondary trauma on professionals working on atrocity crimes.

Firstly, mental health workers or other professionals working in conflict-affected areas may be exposed to lengthy periods of insecurity and be at increased risk to suffer from traumatic incidents or witness such incidents perpetrated against those they try to assist (McCormack & Joseph, 2013; Eriksson et al., 2001). This exposure and the psychological distress related to it can trigger trauma (PTSD) or other chronic stress symptoms. Also, studies showed that the confrontation with war and destruction can complicate relationships and hinder the return and re-integration of aid workers into their family and communities (McCormack; 2009; McCormack & Joseph, 2013). This (temporary) decline of the social support system may lead to a breakdown of one of the most critical coping tools professionals can use to manage the exposure to traumatic material.

Secondly, over the past years there has been growing attention for the challenges around workplace culture in international organizations and judicial settings (see International Bar Association 2018 and 2021). As a lot of the work regarding atrocity crimes takes place in the context of a court, an investigative mechanism or another international organization, the prevalence of a toxic work climate is concerning. In such settings, poor leadership, pervasive harassment, and other forms of misconduct often coincided with a general lack of healthy boundaries and poor gender balance, collectively contributing to an unsafe environment for staff (Rosender et al., 2023). Consequently, staff may be hampered in their capacity to develop peer support, discuss concerns about their well-being or boundaries, or simply acknowledge vulnerability. If left unaddressed, toxicity also undermines trust in the values and the mission of the organization. An unsafe climate may create an uneasy dissonance between the high values of human rights and justice these organizations stand for, and the perceived lack thereof toward staff. If professionals lose their sense of purpose or their sense of belonging to the higher goal the organization pursues, they risk losing an important propeller for their motivation to do this difficult work. Also, those suffering directly from harassment may experience trauma as a result which further affects their capacity to manage their exposure to the traumatic material from survivors. This primary trauma makes them more vulnerable for secondary trauma. Triggered by broader societal developments,[6] fortunately, significant efforts were made in the past years, to fully acknowledge the problem of misconduct and workplace culture in these settings and address the problem systematically through policies and reform.[7]

Thirdly, the presence of a personal trauma history constitutes a risk for professionals who work with traumatic material. This is particularly relevant for mental health professionals, due to the intensity of their exposure when working with survivors, as well as the disproportionately high prevalence of personal trauma histories among mental health workers compared to the general population (Leung et al., 2023). Also for professionals who come from war-affected areas, who may have lived through violent conflict themselves, or may have lost loved ones due to violence, the risk of suffering from primary trauma is real. The additional exposure to vicarious trauma may exacerbate

6 Such as the #MeToo Movement. Secretary General's Bulletin. (2003) Special measures for protection from sexual exploitation and sexual abuse, ST/SGB/2003/1.

7 United Nations (n.d.). *Addressing sexual harassment within organizations of the UN System*, https://shknowledgehub.unwomen.org/en (retrieved December 2 2024); Assembly of States Parties International Criminal Court, (2020). *Independent Expert Review of the International Criminal Court and the Rome Statute System*, https://asp.icc-cpi.int/Review-Court/Review-Mechanism (retrieved 2 December 2024)

trauma-symptoms and suffering and affect their capacity to build rapport with survivors or apply healthy boundaries (Michels et al., 2024, p. 42).

Finally, risk factors created by insecurity, a negative work climate and personal trauma accumulate the risk that is caused by exposure to traumatic material from atrocity crime survivors. The combined risk further depletes the resources and amplifies the negative mental health outcomes for professionals. This will affect their capacity to fulfil their professional role. Increased work-related stress or vicarious trauma is associated with over-involvement and poor boundaries (Leung et al., 2023). Overburdened, apathetic, or over-involved professionals cannot build appropriate rapport, create the necessary safety or show empathy to support or interview survivors or witnesses, which may lead directly to less efficient support, evidence-gathering, or documentation of crimes (Michels et al., 2024).

5 The Power of Protective Factors

And yet, in spite of this substantial list of risk factors, a growing number of mental health workers, legal professionals, and academics dedicate their professional life to assisting, documenting, and researching atrocity crimes and their survivors. This begs the question: what are the factors that drive them, and more importantly, can protect them in this work?

In this regard, there is much we can learn from survivors. Research around the motivations of survivors to testify in trials or truth commissions reveal a remarkable tension between individual distress and collective gain. Survivors are driven by "a compelling need to tell their story" (Stover, 2005, p. 126; Michels et al., 2024) by the need for acknowledgement, their wish to create meaning and regain a sense of control, after having been powerless in the face of unimaginable violence. To reach this goal, they are willing to accept an increase in emotional suffering, at least temporarily (Michels et al., 2024, p. 41).

One explanation for their drive can be found by defining well-being as "a sense of coherence." This is a trait which is associated with successful coping and a strong indicator of well-being. It refers to a person's capacity to make sense of the world, find meaning, and, above all, experience a sense of manageability, predictability, control and agency (Antonovsky, 1993).[8] The re-gained

8 Sense of Coherence consists of three components: Comprehensibility refers to the extent to which individuals perceive stimuli to make cognitive sense, that is, to be ordered, clear, consistent, structured, and predictable. Manageability refers to how individuals perceive the resources at their disposal to be adequate for dealing with stimulus demands. Meaningfulness refers to the extent to which individuals perceive their lives

sense of control, rather than the mere expression of emotion, is what is considered to be at the basis of the therapeutic effect of participation in a justice mechanism (Lens et al., 2015, p. 30). Possibly, professionals could tap into the same resource as the survivors they work with. They may be driven by a sense of purpose, agency, and control, as a counterweight against the unimaginability of the violence of atrocity crimes. The feeling that "their work matters" is a strong motor to endure the difficult confrontation with the accounts of harrowing crimes. This is in line with the more recent research on the importance of "compassion satisfaction," defined as "the feeling of achievement and pleasure derived from doing one's work well and effectively" (Ruiz-Aranada et al., 2024, p. 219). It allows professionals to harness the benefit derived from helping those who are suffering as a tool to withstand secondary traumatic stress.

Also resilience, a personality trait that tempers the negative effect of stress and promotes adaptation, has been identified as an essential protective factor against traumatic events and the effect of adversity on mental health. It plays a key role in alleviating the impact of compassion fatigue and burnout (Ruiz-Aranada et al., 2024, p. 220).

The importance of social support as a protective factor against burnout and other risks for mental health professionals has also been clearly established (Szoke et al., 2023). Also for humanitarian workers "social support may act as a 'buffer' for those with high levels of trauma exposure" (Eriksson et al., 2001, p. 211). Positive social support serves both as a strong protective factor, for example by using a "buddy system" or peer supervision as tool to manage personal boundaries, and as an important deterrent to the development of posttraumatic responses following trauma (Eriksson et al., 2001; McCormack & Joseph, 2013).

Because of the risks inherent to their profession, mental health experts are expected to integrate self-care tools and a strong ethical framework into their work. Research showed that therapists conducting trauma-treatment managed affect through emotional distancing, collegial support, altruism, or drawing on a sense of higher purpose in life, regular exercise, and supportive supervision (Canefield, 2005, p. 98). Learning to apply professional boundaries is one of the fundamental principles for mental health and medical experts to ensure ethical and effective practice. They learn to apply boundaries toward their client relationships, their scope of expertise, the need for informed consent, the use of peer-supervision and confidentiality (Smith, 2003). Boundaries

---

to make sense from an emotional point of view and to what extent they find it worth investing their time, energy, and effort in stressful experiences (Michels, et al., 2024, p. 39).

are needed to protect clients, and are indispensable to protect mental health experts, as they allow them to work from a position of empathy, but contained in a clearly defined framework, without being drained or overwhelmed by the needs of their clients (Michels, 2020, p. 119).

6 The Way Forward: Fostering Safety, Knowledge, Resilience, and Agency

An understanding of the risks, impacts, and protective factors for psychologists working in the field of atrocity crimes can serve as a roadmap for other professions to manage risks and safeguard their well-being in similar work. To strengthen the protection of professionals in this field, four key actions emerge as essential, as they promote the key-components of the sense of coherence and related protective traits.

> **Ensuring Safety** is a fundamental aspect of the duty of care that employers owe to their staff. While physical danger and the resulting stress may be unavoidable in conflict-affected settings, efforts should be made to mitigate these risks to prevent traumatic incidents that may lead to primary trauma for professionals. Psychological protection is equally important, and the responsibility for creating a safe work environment rests primarily with employers. The work context for professionals dealing with atrocity crimes should foster a space where vulnerability is acknowledged. This environment must be one in which social support is readily available, and where professionals are encouraged to recognize and address their own psychological well-being.

> **Developing Knowledge:** Socrates understood that self-knowledge was a key component of living a good life. Similarly, a deep understanding of one's own beliefs, values, and principles is crucial for professionals working in the field of atrocity crimes. It is essential for individuals to understand their own personal boundaries, especially as these boundaries are often challenged when working with survivors of extreme trauma. Insight into one's personal trauma history is vital for understanding vulnerabilities, but it is equally important for comprehending one's motivations and drive to work in a field so deeply imbued with trauma narratives. Academic education in atrocity crimes should place a strong emphasis on self-knowledge, self-care, and personal develop-

ment. Students entering this field should be encouraged and supported to explore their own histories and invest in their personal growth.

A complex issue like atrocity crimes requires a multidisciplinary approach; therefore, the integration of mental health and psychosocial support approaches within the broader frameworks of justice and research on atrocity crimes is highly recommended. To this end, the further development of a theoretical framework for understanding the psychological aspects of working with atrocity crimes is necessary. Such a framework would not only assist survivors but also provide tools to professionals for self-protection. Academic curricula for researchers, legal professionals, and other experts should include the study of trauma as a consequence of atrocity crimes, as well as the risks of secondary and vicarious trauma.

Promoting Resilience: Resilience, a sense of coherence, compassion satisfaction, and self-compassion are vital traits that should be fostered and promoted in professionals working on atrocity crimes. Structural measures within the work environment can support the development of these traits, such as creating opportunities for social support, offering peer supervision, and organizing mandatory debriefings or specialist training. Promoting resilience involves equipping professionals with the tools and strategies to manage their emotional responses and remain psychologically healthy despite the often overwhelming nature of their work.

Allowing Agency: The experience of agency is one of the fundamental conditions that support healthy coping mechanisms in the aftermath of adversity. Agency can also act as a preventative tool when professionals are exposed to traumatic content. When combined with a sense of predictability, agency can counterbalance the feelings of powerlessness that often accompany the brutal realities encountered in this field. The sense of control that comes with agency can mitigate the loss of control typical in trauma responses, where symptoms can appear unpredictably and be triggered by seemingly insignificant stimuli.

Professionals working on atrocity crimes must retain control over their exposure to traumatic material. This means having the choice to engage or not engage with survivors or their stories. Simple strategies, such as the use of trigger warnings, can support this autonomy. On a more fundamental level, it is important for professionals to have the freedom to choose not to engage with certain traumatic content, or parts thereof. Working with atrocity crimes should always be a conscious choice – a personal commitment that requires regular reflection, as it is unlikely to be without psychological consequences. This topic should be openly discussed in academic settings and among practitioners to ensure that professionals are fully aware of the potential impacts of their work.

7 Conclusion

Working with and for survivors of atrocity crimes is not without risks for mental health experts and other professionals. Especially prolonged exposure to traumatic content and the development of an empathetic rapport with survivors can lead to negative mental health outcomes, such as secondary traumatic stress, vicarious trauma, compassion fatigue, or burnout. The distinction between these phenomena is important, as they indicate different psychological processes. The risks stemming directly from the exposure to trauma content can be amplified by factors related to the context in which the work takes place. Environments in which there is physical or emotional insecurity and a high workload amplify distress and hamper the possibilities for professionals to protect themselves against negative impacts. They can also impact their capacity to develop rapport with survivors or witnesses and fulfil their roles in a satisfactory manner.

Protective factors can counterbalance the negative impact of the work on atrocity crimes, and minimize the risks for negative mental health outcomes. Protective personality traits and coping skills include resilience, a sense of coherence or compassion satisfaction. Also factors related to training, social support and a nurturing environment can prevent the development of secondary stress, vicarious trauma, or burnout, and can also foster the development of positive coping skills. Mental health experts traditionally put a lot of emphasis on self-care, within the context of a strong ethical framework. This approach can also assist other professionals working on atrocity crimes to protect themselves. To do so, the development of four key actions is critical: ensuring safety, developing knowledge, promoting resilience, and allowing agency.

References

APA (2013). *Diagnostic and Statistical Manual of Mental Disorders, Fifth Edition.* Arlington, VA: American Psychiatric Association

Antonovsky, A. (1993). The structure and properties of the sense of coherence scale. *Social Science and Medicine*, 36, pp. 725–733.

Canefield, J. (2005). Secondary Traumatization, Burnout, and Vicarious Traumatization. *Smith College Studies in Social Work*, 75(2), pp. 81–101.

Coetzee, S. K., Laschinger, H. K. S. (2018). Toward a comprehensive, theoretical model of compassion fatigue: An integrative literature review. *Nursing & Health Sciences*, 20(1), pp. 4–15.

Danieli, Y. (2009) Massive trauma and healing role of reparative justice. *Journal of Traumatic Stress*, 22(5), pp. 351–357.

Eriksson, C., Vande Kamp, H., Goruch, R., Hoke, S., Foy, D. (2001) Trauma Exposure and PTSD Symptoms in International Relief and Development Personnel. *Journal of Traumatic Stress*, 14(1), pp. 205–212

Figley, C. R. (1995). Compassion Fatigue: toward a New Understanding of the Cosecondary Traumatic Stress of Caring. In B. H. Stamm (Ed.), *Secondary traumatic stress: Self-care issues for clinicians, researchers, and educators*, Baltimore, MD: The Sidran Press, pp. 3–28.

Hamber, B. (2009). *Transforming Societies after Political Violence. Truth, Reconciliation and Mental Health*. Springer.

Human Rights Watch (1999). *Leave none to tell the story*, retrieved 2 December 2024 from https://www.hrw.org/report/1999/03/01/leave-none-tell-story/genocide-rwanda.

International Bar Association (2018). *Us too? Bullying and sexual harassment in the legal profession*, retrieved 2 December 2024 from https://www.ibanet.org/MediaHandler?id=B29F6FEA-889F-49CF-8217-F8F7D78C2479.

International Bar Association (2021). *Mental wellbeing in the legal profession: A global study*, retrieved 2 December 2024 from https://www.ibanet.org/document?id=IBA-report-Mental-Wellbeing-in-the-Legal-Profession-A-Global-Study.

De Jong, J., Komproe, I, Van Ommeren, M. (2003). Common Mental Disorders in Post-Conflict Settings. *The Lancet*, 361(9375), pp. 2128–2130.

Krug, E. G., Dahlberg, L. L., Mercy, J. A., Zwi, A. B., Lozano, R. (2002). *World report on violence and health*. World Health Organization, retrieved 2 December 2024 from https://iris.who.int/handle/10665/42495;

Lens, K., Pemberton, A., Brans, K., Braeken, J., Burnoutgaerts, S., Lahla, E. (2015). Delivering a Victim Impact Statement: Emotionally effective or counterproductive? *European Journal of Criminology*, 12(1), pp. 17–34.

Leung, T., Schmidt, F., Mushquasch, C. (2023) A personal history of trauma and experience of secondary traumatic stress, vicarious trauma and burnout in mental health workers: A systematic literature review. *Psychological trauma: theory, research, practice and policy*. 2023, 15(S2), pp. S213–S221.

McCann, L., Pearlman, L. A. (1990). Vicarious traumatization: a framework for understanding the psychological effects of working with victims. *Journal of Traumatic Stress*, 3(1), pp. 131–149.

McCormack, L. (2009). Civilian women at war: Psychological impact decades after the Vietnam War. *Journal of Loss and Trauma*, 14, pp. 447–458.

McCormack, L., Joseph, S. (2013). Psychological growth in humanitarian aid personnel: reintegrating with family and community following exposure to war and genocide. *Community, Work & Family*, 16(2), pp. 147–163.

Michels, A. (2002). Ils disent que je suis traumatisée – trauma-counselling in Rwanda. *Tijdschrift voor Klinische Psychologie*, 32, p. 181–186.

Michels, A. (2020). the Psychologist-Client Relationship at the ICC: a Road Map for the Development of the Counsel-Victim Relationship. In: R. Jasini, G. Townsend (Eds.) *Advancing the Impact of Victim Participation at the International Criminal Court: Bridging the Gap between Research and Practice*. ICCBA-Oxford: Oxford Law In-house publication, pp. 114–124.

Michels, A. Javidan, P. and Brown, L. M. (2024). Integration of mental health and psychosocial support approaches in accountability mechanisms for atrocity crimes. *Knowledge Platform for Security and Rule of Law*, retrieved 2 December 2024 from https://kpsrl.org/sites/default/files/2024-05/Michels%2C%20A.%20et%20al.%20Integration%20of%20MHPSS%20approaches%20in%20accountability%20mechanisms%20for%20atrocity%20crimes.pdf

Rosander, M., Hetland, J., Einarsen, S., (2023). Workplace bullying and mental health problems in balanced and gender-dominated workplaces. *Work&stress*, 37(3),pp. 325–344.

Ruiz-Aranada, D., Silva-Garcia, B., Fennollar, J. (2024) Therapist self-compassion and compassion fatigue: the mediating role of resilience. *Annals of psychology 2024*, 40(2), pp. 219–226.

SAMHSA (2014). *SAMHSA's Concept of Trauma and Guidance for a Trauma-Informed Approach*. HHS Publication No. (SMA) 14–4884. Rockville, MD: Substance Abuse and Mental Health Services Administration, retrieved 2 December 2024 from: https://library.samhsa.gov/sites/default/files/sma14-4884.pdf

Smith, D. (2003). 10 Ways Practitioners can avoid frequent ethical pitfalls. APA, Monitor on Psychology, *34*(1), retrieved 20 December 2024 from: https://www.apa.org/monitor/jan03/10ways#:~:text=10%20ways%20practitioners%20can%20avoid%20frequent%.

Smith, E. (2020). Victim Testimony at the ICC: Trauma, Memory and Witness Credibility. In: Jasini, R. & Townsend G. (Eds.). *Advancing the Impact of Victim Participation at the International Criminal Court: Bridging the Gap between Research and Practice*, Oxford: Oxford Law In-house publication, pp. 125–136.

Stover, E. (2005). *The Witnesses: War Crimes and the Promise of Justice in The Hague.* Philadelphia: University of Pennsylvania Press.

Szoke, D., Lancaster, C., Hazlett-Stevens, H. (2023). Relationships between burnout, secondary traumatic stress, mindfulness and self-compassion in victim advocates. *Violence Against Women*, 29(12–13), pp. 2551–2568.

UNITAD (2021). *Trauma-Informed Investigations Field Guide*, retrieved 28 July 2025 at chrome-extension://efaidnbmnnnibpcajpcglclefindmkaj/ https://<uri>www.unitad.un.org/sites/www.unitad.un.org/files/general/2104429-trauma-informed_investigations_field_guide_web_0.pdf

UNITAD (2022). *Stanford University Human Rights in Trauma Mental Health Program.* Reference Guide

CHAPTER 9

Working with Victims/Survivors of Genocidal Sexual Violence in Rwanda: *A Personal Journey*

Anne-Marie de Brouwer

1 Introduction

> I was only 12 years old when I was brutally raped during the genocide, at different times by different men. (...) I became a woman without even having a chance to be a girl. I did not know anything about sex; my parents never explained anything to me. I was not prepared to become a mother and take care of a baby. I have never loved my daughter, who was born out of rape, and even though I try my hardest to love her, there is still a long way for me to go. I often wonder why God planned this life for me.
>
> Hyacintha (1982) testimony from 2008 at age 26
>
> DE BROUWER ET AL., 2019, p. 161.

For a very long time, I could not love [my daughter] because she was a constant reminder of my horrifying experiences of the genocide. But this has changed so much over the years. It has been a lengthy process, and three years ago I noticed that my feelings towards my daughter were evolving. It was through the counselling that I received from Mama Lambert at Solace Ministries that I realized that I was not to blame for what had happened to me. In the counselling sessions, I sat with other survivors who also had children born from genocidal rape. We shared our stories and supported each other. We came to understand that the blame fell on the rapists rather than on us. Some survivors had contracted HIV but did not get pregnant, and after the genocide, they were no longer able to conceive children because of the severe sexual violence that they had suffered. When I heard these stories, I felt happy to have a child, even if she was the result of a terrible experience. And I started to wonder why I was mistreating my daughter, after all the abuse I had experienced myself. This was not fair to her; she deserved to be loved, just like every other child. Despite everything, my daughter has always been very wise. Her

> name means "a gift" and I started to see her that way; she is indeed my gift from God. I felt that I should cherish this beautiful gift. Today my daughter is doing very well in school, and she has a good future ahead of her. I love my daughter very much.
>
> Hyacintha (1982) testimony from 2018 at age 36
>
> DE BROUWER ET AL., 2019, p. 168.

The first time I heard more about sexual violence in conflict was during my LL.M. in international human rights law in the UK in 1998–1999, when the conflict in Kosovo was ongoing. At the time, I was 23 years old. The conflict in the former Yugoslavia was still recent (and actually still ongoing in Kosovo and later Macedonia), as was the genocide against the Tutsi in Rwanda. The International Criminal Tribunal for the former Yugoslavia (ICTY) and Rwanda (ICTR) had just started operating. I was wondering what the ICTY and ICTR did, or could possibly do, to provide justice to victims/survivors of sexual violence, as their stories had been in the news (even if sparsely) and were so appalling and brutal. I decided to write my LLM thesis on this topic and to do an internship at the ICTY in The Hague (the Netherlands). I found out that there was still much to understand and to improve in the investigation and prosecution of this crime, and decided to continue to research the topic. I was lucky to secure a Ph.D. position at a university in the Netherlands where I could spend several years writing my book on the prosecution of sexual violence as genocide, crimes against humanity and war crimes before the ICTY, ICTR, and the International Criminal Court (ICC).

As a young researcher, diving into a difficult topic that touches upon the worst of humanity, I was probably not prepared for what I would have to face. After several years of studying the law and reading testimonies and stories of victims/survivors of conflict-related sexual violence (CRSV) for my Ph.D. research, I felt emotionally exhausted and developed a writer's block. I was wondering why I was doing the research and for who. There also had not been a lot written at that time about CRSV prosecutions, making it more challenging. My choice to do an internship at the ICTR in 2003, and my subsequent encounters with victims/survivors of genocidal sexual violence in Rwanda, gave me back my drive to finalize the research and reminded me of the importance of it: to make sure these crimes are understood and that justice is provided for the victims of these brutal crimes.

When I for the first time arrived at the ICTR in Arusha (Tanzania), where the tribunal was located, I was an intern with one of the Prosecution teams. For my Ph.D. research I wished to gain a better understanding of how the ICTR functioned and how it could provide justice to victims/survivors of conflict-related sexual violence. This internship also provided me with the opportunity to meet survivors of genocidal sexual violence in Rwanda itself, as I was given the chance to go to Rwanda with one of the Attorneys of the team I was assigned to and to conduct interviews with people who had been victimized or had participated in the genocide and were about to testify at the ICTR. Some of the people I met in Rwanda and at the ICTR (staff and other interns), greatly inspired me to continue my research. I had many interesting conversations with them that helped shape my thoughts on my research. They also touched me on a personal level; with several I became good friends, and I am still in contact with them up to this day.

My first encounter with Rwanda in 2003 was therefore the start of my continuous involvement with victims/survivors of genocidal sexual violence. First as an academic, writing several articles and books on issues related to CRSV, initially as a Ph.D. researcher, and subsequently as Assistant Professor and then Associate Professor in international (criminal) law. Later, also as a person who set up: (1) a charity that supports Rwandan genocide survivors of sexual violence in a holistic way (as of 2008); (2) an expertise center that addresses injustices for CRSV and human trafficking in a systemic way (research and advise; education and awareness; capacity building and training; and empowerment projects and advocacy) (as of 2017); and (3) a social enterprise that focusses on the socio-economic independence of female coffee entrepreneurs, many survivors of genocidal sexual violence (as of 2019). Today, I am still taking on the many different roles that come with these organizations, including as a teacher, trainer, researcher, entrepreneur, and practitioner.

I started my journey as a law researcher but my encounters with victims/survivors of genocidal sexual violence taught me about the many interrelated issues they are facing, which cannot only be addressed by applying and improving the law. That is why I decided to address CRSV from multiple perspectives and angles (e.g. victimology, criminology, psychology, medical field, IT, history, economy, qualitative and quantitative research methodologies), including by working with others who have a different expertise. Working with others does not only provide support in doing research, it also supports you as a person and professional, in whatever role you are in, allowing you to continue the work you are doing. The resilience of, and direct and recurring contact with, genocide survivors of sexual violence has furthermore given me the energy and strength to continue my work in this field. Today, Hyacintha, whose testimonial you just read, is married and says she feels empowered partly because of the support she has received through the charity I co-founded. She owns cattle and has been able to grow crops that she sells at the market. She also runs her own small business making and selling banana juice. It is people like her, who give me good reason to continue the work that I have been doing in the past 25 years. Survivors of CRSV and colleagues working in this field make me realize, especially in times that the work may become too overwhelming, that one is never really alone.

In this chapter I will discuss my own journey in dealing with these brutal stories of CRSV and how the attention to tackle CRSV has grown over the past years, including on how to interact with victims/survivors in a survivor-centered and trauma-informed manner. I will first, provide a bigger picture of the sexual violence that took place in Rwanda during the genocide against the Tutsi in 1994, including the impact of these crimes on their victims, communities, and societies. Then, I will continue with the different roles that I have been taking up in working with victims/survivors of CRSV and lessons learned. After that, I will discuss the developments in the field of CRSV in the past 15 years or so, whereby CRSV has received greater international attention, including on how to deal with ethics when working with victim/survivors of CRSV. I will end with some lessons learned on how to prevent or mitigate vicarious trauma, and will conclude this chapter with some final remarks and reflections.

2 Sexual Violence in Rwanda during the Genocide against the Tutsi in 1994

Rape and other forms of sexual violence during conflict have been of all times and were viewed in the past as a private matter, seen as collateral damage inconsequential to the larger considerations of wartime politics or justified as an inevitable consequence of war, a necessary bounty for fighting men (Askin, 1997; Brownmiller, 1975). However, the numerous accounts of sexual violence during the genocide against the Tutsi in Rwanda in 1994 and the wars in the former Yugoslavia (1991–2001) captured the world's attention and sexual violence was transformed in people's understanding. It became clear that sexual violence in conflict was often used as a weapon of war, to humiliate, to divide, to destroy, to spread fear, and to terrorize people (Askin, 1997; Viseur Sellers, 2005).

Although sexual violence during conflicts has been documented as both widespread and systematic, perpetrators of these crimes have rarely been held accountable for their actions. However, times are changing, and in the past two decades a clear shift has been taking place, whereby today conflict-related sexual violence is seen as an international crime (e.g. genocide, crime against humanity, war crime) for which perpetrators need to be held accountable, and as a crime that can in fact be prevented.[1]

In order to give some more background information on the crimes we are talking about and dealing with when working with victims/survivors, I will say a few words about the genocidal sexual violence[2] that took place in Rwanda in 1994 and the impact it had and still has on victims/survivors.[3]

2.1 *Sexual Violence in the 100 Days in Rwanda in 1994*[4]

In the 100 days of genocide that ravaged the small East-Central African nation of Rwanda from April until July 1994, about one million Tutsi were killed, and an estimated 250,000–500,000 women and girls as well as an unknown num-

1 For example, in 2009, UN Security Council Resolution 1888 (2009) was adopted, which established the mandate of the Special Representative of the Secretary-General on Sexual Violence in Conflict. This mandate helped in the fight against CRSV, both in terms of prevention and accountability. See: *Concept Note - Commemoration of the 15-Year Anniversary of the Establishment of the Mandate on Sexual Violence in Conflict*, October 2024, https://www.un.org/sexualviolenceinconflict/wp-content/uploads/2024/10/20241023-Concept-Note-Event-15-year-anniversary-of-SVC-mandate-1.pdf (retrieved 21 February 2025).

2 In this chapter, CRSV is used as the umbrella term to refer to sexual and gender-based crimes (e.g. rape, sexual slavery, forced prostitution etc.) that can constitute international crimes, when the common elements of genocide, crimes against humanity and war crimes are fulfilled. In the case of Rwanda, because sexual violence was used as part of the genocide, to destroy the Tutsi population, I refer to genocidal sexual violence (but the terms may at times be used interchangeably in this chapter).

3 There is discussion on the use of the terms "victims/survivors," even if this discussion has not been much taken up in the field of CRSV really. The term victim is most commonly used in the legal settings, and it commonly provides for certain rights (e.g. protection, support), but has been criticized because it has a passive connotation. The term "survivor" has been defined differently by many organizations, national jurisdictions, and also survivors themselves. While in some (mostly English-speaking) countries the term "survivor" is understood as a person who has agency and has or is about to recover from the crime that was committed against that person, in other countries the term does not translate well, and refers to situations of surviving death. It has furthermore been critiqued for enforcing an expectation of growth. Alternative ways of terminology are to refer to the person first, e.g. a person who experienced conflict-related sexual violence, to underline that the CRSV situation does not define a person (it is simply one of the many experiences a person had in life which is referred to as person-first language rather than identity-first language). In the end, it is up to the individual concerned to decide what the preferred language to be used is. Although the term "victim/survivor" is used in this chapter, it is used with full recognition of all of the above.

4 This section is partly based and taken from the book *And I Live On* (2019), chapter 1 (some footnotes omitted).

ber of men and boys were raped (Bijleveld et al., 2009; IPEP 2000, para 16.20).[5] According to a United Nations report, rape was the rule, its absence the exception (UN Commission Human rights 1999, para 16). The sexual violence in Rwanda during the genocide was extreme in its brutality and systematic in its orchestration. Victims were selected predominantly on the basis of their gender and their Tutsi ethnicity. Age did not play a role in who was attacked: Tutsi women and girls of all ages were raped. The targeting of Tutsi girls and women was spurred on in part by anti-Tutsi propaganda preceding the genocide, which alleged that the minority Tutsi population was a threat to the Hutu community (Human Rights Watch, 1996). Rape served as a means to degrade and subjugate Tutsi women. Sexual violence was also directed at Hutu women considered moderates: women who were married to Tutsi men, protected Tutsi individuals or were politically affiliated with Tutsi. Men, primarily of Tutsi ethnicity, were also sexually assaulted, often by the sexual mutilation of their genitals, which were sometimes displayed in public. In some cases, Tutsi men and boys were forced to rape Tutsi women, forced to have sexual intercourse with dead animals, or were raped by Hutu women. Women and girls were subjected to the full range of sexual atrocity. This included rape, gang rape, sexual slavery, forced incest, forced marriage, and amputation or mutilation of victims' breasts, vaginas, and buttocks, or of features considered to be Tutsi, such as small noses or long fingers (Human Rights Watch, 1996). Even pregnant women were not spared. Almost all of the women and girls who did survive the genocide were victims of sexual violence or were profoundly affected by it (IPEP, 2000, para 16.20).

An astounding 70 per cent of survivors were living with HIV after the sexual violence (Amnesty International, 2004, p. 3). An expert panel has reported that some HIV-positive perpetrators intentionally tried to transmit the virus by raping Tutsi women (IPEP, 2000, 16.19). In the eyes of the Hutu perpetrators, infecting a Tutsi woman with HIV served as an effective means to infect her future sexual partners and any children she bore as well as to eventually kill her and leave her dependents without her support (Nduwimana, 2004, p. 18). Some women abducted to be the personal slaves, or "wives," of Hutu men were forced to remain with their rapists after the genocide, in some cases moving to neighboring countries with their captors.

Compared with conflicts in other places, the sexual violence in Rwanda became notorious because of the organized propaganda, which contributed

5 A 2009 study estimated the number of women raped during the genocide against the Tutsi in Rwanda was just over 350,000, and most of them Tutsi, which was held to be most likely an underestimate (Bijleveld et al., 2009).

significantly to fueling sexual violence against Tutsi women, the very public nature of the rapes and the level of ruthlessness directed toward women.[6]

2.2 *Impact of CRSV*

In the immediate aftermath of the 1994 genocide against the Tutsi in Rwanda, the profound impact on survivors was difficult to fathom. This was particularly so for survivors of genocidal sexual violence, who (initially) felt obliged to hide their pain because of the stigma associated with sexual violence, and were left to wrestle with illness, poverty, and trauma in isolation. The UN General Assembly passed a resolution in 2004 affirming that survivors of sexual violence are among those who face the greatest hardship in post-genocide Rwanda.[7]

The impact of CRSV involves a number of consequences: physical, psychological, socio-economic, and legal. It will be outside the scope of this article to go much in detail about all the impacts, but I will elaborate here on a few (Denov et al., 2020). It is important to understand these, especially when working with victims/survivors of these crimes.

> *Physical impact*: CRSV is characterized by a high level of brutality that causes damage to body tissues and organs that can be life-threatening, such as traumatic genital injury and physical trauma to reproductive organs (e.g. bleeding, fistula, loss of ability to procreate), HIV, and secondary illnesses (e.g. cancer, TBC).
>
> *Psychological impact*: CRSV has a destructive psychological, emotional, and spiritual impact on victims/survivors, and a number of difficult, and often long-lasting, psychological consequences can be catalyzed. Among these are trauma-related conditions (e.g. PTSD, anxiety disorders), impacts on mood and emotion (e.g. grief, fear, disgust, emotional detachment), and identity, relational and sexual consequences (e.g. low self-esteem, shame, distrust, neglect of self or children born as a result of CRSV).
>
> *Socio-economic impact*: CRSV not only has an impact on the individual, but also forces families, communities, and societies to process a collective

6 See testimony of Binaifer Nowrojee, expert witness before the International Criminal Tribunal for Rwanda, in *The Prosecutor v. Théoneste Bagasora and others: Transcripts*, ICTR-98–41-T (Judgement, 12 July 2004), p. 34.

7 UN General Assembly, *Resolution 59/137 of 10 December 2004 on Assistance to Survivors of the 1994 Genocide in Rwanda, Particularly Orphans, Widows and Victims of Sexual Violence* (A/RES/59/137), 10 December 2004.

trauma that has left them shattered. CRSV may cause socio-economic consequences related to erosion of community/social cohesion (e.g. stigma-induced social isolation, ostracization, further violence) and economic hardship and disruption of livelihoods (e.g. reduced economic opportunity due to health problems and withdrawal from education).

Legal impact: CRSV may results in harm and disputes which for many survivors means that they need access to legal and other forms of justice and legal aid. Victims of CRSV and their children may, however, be unable to claim legal 'victimhood' identities and receive little opportunity to access justice and reparation (e.g. going to court for the harm experienced, inheritance disputes).

While women and girls were the primary targets of the rape campaign, boys and men also suffered brutal sexual violence during the genocide and generally had more difficulty to speak out. Of course, sexual violence was invariably only one element in a succession of traumatic episodes, including other forms of abuse, torture, killing of loved ones, and destruction of property. Most survivors, therefore, experienced cumulative trauma, which was difficult, if not impossible, to deal with in the aftermath. More than thirty years later, the devastating consequences of sexual violence on survivors remain palpable. How to live on when having faced these devastating and brutal acts committed against you?

3 Working with Victims/Survivors in Different Capacities

Despite the severity of the consequences of the genocidal sexual violence, tremendous strides have been made in addressing survivors' many needs. The Rwandan government, non-governmental organizations, and the international community have undertaken a host of initiatives and programs to support survivors, many with promising and impressive outcomes, particularly in the realms of HIV and healthcare, justice and reconciliation, socio-economic support, and survivors' healing process (De Brouwer et al., 2019, pp. 217–231). A holistic and survivor-centered approach is indeed needed in light of the many impacts CRSV has on a person's life and the broader community and society survivors are part of. In this section I will elaborate on the roles and opportunities I have/had in supporting and working with genocide survivors of sexual violence.

3.1 *The Work of an Academic*

As mentioned, when I started to work as a Ph.D. researcher on such a heavy topic, there was nothing really in place to accommodate possible coping strategies when facing trauma or how to ethically conduct research with such a vulnerable group of people. It was the year 2000, and there was not much thought on this yet. I was one of the very few working on this topic worldwide,[8] without institutional support on these matters. What helped me mentally was the encouraging support from one of my fellow-Ph.D. researchers (who was working on another topic), my partner Freek Dekkers, and, as mentioned, the support from other interns and some staff at the ICTR as well as input from a practitioner working at the ICTY. Working on a Ph.D. can be quite lonely sometimes, and I realized that, it is important to build a network around you of people you can discuss your work with. You need to search for people with whom you can share your work and struggles, rather than complain about the absence of such support, which I sometimes did in those early years and which only took away energy that I actually needed to do my work.

After I completed my Ph.D. research in 2005 (De Brouwer, 2005), I continued to write academic articles and books about, for instance, the justice process in Rwanda and before the ICTR in the years that followed (De Brouwer, 2009; De Brouwer & Smeulers, 2016; De Brouwer & Kaitesi, 2016). For my work on the gacaca, the local courts where genocide cases were dealt with in great numbers, I conducted interviews with genocide survivors who had testified before these courts, including survivors of sexual violence (De Brouwer & Ka Hon Chu, 2012; de Brouwer & Ruvebana, 2013). Doing qualitative research helped me to better understand the impact of justice on their lives. I made sure that I was well prepared before conducting the interviews (e.g. types of questions, interview setting, translation, interpretation), had survivors sign and understand the contents of consent forms, ensured I interviewed survivors with respect and integrity (e.g. to listen, without bias or judgment, taking the time), and to think about how they could (safely) participate (e.g. venue; availability of support, including counselling; fee to cover transport and stay) as well as for them to hear back the results of the research. Putting the interests of the survivors in the interviewing process first, helped

8 One very important work that dealt with this topic on a Ph.D. level was the work of Kelly Askin (1997) and her contribution to the field helped me a lot in my own research. Other contributions from practitioners and academics that were very helpful in those early years came from, inter alia, Patricia Viseur Sellers, Valerie Oosterveld, Kim Thuy Seelinger, Susana SaCouto, amongst others. Still today they work in this field and have inspired future generations with their ongoing work and contributions developing the field of CRSV prosecutions.

to conduct the interviews in a dignified manner even though protocols on survivor-centered and trauma-informed interviewing with regard to survivors of CRSV, such as the Murad Code, did not yet exist at the time. Working together with an organization that supported the survivors already (Solace Ministries), helped a lot because of the trust that had been built between the victims, the organization and me.[9]

Of course, I also conducted further research into CRSV and how best to prosecute this crime, not only in relation to Rwanda, but more generally and from a global perspective. Highlights during my time as an academic were the several international conferences I organized in later years, together with colleagues, in particular the ones in Rwanda in 2009 and 2013, where we discussed victimological, criminological, and research approaches to international crimes. Where better to do so then in Rwanda? By this time, we were with a bigger group of 'like-minded' people who were interested in this topic, which, as mentioned, is very helpful when dealing with emotions and ethics involving CRSV research and interviews with survivors.

3.2 *The Work of Solace Ministries and the Mukomeze Foundation: A Holistic Approach*

Coming into contact with the organization Solace Ministries in Rwanda, and its founder Jean Gakwandi, had a big influence on my professional and personal life. By chance, I met Jean on 1 January 2004, when I had just completed my internship at the ICTR. In order to explain how exactly this encounter influenced me, it is important to say a few words about Solace Ministries as well as the charity I, together with my partner, subsequently set up in 2008 in the Netherlands (named "Mukomeze," meaning "Empower her/him"), which works in close collaboration with Solace Ministries.

3.2.1 Solace Ministries

Solace Ministries is a Rwandan ecumenical non-governmental organization dedicated to meeting the needs of widows and orphans of the 1994 genocide against the Tutsi in Rwanda.[10] Jean Gakwandi, a genocide survivor himself, established the organization in December 1994, and it continues to be run by genocide survivors today. The sorrow that plagued Jean during and following the genocide, as well as the love he felt for his fellow survivors and his devout Christian faith, motivated him to dedicate his life to comforting others.

---

9 See more below on Solace Ministries, the Murad Code, and interviewing ethics generally.

10 This section is partly based on De Brouwer et al. (2019), chapter 3.

Solace provides its members with counselling, community development programs, medical care, education, and employment support. Those who have the capacity to work also receive micro-credits for agricultural or business endeavors. These services are uniquely tailored to the needs of genocide survivors. The organization's holistic approach is informed by the belief that the first step in the healing process requires survivors to feel that they are truly being heard. Trauma counselling, in both individual and group sessions, is vital. In Solace's experience, survivors are generally unable to adequately care for themselves or resume other activities without this crucial first step. Even after survivors have received counselling, trauma related to the genocide is deep-rooted, enduring and may affect subsequent generations (Eichelsheim et al., 2019). The healing process unfolds over many years.

Solace has five regional centers around Rwanda, with a total of around sixty staff. Solace supports more than eight thousand families (about forty thousand people) across Rwanda, in sixty Solace communities ranging in size from fifty to several hundred members. The organization strives to become an alternative family for survivors, to restore survivors' sense of dignity and to create support networks for those who are traumatized, isolated, poor, and crave hope in the face of an uncertain future.

In 1999, at the initiative of a group of women within the organization, Solace began providing specific services for survivors of sexual violence. It was soon evident that there were many genocide survivors of sexual violence, most of them living with HIV, who had feared speaking up about their experiences. They were afraid of the reactions of their relatives and community members. Within the year, Solace had set up specialized individual and group counselling sessions with Mama Lambert as the then main counsellor and a genocide survivor herself. Mama Lambert, Jean Gakwandi, and other Solace staff listened to survivors' stories and provided them with comfort and advice.

In 2002, Solace established a private clinic in Kigali, where women could be tested for and counselled about HIV in a safe and private environment. In 2011, Solace converted the private clinic into a public one, in part because public education campaigns by the Rwandan government to address HIV-related discrimination helped reduce the need for the private clinic setting. At the public clinic, twenty-nine Solace staff now serve tens of thousands of people from the region, including survivors of genocidal sexual violence.

By 2004, Solace Ministries had documented among their membership more than eight hundred survivors who were subjected to sexual violence during the genocide, and this number continues to grow. Even today – more than 30 years after the genocide – Solace continues to encounter survivors who have never spoken about their experiences of sexual violence during the genocide.

Throughout the years, Solace has supported survivors as they faced a myriad of consequences related to their experiences of sexual violence. Among other things, the organization has helped survivors grapple with medical complexities associated with HIV, as well as other illnesses linked to the sexual violence they suffered; in some cases, survivors succumbed to their illnesses. Solace also created a safe space for male survivors of sexual violence, who faced – and continue to face – significant challenges in recounting their experiences. Moreover, the organization has helped to heal dysfunctional relationships between mothers and their children who were conceived from sexual violence inflicted during the genocide. Over the years, Solace has grown to accommodate survivors' needs, as they navigate the devastating ramifications of genocide.

As Mama Lambert said in 2018: "In our culture, talking about sex is very private. That is why it was very hard for survivors to come up and reveal that they were raped. Some even killed themselves following the genocide. But nowadays things are changing slowly. We believe that we should not keep quiet; we should speak the truth so that justice could take its course. If you speak out, it can be a lesson to others. When you release your burden, you release your heart" (De Brouwer et al., 2019, p. 230).

Thousands of genocide survivors of sexual violence have benefited from Solace's comprehensive, compassionate, and dedicated approach to healing. Despite a host of often-debilitating obstacles, survivors of sexual violence are active and many have taken on leadership positions in their communities. The survivors are overall proud of their accomplishments.[11]

3.2.2 The Mukomeze Foundation

Solace partners with different organizations, both inside and outside of Rwanda. One of these organizations is the Mukomeze Foundation, based in the Netherlands.[12] After the encounter with Jean Gakwandi in 2004, my partner and I visited Rwanda numerous times to better understand the work of Solace Ministries and to meet widows, orphans and HIV-infected women, the people Solace Ministries supports. In particular, the sexual violence inflicted on women and men during the genocide, its impact on their lives and the (then) limited (inter)national support for this, made us believe that this group of survivors deserved extra support. Mukomeze therefore supports genocide survivors of sexual violence, in an effort to help them regain their

11 For more information about the work of Solace Ministries, see Gakwandi and Heidrich (2015); Mama Lambert (2024) and De Brouwer et al. (2019).

12 See on the Mukomeze Foundation: www.mukomeze.nl (retrieved 21 February 2025).

sense of dignity, hope, and economic independence. Most of the people supported by Mukomeze live in southern Rwanda, where fewer services and facilities are available.

Mukomeze coordinates individual sponsorships and group projects, intended to support survivors of genocidal sexual violence in rebuilding their lives. Survivors spend their sponsorship funds in different ways, including by repairing or purchasing their own homes, paying for their children's school materials and fees, supporting their own post-secondary education, setting up small businesses (e.g. handicraft-making and sewing), and engaging in livestock farming or agriculture. To date, around 90 women and some men have benefited from the Mukomeze sponsorship program, and several hundred Rwandans have also received support through a variety of projects. Mukomeze regularly coordinates meetings between Rwandan survivors and sponsors, donors and others. By raising awareness of survivors' living conditions, resilience and strength, and by promoting cross-cultural exchange (including trips to Rwanda), the Mukomeze Foundation strives to provide a global platform for genocide survivors of sexual violence. Mukomeze is run by a board of volunteers (who strategize and implement the work) and has several advisory board members and ambassadors, including from Rwanda.

Getting into contact with Jean and his organization and staff opened up a whole new world for me. As I had until then been mostly focused on reading testimonials of victims/survivors of sexual violence and looking at legal avenues to address the injustices committed against them, Jean helped me to see the reality these women and men were dealing with post-genocide. When you visit people at their homes and sit down with survivors, it is where one starts to really understand the crime of CRSV. Its brutality and impact.

Even several months before the Mukomeze Foundation officially started, I worked – together with two Canadians, one of which who was my colleague at the time at an NGO where we worked on gender justice before the ICC and globally – on a project to collect the testimonials of genocide survivors of sexual violence, sixteen women and one man. This project, which we undertook in our own time, has been one of the most intense, yet rewarding, ones in my life. By interviewing the women and man for their stories to be later on published in a book that would be named *The Men Who Killed Me* (De Brouwer et al., 2009), I learned many life lessons from the survivors as well as the staff members of Solace. They became my friends and teachers for life, teaching me about integrity, friendship, giving back, being humble, resilient, to not give up, and forgiveness. All survivors in the book requested to be in there themselves; it was their own wish that we only helped to implement. By telling their stories, together with their photographs, they wished to tell the world what had happened to them; to make people listen, to get justice and ask for prevention. At the time, in 2008, it was very early days for genocide survivors of sexual violence to open up so publicly, not only within Rwanda but also globally. As mentioned above, the interviewing process was carefully done, with the support of Solace Ministries, who already supported them as they were beneficiaries of this organization. The testimonials were taken several times and read back in order to make sure that it was correct and survivors agreed; a similar procedure applied to the photos.

The book has been used all over the world (e.g. in courses, theatre, a song) and people have also written back to survivors or made paintings/drawings about the survivors, as they were so touched by their stories. It even helped them sometimes in their own recovery: one Canadian student who read the book in college had stood up in class to say that she was a victim of sexual violence herself and that the stories of the people in the book had helped her to talk about it. As we had started the Mukomeze Foundation in 2008, and the people in the book also got into our sponsorship program (and received proceeds from the book), we were able to continue our close cooperation and friendship and to actually let the Rwandan victims/survivors know that their stories made an impact on people around the world. I still remember the words of the one man in the book, Faustin, when he said that many people from abroad only come to hear their testimony to use it for their own career and never come back again to talk about its impact. Indeed, when interviewing people, it is important to ask yourself whether you are really adding value with your work for survivors (see e.g. Schulz & Anne-Kathrin Kreft, 2021).

Being part of Mukomeze and working together with Solace Ministries meant that we gotten to know many people, both staff working at Solace but of course also the survivors of sexual violence we supported together with Solace. We visited them in their houses, we saw how projects had been implemented, and attended group counselling sessions, among other things. Visiting Rwanda and the people in our program often made that we gotten to know each other well, and that we also became part of the alternative Solace family. Our cooperation had always been based on honesty and trust, whereby we worked from a bottom-up approach: Solace staff knows who or what needs attention first and foremost. Communication in each cooperation is key; that was not different in ours. We learned that some people would also lie about being a survivor of sexual violence just to receive a sponsorship or that people who we considered empowered nevertheless left the program being unhappy. Also, sometimes people who were given items, had these stolen from them, or investment in someone's business qualities did not turn out as positive as one would have hoped. When confronted with these types of situations for the first time, it may be hard to accept, but when thinking about it more we realized it was perhaps logical taking into account the difficult life conditions people are facing. Furthermore, not each and every person/survivor is the same, has different characteristics and backgrounds and different responses to what happened to them, which one cannot overlook. Honest and clear communication between our organizations, and getting back to each other when things were not well understood, made that we communicated well with each other, and could really listen to each other. We also realized that putting some people from the Netherlands in contact with our partner organization is not always a recipe for success: not every person is capable of really understanding the impact and needs of survivors, becomes too traumatized, or has different communication styles that may not fit with the way we as Mukomeze and Solace work together.

Coming back to the book project *The Men Who Killed Me*. In 2018, ten years after its publication, we decided – partly through the organization Impact (see below) and in consultation with the survivors – to add the stories of the survivors' lives in the years 2008–2018 to the book as we realized that many readers were under the impression that their lives had stood still. This resulted in the book with the new title *And I Live On* (De Brouwer et al., 2019) describing the change from 14 years after the genocide (2008) to 24 years later (2018) and how organizations such as Solace Ministries and Mukomeze had and can support in this. It also showed the long-lasting impact of CRSV on people's lives, as some people had in the meantime passed away due to the consequences of genocidal sexual violence (e.g. HIV/AIDS and secondary diseases, such as cancer), an often-overlooked aspect of CRSV, leaving other family members (often the children) on their own. Furthermore, the aging of widows is today an additional issue as they generally do not have a pension. Although the interviews with survivors went well, like previously, we realized that increasing use of and access to social media had an impact on the survivors and their families; several of them indicated that they did not wish their photos to be displayed on social media.

Working again with the people in the book has been a privilege. It is rare to read about the lives of victims/survivors of CRSV beyond the first publication of a book (or article for that matter). Yet, in order to understand how people's lives may evolve, or what the impact of CRSV is on peoples' lives, it is important to understand and address the long lasting consequences.

3.3 *The Work of* IMPACT*: Center against Human Trafficking and Sexual Violence in Conflict*

In 2017, I left the university to start – together with Eefje de Volder, who was also working at the university at the time and with whom I worked in Mukomeze – our own organization called Impact: Center against Human Trafficking and Sexual Violence in Conflict.[13] Eefje and I wanted to create more impact than we thought we could do while working at the university by focusing on two themes we felt very passionate about: human trafficking (a topic Eefje had been working on) and CRSV.

With Impact we focus on CRSV, human trafficking and their nexus as we believe there are many similarities between both crimes. The focus is not only on Rwanda, but worldwide. We conduct research and advise; education and awareness; training and capacity building; and empowerment projects and advocacy. We apply a systemic and interdisciplinary approach in our work by targeting different stakeholders with different backgrounds. For example, we have been able to develop Summer and Winter Schools on justice for victims of human trafficking and conflict-related sexual violence, whereby we are able to teach and inspire the younger generation to work in this field. We approach the topic from a theoretical and practical point of view, and invite guest speakers, including those who survived the crimes, also from Rwanda. As the topic of the course is often not or only cursory mentioned in the curricula of universities, we believe it is important that students have the opportunity to learn more about it. This is also what we hear back from them, and some have even continued their professional work in this area after attending our course. Yet, it may not always be easy to talk about this kind of topics and may even be traumatizing for students. Because of this, we always discuss the possibility of support in case this might be needed (e.g. talk to one of us in private or a psychologist, who is also a guest speaker in our course).

As we are conscious of the sensitive field we work in, we want to ensure that each person or organization we work with – as a partner, a donor, a board member, a staff member, a student, a victim/survivor or otherwise – is treated with respect and dignity. To underline our mutual commitments in this respect, Impact has an Integrity Protocol.[14] As a result, we need to be extra careful in guaranteeing equality, respect, confidentiality, (data) integrity, and a protective environment. When working with victims/survivors, we commit ourselves to the Murad Code (see next paragraph) which distils existing mini-

13 See on Impact: www.impact-now.org (retrieved 21 February 2025).

14 Impact Integrity Protocol (2023), see: https://impact-now.org/wp-content/uploads/2023/09/Integrity-Protocol-FINAL-VERSION.pdf (retrieved 21 February 2025).

mum standards for the safe, effective, and ethical gathering and use of victim/survivor information. Although many organizations still do not have Integrity Protocols, especially the smaller ones, we notice that more and more organizations are becoming aware of the importance of having them in place.

3.4 *The Work of Bèkske: Rwandan Empowerment Coffee*

Finally, in 2019 I co-founded an organization called Bèkske: Rwandan Empowerment Coffee.[15] This is a social enterprise that aims to empower Rwandan female entrepreneurs who grow high quality coffee berries in the countryside of Rwanda. We – Eefje de Volder (my colleague also at IMPACT) and I – sell the beans in the Netherlands and from the sales the women receive a fair price. In general, they receive 4 times more from Bèkske in comparison to most other coffee businesses.

We partner with 75 women who grow the coffee (all genocide survivors, most also of sexual violence), a washing station, and Solace Ministries that trains the women on doing business and agriculture, and coordinates much of the work to be done. With Bèkske we stand for quality coffee (as it is "specialty coffee"), honest coffee (fair prize), sustainable coffee (good for nature and humans), and transparency about what we do and how much all stakeholders earn in the chain. We work toward achieving Social Development Goals numbers 1 (no poverty), 4 (quality education, especially for the women's children), 5 (gender equality and women empowerment), 8 (fair work), and 12 (sustainability) in particular.

Bèkske is run by women for women, which is today still a novelty in the male dominated coffee business. Furthermore, the UN has praised us for being one of the few, if not only, enterprise outside of a conflict situation that socio-economically supports CRSV victims/survivors as a target group specifically; something more enterprises could do they say.[16] The work we do to make Bèkske a success has taught us to become even more entrepreneurial as we are dealing with a product that needs to be imported, sold and be profitable. As we do not have a sales and marketing background, this proved to be challenging. Yet, the mission and vision of Bèkske aligns so much with what we already do – "supporting survivors of CRSV in a holistic and survivor-centered way" – that supporting them socio-economically is a very important, if not

15 The website of Bèkske can be found here: www.rwandanempowermentcoffee.com (retrieved 21 February 2025).

16 UN Action Against Sexual Violence in Conflict, *Addressing Conflict-Related Sexual Violence: Private Sector Opportunities for Engagement*, 2022, https://www.stoprapenow.org/wp-content/uploads/2022/09/Addressing-CRSV-Private-Sector-Opportunities-for-Engagement-Full-Paper.pdf (retrieved 21 February 2025).

crucial, way, we think, for them to live on, take their own decisions, and be self-supportive and proud of themselves and the work they do. Bèkske has taught us to become more entrepreneurial in our cooperation with partners, including in thinking about ways to grow our business and attracting investors (so that we can, for instance, attract staff with a background in sales and marketing). Although our cooperation with the survivors and Solace Ministries is solid in light of the many years we are already working with them, in this new entrepreneurial setting with many different partners and interests, we need to make even more sure that we continue to listen to the survivors and involve them in the decision making every step of the way.

4 Developments in the Field of CRSV as an International Crime and Ethical and Survivor-Centered Approaches: A Short Overview

When I started my journey addressing CRSV at the international criminal tribunals from a legal and victimological point of view by the end of the 1990s, there was not much in terms of how to properly document these crimes and how to interact with victims/survivors of conflict-related sexual violence in a survivor-centered manner. The Tribunals had just started and staff had a lot on their plate, and CRSV was generally not seen by many to be as severe as some of the other international crimes.

With time, important achievements have been made in the field of CRSV. For example, a gender advisor and other staff members, who understood the importance of justice to victims of CRSV, were instrumental in developing the law and procedures around it; sexual violence was, for the first time, recognized as an act of genocide (in the monumental ICTR Akayesu Judgment in 1998) as well as under crimes against humanity (including enslavement) and war crimes; several sexual violence crimes are now explicitly laid down as international crimes (e.g. rape, sexual slavery, enforced prostitution, forced pregnancy as crimes against humanity and war crimes), gender persecution is recognized as a crime against humanity, and so is forced marriage (under "other inhumane acts"), all in the ICC Rome Statute.[17] These crimes are prosecuted against both male and female perpetrators, the victims can be female, male, or any other gender identity (both adults and children), and there is more attention to reproductive crimes (e.g. forced pregnancy, forced impreg-

17 Articles 6, 7, and 8 of the ICC Rome Statute, www.icc-cpi.int/sites/default/files/2024-05/Rome-Statute-eng.pdf (retrieved 21 February 2025). For the Akayesu case and Judgments see: https://ucr.irmct.org/scasedocs/case/ICTR-96-04#eng (retrieved 21 February 2025).

nation) and intersectionality (e.g. victims can be targeted due to a number of reasons, such as ethnicity, gender, age, nationality) (Women's Initiative for Gender Justice, 2023; Altunjan, 2021).

The ICC Office of the Prosecutor has installed special advisors and developed policies to guide its investigations and prosecutions on topics pertaining to Sexual and Gender-Based Crimes (SGBC), Slavery Crimes, Children and Gender Persecution, some of which is based on similar manuals of the ICTR and ICTY.[18] It could be argued that these documents find its origin in the Pruit Memo, prepared by Lisa Pruit, who drafted the very first guidelines on how to conduct appropriate interviews with victims/witnesses of CRSV before the ICTR, i.e. with dignity, respect and in safety.[19] She laid the foundation of today's views on how to interact with victims/survivors of sexual violence. For example, the ICC now has a Code of Professional Conduct for Counsel and a Code of Judicial Ethics, which sees to respectful behavior inside the courtroom, including by not interfering in a discriminatory and intimidating manner with victims appearing before the Court.[20]

From this quick overview of developments, despite some severe setbacks in witness intimidation, threats and revictimization at times (De Brouwer, 2005; De Brouwer 2015), it is clear that much has been achieved since the 1990s, whereby many people from within and outside the Tribunals have contributed. That does not mean, however, that not more needs to be done, on the contrary: the track record of accountability for CRSV is still minimal. Even at the ICC, in the more than 25 years since its existence, only two cases resulted in convictions for CRSV.[21] At the political level, important achievements have been made as well. There are, for instance, seven UN Security Council Resolutions addressing the prevention and response to CRSV, starting with UNSC Resolution 1820 (2008). One such resolution led to the establishment of a separate UN Office with a Special Representative for CRSV and a Team of Experts

18 See for the list of Special Advisors at the ICC: https://www.icc-cpi.int/about/otp/special-advisers-to-the-prosecutor (retrieved 21 February 2025). See for the ICC's SGBC Policy (2023): https://www.icc-cpi.int/sites/default/files/2023-12/2023-policy-gender-en-web.pdf (retrieved, 21 February 2025). See for the ICTR Manual (2014), https://unictr.irmct.org/sites/unictr.org/files/legal-library/140130_prosecution_of_sexual_violence.pdf (retrieved 21 February 2025).

19 See the documentary "The Uncondemned" (2015), https://www.imdb.com/title/tt4082346/ (retrieved 21 February 2025).

20 See, for these ICC Codes: https://www.icc-cpi.int/resource-library#counsel (retrieved 21 February 2025).

21 These convictions resulted in the Ntaganda and Ongwen cases. The difficulty seems to lie mostly in linking high-level accused to the crimes.

deployed around the world to improve the rule of law response to CRSV.[22] The Preventing Sexual Violence in Conflict Initiative (PSVI), which was founded in 2012 and is part of the UK's Foreign, Commonwealth & Development Office, has been another important achievement.[23] The aims of the PSVI is to raise awareness of the extent of sexual violence in conflict and rally global action to end it. The PSVI also has a Team of Experts, of which I am a member. The team consists of "a flexible and diverse pool of skilled individuals" who deploy to fragile and conflict-affected states to assist the UK government delivery of national security priorities.[24] Before deployment, they (and others) undergo training to prepare them to possible hostile situations, and the training also includes training on CRSV and trauma responses. The PSVI has developed several important declarations and documents, including the 2017 International Protocol on the Documentation and Investigation of Sexual Violence in Conflict, which includes guidance on ethical and survivor-centered interviewing techniques, and the 2022 Political Declaration.[25]

Finally, in the past decade a survivor-centered/led approach has become more or less part and parcel of legal and civil society approaches; however, with different interpretations and applications (Dolan et al., 2024). This shift has been greatly inspired by Dr. Denis Mukwege (a Congolese gynecologist and women's rights activist) and Nadia Murad (UNODC Goodwill Ambassador and survivor of genocidal sexual violence by ISIS against the Yazidis), both Nobel Peace Prize winners in 2018 for their work for victims/survivors of CRSV. For example, the Dr. Denis Mukwege Foundation is an international human rights organization working together with survivors of conflict-related sexual violence around the globe to make sure that survivors receive the holistic care

22 See Office of the Special Representative of the Secretary-General on Sexual Violence in Conflict, https://www.un.org/sexualviolenceinconflict/ (retrieved 21 February 2025). See also: UN Security Council Resolution 1888 (2009).

23 See Gov.UK, Preventing Sexual Violence in Conflict Initiative: www.gov.uk/government/organisations/preventing-sexual-violence-in-conflict-initiative (retrieved 21 February 2025).

24 See Gov.UK, PSVI Partners: https://www.gov.uk/guidance/psvi-partners#the-psvi-team-of-experts (retrieved 21 February 2025).

25 See Gov.UK, Preventing Sexual Violence in Conflict Initiative: https://www.gov.uk/guidance/psvi-library; and https://www.gov.uk/government/publications/conflict-related-sexual-violence-political-declaration-at-the-2022-preventing-sexual-violence-in-conflict-initiative-conference/preventing-sexual-violence-in-conflict-initiative-psvi-conference-2022-a-political-declaration-on-conflict-related-sexual-violence (retrieved 21 February 2025).

they need, can participate in everything that concerns them (before, during, and after a project or event), and obtain reparations.[26]

Also Nadia Murad set up her own organization called Nadia's Initiative, which is dedicated to rebuilding communities in crisis (in particular the Yazidi homeland in Sinjar, Iraq) and advocating globally for survivors of sexual violence.[27] One important document named after Nadia Murad is the Murad Code, a code – as mentioned earlier – which sets out the ways in which victims/survivors of CRSV can be ethically and survivor-friendly interviewed by different stakeholders. This is highly needed in light of past and still current unfriendly practices, such as repeated and unnecessary interviewing, harmful interviewing, absence of follow-up medical or psycho-social support in place, and questions around consent, including for sources found in the digital space (also: Boesten et al., 2018; Koenig et al., 2024). The Code's key objective is to respect and support survivors' rights and to ensure work with survivors to investigate, document and record their experiences is safe, ethical and effective in upholding their human rights.[28] The Murad Code, builds on previous guidelines in this respect (such as the PSVI's International Protocol), and provides guidelines on how to properly do this kind of work by focusing on 10 principles: (1) understanding survivors as individuals; (2) respect survivor control and autonomy; (3) be responsible and have integrity; (4) add value or don't do it; (5) preparation is the foundation; (6) know and understand context; (7) build systems, competency and support (all preparation principles); (8) gather CRSV information from other sources; (9) take the time, create the space; and (10) respectful and safe interactions. Of course, the Code will only work in practice if the different stakeholders working with victims/survivors of CRSV also know how to use it and are (continuously) trained in it. It is precisely this, where a lot still needs to improve: although many organizations claim they are survivor-centered, the interpretation and level of survivor-centeredness varies still significantly across organizations (Dolan et al., 2024).

---

26 See Mukwege Foundation: https://www.mukwegefoundation.org/ and the other organizations that were set up subsequently in support of survivors of CRSV: SEMA (https://www.semanetwork.org/) and Global Survivors Fund (https://www.globalsurvivorsfund.org/) (retrieved 21 February 2025).

27 See Nadia's Initiative: https://www.nadiasinitiative.org/ (retrieved 21 February 2025).

28 *Global Code of Conduct for Gathering and Using Information about Systematic and Conflict-Related Sexual Violence*, (2022), https://static1.squarespace.com/static/5eba1018487928493de323e7/t/671bec2693eac7048c0518b8/1729883174597/220413_Murad_Code_EN.pdf (retrieved 21 February 2025).

5 Vicarious Trauma: The Importance of Self-Care

Without a doubt, persons working in the field of CRSV will need a healthy dose of resilience. Self-care is, in any case, always important when conducting research involving international crimes, such as CRSV, and probably even more so when interacting with victims/survivors of these crimes. After all, the risk of vicarious trauma for those interacting with survivors of CRSV is always lurking: i.e. a process of change that occurs when being empathetically engaged with survivors of such horrific crimes, which may result in, for instance, feelings of anger or sadness, loss of hope, pessimism, cynicism, distancing, numbing, compassion fatigue, becoming overly involved emotionally with the person concerned (Rullman, 2022).[29] Even the most resilient persons who have been absorbing traumatic, violent content for many years on row will eventually become affected by it to some degree.

Yet, how does one do that; how does one prevent or mitigate vicarious trauma? When I started my research on CRSV there was not really any thought put into this. I had not even heard about the term "vicarious trauma" before. There were still few people working in this field, either in academia or practice, and the attitude was more one of putting your shoulders to the wheel. This is slowly changing now, but giving proper attention to preventing or mitigating vicarious trauma is still not very common in certain work environments. In the past five years, some researchers on CRSV and international crimes have opened up this discussion, arguing that more attention should be given to how to cope with trauma when working on such heavy topics in academia or when going to the field to interview survivors (O'Brien, 2021; Schulz & Kreft, 2021; Kreft, 2019). They argue that, generally speaking, it is difficult to talk about the impact this kind of research can have on individual researchers' mental health (e.g. depression, look at life), including on how this may have impacted the research process itself, and therefore is often avoided (Schulz & Kreft, 2021; Skjelsbaek, 2018). In general, CRSV is indeed not a topic that is easily discussed with friends or family at the dinner table, and this is sometimes also the case at the workplace, especially if you may be the only person working on the theme. Even people who may work in this field on a frequent basis, such as Judges or Prosecutors, may feel discomfort to talk about CRSV or dealing with victims/

29 See, e.g., British Medical Association, Vicarious Trauma: Signs and Strategies for Coping https://www.bma.org.uk/advice-and-support/your-wellbeing/vicarious-trauma/vicarious-trauma-signs-and-strategies-for-coping (retrieved 21 February 2025). In addition, in case the interviewer has experiences of sexual violence him/herself, it is important that that person has been able to cope/deal with that past situation in order not to cause re-traumatization with survivors interviewed.

survivors of CRSV (Sharatt, 2020; De Brouwer, 2015). One author framed the answer to this reluctance as follows: "from speaking with the victims the fear of hearing the worst overshadows us" (Kaitesi, 2014, p. 166). Yet, when dealing with these crimes and working with the survivors, it is important to face the reality of these crimes, not only to make sure that justice is done, but also to mitigate vicarious trauma. Some researchers and practitioners have, therefore, asked for a more honest and open conversation on the impact of working on the topic of CRSV or international crimes generally (Schulz & Kreft, 2021).[30]

Indeed, doing this kind of work – in all kinds of capacities – may impact how you may view the world and look at things in life. For example, when you are constantly working on CRSV, seeing how violence against women and girls is a broader issue which impacts women and girls all around the world (whether in the form of sexual harassment, femicide, human trafficking, or sexual violence in peace time), you may become angry or even numb from time to time, feeling like the work does not pay off. You start to wonder about the pervasiveness of violence against women and girls, no matter where you live in the world. I also started to think of some #MeToo moments of myself, and sometimes start to wonder how come that nowadays, this is still an issue our children will have to deal with too, even when in some parts of the world more attention seems to be given to it and, in some instances, public rejection and prosecution are more noticeable.

How does one prevent becoming mentally, physically and emotionally exhausted when working on the topic of CRSV and interacting with survivors of these crimes? One thing I realized is that certain emotions, such as anger or sadness, are also not necessarily bad. It is important to feel them, and to let them exist, because these emotions also make you feel that you care. They also motivate you to do your job and to fight for what you are passionate about. Expressing my anger with my colleague Eefje who understands where I am coming from, can already help me to deal with it. The emotions should, however, not become too much present in the sense that you simply can no longer do the job or 'do not care anymore'.

It is therefore important to keep and maintain an 'emotional balance' and to avoid, or reduce, the risks of vicarious trauma. For example, by taking care of yourself emotionally and physically (nurture self-care); maintaining a healthy work/life balance (having outside interests); taking regular breaks; being realistic of what you can accomplish; seeking social support from friends,

30 Listen to the two episodes (118 and 119, December 2024) of Asymmetrical Haircuts on "Dealing with Secondary Trauma" on Spotify, for people working in the international criminal justice sector.

colleagues, including debriefing sessions, and by getting therapy, if needed (Rullmann, 2022; Theidon, 2014).[31] It is important to know yourself, to listen to yourself, when you, for instance, start to feel down. If you can detect those emotions, you can also do something about them, by for instance taking a break and going for a walk, if that is a response that helps you. There can also be things you may not wish to do anymore. In my case, that is watching extremely violent movies, including sexual violence scenes, as I feel that these movies are often real scenarios and not simply movies. Watching that makes me depressed and I have started to avoid these kinds of movies. Knowing your own triggers and limits is important.

What has helped me in particular to continue this work is not only to take time for myself to digest but also to be with survivors of CRSV. What has helped me a lot was that I did my interviews with survivors who were part of an organization (Solace Ministries) that supported them already. Staff of the organization were present when counselling was, for instance, needed. For me, coming back often to Rwanda, and meeting with the survivors on a continuous basis, has also helped me so much in coping with my emotions. Through my many different roles and meetings with survivors, I got to know the survivors well, and I could both cry and laugh with them, acknowledging the bad past but also looking to a brighter future. I literally could see the change in them due to the work of our partner organization and our organizations working with them; this gives me strength and a purpose to work for. It is certainly not a good idea to cry a lot when you are in a role of conducting interviews (as you probably have certain other issues of your own to deal with). However, when I attend counselling sessions of victim/survivors or make home or community visits, especially in my Mukomeze role, and survivors share their stories and cry, I sometimes cry too. It is because I care. Besides, I know from survivors that it also helps them seeing others express their emotions, to see that others care. Showing your emotions is not a sign of weakness as some people sometimes seem to think, but a sign of compassion, a way to release your emotions, and furthermore a signal that motivates me to continue to fight for a cause worth fighting for. I realize that due to my many different roles I have been privileged to meet with the survivors on a continuing basis, something which is not always possible for everyone involved in this kind of work.

Besides my continuous interactions with survivors themselves, of great importance are my interactions with staff at the organization (Solace Minis-

31 The CE-CERT Model of Brian Miller with Components for Enhancing Clinical Experience and Reducing Trauma is, for instance, helpful for yourself and (when supporting) your colleagues. See: https://www.cecertmodel.com/home (retrieved 21 February 2025).

tries) we work with. Being part of their organization for many years, together with the survivors they themselves are and serve, has made us also become part of their alternative family. Seeing how they work together to make a positive impact in the lives of the genocide survivors of sexual violence is very motivating. I learned a lot from them, in particular I learned a lot from Jean Gakwandi and Mama Lambert. Important lessons that I can use in my own life (both professional and private) that I learned from Mama Lambert are, for example, that is important to fight for what you belief in; two is better than one (i.e. work together); to be patient; to be compassionate; to forgive is not to forget; and when you release your heart, you release your burden. Very sadly, Mama Lambert passed away in September 2024. She touched the lives of literally thousands and thousands of people in Rwanda and all around the world. She wrote a book called *For those who do not believe in miracles* in which she described her own life story and taught us about how to deal with trauma, after having experienced the worst (Mama Lambert, 2024). To me she was a very important person in my life, both personally and professionally, and it is very difficult to accept she is no longer with us. She was a big inspiration to me to do the work I do. I grief and feel traumatized by losing her. But I believe that she and the lessons she taught me will help me to continuously look for the positive things we can all do to make a change in the lives of people who have suffered immensely and to work on preventing the crimes all together.

6 Final Remarks

We have come a long way in the field of preventing and addressing CRSV in a survivor-centered and trauma-informed manner. Many achievements have been made and there are today many people who are committed to the cause, with the field still expanding. When realizing this, you see that you are never really alone, and in fact standing on the shoulders of so many people who have contributed to this cause. Despite the numerous achievements, CRSV is however still a pervasive crime which needs to be addressed better. As those working in this field will have to deal with traumatic stories, it is important that they are aware of the potential impact working in this field may have on themselves and their surroundings. This requires self-reflection and self-care. In addition, it is important that work environments take into account the possible impact working in this area may have on a person and that they provide institutional support, an understanding that has only recently emerged. This can be done through trainings where attention is paid to the possible impact of dealing with these crimes (mental well-being), setting up support networks within the organization (or outside), and offering peer support or counselling. Finally, it is important that people working in this area also get the support from governments and other leaders in the world (also financially) so that they can continue to tackle one of the greatest injustices in the world.

I thank the editors of this book for putting the spotlight on the under researched and addressed topic of emotions and ethics when dealing with mass atrocity crimes. Writing this book chapter furthermore provided me with the opportunity to take some time to reflect on my own journey, current state and possible future initiatives and challenges to undertake and tackle.

References

Altunjan, T. (2021). The International Criminal Court and Sexual Violence: Between Aspirations and Reality. *German Law Journal*, 22(5), pp. 878–893.

Askin, K. (1997). *War Crimes against Women: Prosecution in International War Crimes Tribunals*. Leiden: Martinus Nijhoff Publishers.

Amnesty International (2004). *Rwanda: 'Marked for Death,' Rape Survivors Living with HIV/AIDS in Rwanda*, 5 April 2004.

Bijleveld, C., Morssinkhof, A., Smeulers, A. L. (2009). Counting the Countless: Rape Victimisation During the Rwandan Genocide. *International Criminal Justice Review*, 19(2), pp. 208–224.

Boesten, J., Henry, M. (2018). Between Fatigue and Silence: The Challenges of Conducting Research on Sexual Violence in Conflict. *Social Politics: International Studies in Gender, State & Society*, 25(4), pp. 568–588.

Koenig, A., Ghaly, A. Lieban Levine, S. (2024). Merging Responsibilities: Ethical Considerations for Securing Consent in Open-Source Investigations of Conflict-Related Sexual Violence, *Journal of International Criminal Justice*, 22(2), pp. 263–280.

Brownmiller, S. (1975). *Against Our Will: Men, Women and Rape*. New York: Simon & Schuster.

De Brouwer, A. M. (2005). *Supranational Criminal Prosecution of Sexual Violence: The ICC and the Practice of the ICTY and the ICTR*. Antwerp: Intersentia.

De Brouwer, A. M. (2009). Gacumbitsi Judgement. In: G. Sluiter, A. Klip (Eds.). *Annotated Leading Cases of International Criminal Tribunals: The International Criminal Tribunal for Rwanda 2005–2006*, XXIV. Antwerp: Intersentia, pp. 583–594.

De Brouwer, A. M. (2015). The Importance of Understanding Sexual Violence in Conflict for Investigation and Prosecution Purposes. *Cornell International Law Journal*, 48, pp. 639–666.

De Brouwer, A. M., Ka Hon Chu, S. (2012). Gacaca Courts in Rwanda: 18 Years After the Genocide, Is There Justice and Reconciliation for Survivors of Sexual Violence?, *IntLawGrrls*, 7–9 April 2012.

De Brouwer, A. M., Ka Hon Chu, S., De Volder, E., Muscati, S. (2019). *And I Live On: The Resilience of Rwandan Genocide Survivors of Sexual Violence*. Tilburg: Wolf Legal Publishers.

De Brouwer, A. M., Ka Hon Chu, S., Muscati, S. (2009). *The Men Who Killed Me: Rwandan Survivors of Sexual Violence*. Vancouver: Douglas & McIntyre, 2009.

De Brouwer, A. M., Kaitesi, U. (2016). Sexual Violence: The Legacy of the ICTR, In: A. M. de Brouwer, A. L. Smeulers (Eds.). *ELGAR Compagnion to the International Criminal Tribunal for Rwanda*, Cheltenham: Edward Elgar Publishing Ltd, pp. 171–201.

De Brouwer, A. M., Ruvebana, E. (2013). The Legacy of the Gacaca Courts in Rwanda: Survivors' Views. *International Criminal Law Review*, 13(5), pp. 937–976.

De Brouwer, A. M., Smeulers, A. L. (Eds.) (2016). *ELGAR Compagnion to the International Criminal Tribunal for Rwanda*. Cheltenham: Edward Elgar Publishing Ltd.

Denov, M., Eramian, L., Shevell, M. C. (2020). "You Feel Like You Belong Nowhere": Conflict-Related Sexual Violence and Social Identity in Post-Genocide Rwanda. *Genocide Studies and Prevention*, 14(1), pp. 41–59.

Dolan, C., Hovil, L., Pasquero, L. (2024), "Translating Survivor-centredness into Pedagogical Approaches to Training on Sexual Violence in Conflict and Emergency Settings: A Case Study. *International Review of the Red Cross*, 106(926), pp. 679–702.

Eichelsheim, V. I., Berckmoes, L., Hola, B., Rutayisire, T., Richters, A. (2019). Before My Time? Addressing the Intergenerational Legacies of the Genocide Against the Tutsi in Rwanda. *Intervention*, 17(1), pp. 31–39.

Gakwandi, J., Heidrich, K. (2015). *Solace: The Story of Solace Ministries*. Bielefeld: Stiftung proWerk Bethel.

Human Rights Watch (1996). *Shattered Lives: Sexual Violence during the Rwandan Genocide and its Aftermath*.

International Panel of Eminent Personalities (IPEP) (2000), *Rwanda: The Preventable Genocide*. Addis Ababa.

Kaitesi, U. (2014). *Genocidal Gender and Sexual Violence: The Legacy of the ICTR, Rwanda's Ordinary Courts and Gacaca Courts*. Antwerp: Intersentia.

Kreft, A. K. (2019). *On Difficult Research and Mental Wellbeing*, retrieved 18 November 2024 from https://anne-kathrinkreft.com/2019/03/14/on-difficult-research-and-mental-wellbeing/

Mama Lambert, (2024). *For Those Who Do Not Believe in Miracles: The Resilience of a Rwandan Woman Who Survived the Genocide*. 4th updated edition, Published in house and available via www.mukomeze.nl.

Nduwimana, F. (2004). "The Right to Survive: Sexual Violence, Women and HIV/AIDS", *International Centre for Human Rights and Democratic Development, Rights and Democracy*.

O'Brien, M. (2021). Coping with Trauma from Research Content: Conducting Genocide Research. *Voices of Academia*, retrieved 18 November 2024 from https://voicesofacademia.com/2021/07/16/coping-with-trauma-from-research-content-conducting-genocide-research-by-melanie-obrien/

Rullmann, J. (2022). How to Maintain Mental Health as a Professional Working with Survivors of Human Trafficking and Conflict-Related Sexual Violence? *Journal of Human Trafficking, Enslavement and Conflict-Related Sexual Violence*, 3(2), pp. 199–205.

Schulz, P., Kreft, A. K. (2021). Researching Conflict-Related Sexual Violence: A Conversation between Early-Career Researchers. *International Feminist Journal of Politics*, 23(3), pp. 496–504.

Sharratt, S. (2013). Voices of Court Members: A Phenomenalogical Journey – The Prosecution of Rape and Sexual Violence of the ICTY and the BIH, in: A. M. de Brouwer, C. Ku, R. Romkens, L. van den Herik (Eds.), *Sexual Violence as an International Crime: Interdisciplinary Approaches*. Antwerp: Intersentia.

Skjelsbæk, I. (2018). Silence Breakers in War and Peace: Research on Gender and Violence with an Ethics of Engagement. *Social Politics: International Studies in Gender, State & Society*, 25(4), pp. 496–520.

Sylvester S. S. (2021). *Linking High-level Accused to Sexual and Gender-Based Crimes in International Criminal Law* (University of Groningen, Ph.D. thesis).

Theidon, K. (2014). *How Was Your Trip?' Self-Care for Researchers Working and Writing on Violence*, DSD Working Papers on Research Security, No. 2, retrieved 18 November 2024 from https://kimberlytheidon.com/2015/11/18/how-was-your-trip-self-care-for-researchers-working-and-writing-in-violence/

UN Commission on Human Rights (1999), *Question of the Violation of Human Rights and Fundamental Freedoms in Any Part of the World, with Particular Reference to Colonial and Other Dependent Countries and Territories: Report on the Situation of Human Rights in Rwanda, submitted by Mr. René Degni-Segui under paragraph 20 of resolution S-3/1 of 25 May 1994* (E/CN.4/1996/68), 20 January 1999.

Viseur Sellers, P. (2005). *The Prosecution of Sexual Violence in Conflict: The Importance of Human Rights as Means of Interpretation*. OHCHR paper, retrieved 18 November 2024 from https://www.ohchr.org/sites/default/files/Documents/Issues/Women/WRGS/Paper_Prosecution_of_Sexual_Violence.pdf

Women's Initiatives for Gender Justice (2023). *Judicial Approaches to Sexual and Gender-Based Crimes at the International Criminal Court: Structural Shortcomings, Critical Improvements and Future Possibilities of Intersectional Justice*, retrieved 18 November 2024 from https://4genderjustice.org/wp-content/uploads/2023/11/Judicial-Approaches-to-Sexual-and-Gender-Based-Crimes-at-the-ICC.pdf

CHAPTER 10

'Wounded Healer': Symptoms in Professionals Deployed in the Context of International Crisis Response

Caecilia Johanna van Peski

1 Introduction: Deployed in the Context of International Crisis Response

> To some, the concept of the wounded healer might sound morbid and unhealthy. They might feel that the ideal of self-fulfillment is replaced by an ideal of self-castigation, and that pain is romanticized instead of criticized. I would like to show how the idea of the wounded healer does not contradict the concept of self-realization, or self-fulfillment, but deepens and broadens it.
>
> HENRI J.M. NOUWEN. In: 'The Wounded Healer' (1979, pp. 96–97)

I returned to the Netherlands in the fall of 2017 after my three-year deployment to Ukraine. I had been serving in the most eastern *Oblast* (Province) of the country, initially as a Monitoring Officer, subsequently as Deputy Commander in the OSCE Special Monitoring Mission to Ukraine (OSCE SMM).[1] My deployment years were spent between the cities of Donetsk, Mariupol, Kherson, and Odesa. Our geographical movements as a team were determined by the movements of the separatist groups, members of the self-proclaimed Donetsk People's Republic (DNR)[2] Armed Forces, and the Ukrainian Armed

1 The OSCE Special Monitoring Mission to Ukraine (OSCE SMM) was put in place to contribute to the reduction of tension in the region, the finding of facts in the context of war crimes, mass atrocities and crimes against people, and to the facilitation and fostering of peace and stability in Ukraine. The mission was deployed on 21 March 2014, following the Russian annexation of Crimea and the outbreak of open conflict in eastern Ukraine. On 31 March 2022, the OSCE SMM ended following the Russian invasion of Ukraine. Source: OSCE SSM Homepage (no longer available upon closure of the mission).

2 The Donetsk People's Republic (Donetskaya Narodnaya Respublika), or DNR, comprises the occupied parts of eastern Ukraine's Donetsk Oblast with its capital in Donetsk. In February 2014, Russia annexed the Crimean Peninsula from Ukraine, while armed separatists seized government buildings and proclaimed the Donetsk People's Republic and Luhansk

Forces. The latter were opposing the first two in their defense of Ukraine's territorial integrity.

My years as part of OSCE SMM were much more challenging than I anticipated when I commenced the mission in February 2014. That winter, while frosty north-eastern winds were blowing from the Ural Mountains, waves of civil protests were spreading across the country. Despite these troublesome events, nothing indicated the onset of a full-blown war just weeks further in time. The civil protests in Kyiv would later be referred to as *Yevromaidan* (Euromaidan),[3] or the Maidan Uprising. Maidan is the name of the central (Independence) square in the heart of Kyiv. It was here where protests erupted in November 2013, after Ukraine president Viktor Yanukovych's unexpected decision to refuse the signing of the European-Union Association Agreement. As an alternative, President Yanukovych opted for tightening the bonds with the political leaders in Moscow's Kremlin Citadel.

In February of 2014, after weeks of protesting on Maidan Square, Yanukovych and the parliamentary opposition signed an agreement to bring about an interim unity government, constitutional reforms, and early elections. Police abandoned central Kyiv that afternoon, and his government ministers fled the city in the evening. The next day, parliament removed Yanukovych from office (later titled the 'Revolution of Dignity') and installed an interim government. The Maidan Uprising was followed by the Russian annexation of the Crimean Peninsula and pro-Russian unrest in eastern Ukraine, eventually escalating into the Russo-Ukrainian War. The conflict also led to the displacement of thousands of people, animals, and goods.

With these events taking place just weeks before my arrival in OSCE SMM, it could have been expected – at least in hindsight – that my life on the mission would have many challenges. And so it was, all three years long. Challenging for my colleagues and I, but much more so for the local population that would be living through the onset and further escalation of a nightmarish war that – as we know now – would last over a decade.

People's Republic (*Luhanskaya Narodnaya Respublika*), or LNR, as independent states. The DNR and LNR received no international recognition from any United Nations member state before 2022. On February 21, 2022, Russia recognized the DNR and LNR as sovereign states. Three days later, Russia launched a full-scale invasion of Ukraine, partially under the pretext of protecting the two republics (Ledur, 2022).

3 During the climax of Yevromaidan Uprising (18–20 February 2013), when battles took place in Kyiv between Maidan protesters and Kyiv Metropolitan police. See Radio Free Europe/Radio Liberty (2024). *Ukraine Opposition Vows to continue Struggle after Yanukovych Offer*, https://www.rferl.org/a/protesters-police-tense-standoff-ukraine/25241945.html (retrieved 10 February 2024).

1.1 *Military, Police and International Civil Servants: A Foreign Legion*

My group of colleagues consisted of former military (many of whom had opted for further international deployment after their early retirement from the armed forces), of professionals with a policing or border protection background, and international civil servants. The latter group of civilian colleagues (e.g. colleagues who are not serving within the armed forces or police) was least homogeneous. Some civilian colleagues (e.g. colleagues that were not actively serving within the armed forces, or the police corps) held a background in law, communications, governance, psychology, sociology, anthropology, history, diplomacy, or (war) journalism.

I could best be defined as a social scientist from my studies in cultural psychology and civil-military interaction, but I also had military experience as a reservist with the Royal Netherlands Army. I studied at the German *Bundeswehr* University and have formerly been deployed to Afghanistan, Pakistan, Tajikistan, Uzbekistan, Kazakhstan, Kyrgyzstan, Ukraine, Kosovo, Armenia and Georgia, among others.

By the time I turned 48, I was a well-seasoned, experienced professional in peace and security with plenty of anecdotal knowledge from the field. I had come to understand that in times of conflict, previously learned 'rules of engagement' can never be (re-)applied directly (or even indirectly) to another context because no two situations offer identical (or even similar) conditions. In the end, this meant that my group had to re-invent ourselves time and time again to be able to maintain the professional standards that our ever-changing environment demanded from us. Maintaining a high level of flexibility took effort, but it grew our mental fortitude and shaped us to be more resilient against sudden shocks.

In one way, our troop formed an entity which did not differ much from that of the *Légion étrangère* (the French Foreign Legion). We had made ourselves readily available for deployment to many conflicts and under many flags (albeit, most of the time a flag with a shade of blue). Some of us did so because they were missionaries driven by idealistic motives or spiritual values. Many of these members believed that one person had the power to change the world. Others in the troop were mercenaries who, irrespective of the cause, were interested primarily in making their 'mission millions'. And a few were madmen, no longer capable of holding a desk-job back home (if that had ever been possible considering their outlier personalities). And some of them were all three at the same time.

In my case, it meant that I would be – for at least a decade more – serving 'the blue flag(s)' based on my belief that I could make a difference in the world. Or at least, I believed that that was my underlying motivation. The phrase 'serving the blue flag' is usually used to refer to people who serve the blue flag of the United Nations. However, it could also be used to reference the (dark blue) OSCE flag, the (even darker blue) NATO flag, and the (relatively light blue) EU flag. And, because I am Dutch by birth, it also means serving the blue flag of my own country, the Netherlands, even though I only spent a few years there due to my deployment abroad and because I was raised in a different country.

1.2 *The Package of Measures for the Implementation of the Minsk Agreements (Minsk I and II)*

Back to the Ukraine days in early 2014. My OSCE SMM team was based at the buffer zone running from Kharkiv in the north, to the Azov Sea in the south. The zone had been shaped by the movement of troops as well as by the attempts to peacefully settle the dispute. The Minsk I Agreement, and subsequent Minsk II Protocol and Package of Measures, were of pivotal, instrumental value. These Minsk Agreements would direct our OSCE SMM work during all my deployment in the Donbass.

Russia forced Ukraine to sign the Minsk Protocol I after a defeat in August 2014 at Ilovaisk, Donetsk *Oblast*. This protocol was drafted by the Trilateral Contact Group on Ukraine, to which I functioned as a liaison on behalf of the OSCE SMM team. At the time, the Trilateral Contact Group on Ukraine consisted of Ukraine, Russia, and the OSCE, with mediation by the political leaders of France and Germany within what was called the 'Normandy Format.'[4] After extensive talks in Minsk, the agreement was signed on 5 September 2014 by representatives of the Trilateral Contact Group (TCG) and, without recognition of their status, by the leaders of the self-proclaimed Donetsk People's Republic (DNR) and Luhansk People's Republic (LNR).[5]

Unfortunately, the protocol bitterly failed to stop the fighting in Ukraine's far-east *Oblasts*. Matters grew unmeasurably more complex when in March 2015, Russia sent a large batch of their military to the border with Ukraine, aggravating the already unstable situation. Following the Russian victory at

4 The Trilateral Contact Group (TCG) on Ukraine is a group of representatives from Ukraine, the Russian Federation, and the Organization for Security and Co-operation in Europe, that was formed as means to facilitate a diplomatic resolution to the war in the Donbass region of Ukraine. See Belarus News (2020). *Subgroups of Trilateral Contact Group on Ukraine in talks in Minsk*, https://eng.belta.by/politics/view/subgroups-of-trilateral-contact-group-on-ukraine-in-talks-in-minsk-128904-2020/ (retrieved 29 April 2023).

5 See: Organization for Security and Co-operation in Europe (2014). *Chairperson-in-Office welcomes Minsk Agreement, assures President Poroshenko of OSCE support*, https://www.osce.org/cio/123245 (retrieved 14 May 2024).

Donetsk Sergei Prokofiev International Airport and in defiance of the Minsk Protocol, Russia invaded with fresh military forces and attacked Ukrainian forces at Debaltseve, Donetsk *Oblast*. At Debaltseve, Ukraine subsequently suffered a major defeat.

Minsk II was signed February 12, 2015, and consisted of a 'Package of Measures' including a ceasefire, withdrawal of heavy weapons from the front line, release of prisoners of war, constitutional reform in Ukraine that granted self-government to areas of Donbass, and restored control of the state border to Ukraine. Fighting subsided following the signing, but the battles never ended completely, and the agreement's provisions were never implemented in full. In the end, the fundamental disagreement over sovereignty could not (and still cannot) be dodged. Either Ukraine is sovereign, or it is not. There is no middle way. At its very core, this is what remains in the way of complete Minsk II implementation today.

2 Eye-Witnessing the Manifestations of Mass Violence and Crimes against People

> Who can save a child from a burning house without taking the risk of being hurt by the flames? Who can listen to a story of loneliness and despair without taking the risk of experiencing similar pains in their own heart and even losing their precious peace of mind?
>
> HENRI J.M. NOUWEN. In: 'The Wounded Healer' (1979, p. 79)

2.1 *The Shyrokyne (Mariupol Raion, Donetsk Oblast) Standoff (February–July 2015)*

Meanwhile, I had been promoted to the rank of Deputy Commander of the OSCE SMM Patrol Hub Mariupol, Donetsk *Oblast*. In this capacity, my team was observing, monitoring, and reporting manifestations of mass violence and crimes against people. The events they were privy to caused horrendous suffering on the side of the Ukrainian population. Often, these events also had a significant impact on members of the OSCE SMM team. I recall an occasion in Shyrokyne during spring of 2015:

Shyrokyne was a quaint village sitting on the shore of the Azov Sea. In February 2015, intense fighting pushed the Shyrokyne population to evacuate their village, after up to 80 *per cent* of the village houses had become damaged beyond repair. I took part in the OSCE SMM patrols overseeing the process of civilian evacuation. As the sounds of the firing T-64's crept closer to the village from the east, the incidence of shelling by the Ukrainian troops also grew in strength. The Shyrokyne citizens and our OSCE SMM patrol were caught in the middle. Late in the afternoon, buses were brought in from Mariupol to collect citizens. Mothers, fathers, children, the elderly... all stood ready to board the coaches, hastily.

The situation was tense. An elderly gentleman – a farmer dressed in blue dungarees – stood waiting in line to board the bus. He was trying to let his grandson go before him, wanting to make sure that the boy gets a seat on the bus. Grandfather is holding two 'Big Shopper' bags, one in each hand. Ironically, these bags – within the jargon sometimes referred to as 'refugee bags' – defined Grandfather's status all too well. I ask Grandfather whether he was comfortable enough to travel.

"I have done this before," Grandfather replied. "Thirty years ago, I was evacuated in a frenzy too. I used to live in the *atomgrad* (closed city) near Pripyat. Many of my Shyrokyne neighbors lived in the *atomgrad*. When, in 1986, Chernobyl power plant melted, we were all evacuated from our city, to be re-placed in Shyrokyne. In 1986, we were forced to give up our homes, our jobs, our lives, our customs and traditions. But we built new lives in Shyrokyne. We left our possessions, the farmlands that our ancestors had cultivated, and our livestock that were contaminated. But we did bring our neighbors." Nodding in the direction of the bus, Grandfather added: "Here we go again, side-by-side with our neighbors."

A handful of people stayed behind in Shyrokyne, refusing to evacuate: the priest of the Orthodox church (who stayed behind to protect the *iconostasis*); two twin sisters in their nineties (who had never gone a day without each other); a recluse with a history of mental illness and his young son (whom the hermit was the sole provider for); an elderly pigeon breeder (unwilling to give up his pedigree line of prizewinning doves); and the young athletic man who had come to Shyrokyne from Taganrog, Russian Federation, just months earlier (and whom we suspected to be fighting for Ukraine's opponent...). Over the following weeks, these seven people would become well-known among my team and I, because we would be trying to meet with them in Shyrokyne to monitor their status and well-being, as well as to collect information from them.

On many occasions, the intensity of the fighting in and around Shyrokyne prevented our OSCE SMM patrol from entering the village. But we did manage to look up the 'Shyrokyne Seven.' We handed them all food parcels and provided diabetes medication for the twin sisters. We also gave the child Plumpy Nut, a therapeutic paste formulated to treat children with acute malnutrition. I felt good about being able to provide actual life-saving support. Shyrokyne's Seven grew close to my heart, including the athletic young man whose intentions remained unclear. With time, I began to understand their reasoning for staying behind. Getting to know them better made it all the more painful to witness, week after week, the slow attrition of Shyrokyne's Seven. One by one, we found them helpless, lifeless in their homes that were shelled to pieces. In the end, none of them survived the Shyrokyne standoff.

2.2 *The Lost Children of Hranitne* (*Volnovakha Raion, Donetsk Oblast*) (*October 2014*)

Situated on the (west) bank of the Kalmius River, Hranitne is a granite quarry town (hence the name of the village: 'granite'). In August 2014, during the war in Donbass, the Kalmius River became the boundary between DNR-controlled territory on the east bank and Ukrainian government-controlled territory on the west bank. I also recall the events that took place that fall in Hranitne:

By October of 2014, Hranitne had endured constant shelling for several weeks. It was nearly impossible for our OSCE SMM patrol to enter the village because the entry road was blocked by Toblerones (defense lines) and we needed to ensure the safety and security of our own personnel. We would place our patrol strategically in a stationary position far from the trajectory of cannon fire. While Hranitne villagers were being held prisoner in their own town, our access to information about what was happening on the inside grew limited.

We would engage in acoustic monitoring (tallying what we could overhear about the number of firing impacts), and visual monitoring (viewing the impact of firing and assessing the launch directions, taking pictures of the smoke fumes circling-up from the burning houses). Every now and then, a villager or a Ukrainian emergency worker would be spotted entering or exiting Hranitne. In such cases, we would flag them down. We would then receive updated information regarding the current security and humanitarian situation. We came to suspect that three T-72 tanks were hidden in the village. We had not detected any firing from inside the village toward the village surroundings, but the intensity in which the (non-strategically located) village was being shelled made us presume that something valuable was being held there (out of sight, obviously, because this would be in violation of the Minsk Agreement to withdraw heavy weaponry).

Toward the spring of 2015, the troops started to retreat. This made it possible for our patrol to enter the village. We met with villagers, mapping their security as well as life-support needs. Springtime brought an abundance of flowers to the fields around Hranitne, with chamomile, poppies, and clover growing left, side and center and on the ruins of burned-down houses. Schoolchildren could be seen with a jump rope, resuming some kind of normalcy.

One spring morning, our patrol came cruising from around a bend in the road near the entrance to Hranitne. Five of the children that we had often seen playing were now laying on the sandy road, motionless as far as I could see. Some villagers were standing near them. We halted our patrol and entered the scene, trying to establish what had happened. Were the children engaging in some sort of hide-and-seek game? But all five children were lifeless, their frail frames laying on the road as if in some eternal children's game. "All in, all in, everybody out there all in free!", I was waiting for these words to sound, but the call never came for all five children had been lethally hit by an electricity wire that had come down from a *Donbassenergo*[6] high-voltage power pole. It had collapsed because of shelling damage during the Hranitne winter blockade. The massive surge of voltage coming from the electricity wire had snapped the life out of the children turning them into celestial faced, opaque skinned, unanimated dolls.

2.3 *The Withdrawal of Heavy Weaponry at Kostiantynivka Quarry (Kramatorsk Raion, Donetsk Oblast) (February 24, 2015)*

Kostiantynivka is an industrial city located on the Kryvyi Torets river. During Soviet times, the city developed into a hub for the production and processing of iron, zinc, steel, and glass. I recall an event that took place, February 24, 2015, in close vicinity of Kostiantynivka:

It happened at 4 a.m. on a freezing Tuesday. A freezing cold winter morning, in a field near Kostiantynivka. Our OSCE SMM patrol had mounted itself in a stationary position alongside the road. Earlier that night, we received a *frago*[7] stating that we were to receive a military convoy made up of towed artillery guns and additional tracked vehicles, including tanks. Ten days earlier, the Ukrainian government and separatist groups in the east had agreed to pull-back heavy weaponry from the frontline in accordance with Minsk II. Work was supposed to resume the following Sunday, but it had been unclear when the withdrawal would commence – if ever. Although our OSCE SMM patrol is ready to receive what or whoever turns-up from over the horizon, not many of us believe that we will be receiving anything more than the sounds of the early

6 *Donbassenergo* is a regional power generation company in the eastern part of Ukraine. See website *Donbassenergo*, de.com.ua (retrieved 30 September 2024).

7 A fragmentary order is a military term for an operation order issued on a day-to-day basis that eliminates the need for restating information contained in a basis operations order. Fragmentary orders are often necessary due to a change in action by belligerent parties or an enemy.

birds this morning. It had only been two days since the signing of the agreement, and the deadline for the retreat was set on 8 March. If any movement could be detected, it would not happen before we approached that final date. In the fog of war, on this early February morning, I expected no party to make the first move in tearing-out their tanks. Nevertheless, the OSCE SMM patrol was eager to engage, for if the pull-back did materialize, it would mean a breakthrough vis-à-vis the current stalemate, and the potential saving of many civilian and military lives. After five hours of waiting alongside the deserted country road, to our great surprise, we heard a deep, drilling sound that grew in intensity over time. Never could I have imagined the scene materializing in front of our eyes: from far beyond the horizon, a column of tanks – 40 or 50 of them – were slowly moving in our direction. Soon the sound of their diesel engines became so loud that I was no longer able to hear my own elevated heartbeat. When the column reached us, it halted, as if it were a line-up for some bizarre reception, with the foremost tank stopping first and the rest following the halt. With the engines remaining on full revolving mode, the sound of 50 blasting tanks prevented any spoken word to be exchanged. I did not know what to expect next. A hatch door opened on top of the first tank and a Russian commander stuck out his head. He looked me in the eyes. Him and his men had just spent several weeks behind the slack hills of relic iron ore quarries. Our OSCE SMM patrol were the first other human beings these men had encountered in many weeks. With no words spoken, I understood I was looking into the eyes of an intensely worn-out man, a man closer to death than to life. Eyes with a bottomless gaze, that had witnessed things no one should ever see.

3 Life Imitates Art

> Men are not made for safe havens. The fullness of life is the hazards of life.[8]
>
> AESCHYLUS 525–456 B.C.

My first week home after my three-year OSCE SMM deployment was in fall of 2017. I reflected on how I had left behind Ukraine's Donbas and the Donbas people. I knew I had left them in a state of utter despair, in a situation charac-

8 Aeaschylus (525–456 B.C.), ancient Greek tragedian who expanded the number of characters in the theatre and allowed conflict among them. In: Oresteia (458 B.C.)

terized by asymmetric warfare and the great disarray that warrying parties cause when all claim to be the rightful holder of legitimate power. Over my years in mission, the situation had led to high numbers of casualties. End-of-Mission times, in my opinion, are meant to wish colleagues farewell, to process experiences, and catch up with family and friends for whom too little time was available during deployment and to engage in those activities needed to recover one's health, mental, physical and spiritual strength, and emotional well-being. End-of-Mission times also require searching for the next post to prevent becoming unemployed because as most non-military deployments are based on temporary contracts.

While I had spent my first week home from mission reviving my Dutch dwellings and catching up with family and friends, I was too early in the process of (temporary) re-uptake to my domestic life to be engaging in the deep-processing of the last three years of mission experiences. As a mission veteran, I have come to experience that that deeper processing of those experiences would develop only with time, with many contemplative moments sometimes occurring years, or decades later.

3.1 *'Kill Me Today, Tomorrow I'm Sick'*

In the early post-deployment stages back in 2019, I was profoundly struck when viewing a YouTube clip, the link for the clip sent to me by a Swedish mission-colleague. This clip set in motion deeper reflections of my recent mission. The clip was a trailer for a newly released film produced by Joe Schröder titled *Kill Me Today, Tomorrow I'm Sick*. The film stars Henryk Broder as a drunken and cynical journalist, and Joachim Steinhöfel as an ice-cold, self-absorbed OSCE Head of Mission. It was set to be released in 2019 and subsequently won the prestigious Silver Zenith Award at the Montreux Film Festival in Switzerland. The tragicomedy ruthlessly addresses the role of international organizations in crisis regions around the world. It is a typical German movie, presenting nudity in abundance and many sex scenes. The film also offers a smart, *film noire*-sense of humor that brings viewers to tears rather than making people laugh. Not only did the film make an impact on the jury at the Montreux Film Festival, it also impacted me.

The film features a blond, blue-eyed, attractive young professional as a female heroine who is an ambitious international civil servant on a new deployment to war-torn Kosovo. Our female protagonist is a pure, good-hearted, and highly committed professional. For our heroin, the good cause always comes first. The unmarried, child-free woman is deeply motivated by what she sees as her personal responsibility to 'do the right thing.' The 'right thing' to her included standing up for the safety, dignity, and human rights of all those who fall victim to oppression, conflict, and war.

Our female hero stands in contrast to the self-absorbed Head of Mission, who is trying to uphold his *Sauberman*-image (an impeccable, clean-hands, highly biased projection of himself) against the backdrop of the very dirty, highly troubled context they work in. They represent fictitious characters in a fictitious OSCE mission that never took place. Still, the context does hold similarities to OSCE, or any other 'blue flag' peacekeeping missions and mission deployments related to international crisis response.

3.2 *Fictive Mission Scenario's*

In the opening scene of the film, viewers are introduced to Anna Neubert, the angelic heroine, when Anna enters the Pristina-stage upon her arrival in Kosovo. As part of her work, Anna interviews victims of mass atrocities and violence against Kosovo's population.[9] In addition, Anna is also expected to visit local morgues and to investigate, together with forensic experts, the cause of death of persons who are brought in.

During that opening scene, when Anna is searching for a taxi to bring her to the hotel, she runs into a local, German-speaking man who offers to help. This dark-haired, brown-eyed smoking and drinking German-speaking man soon becomes Anna's *objet d'amour*, as well as her protagonist. Throughout the film, Anna's male counterpart, her 'fixer,' introduces her to deeper layers of Kosovo's society and conflict-context. He continually refers to Anna as *Frau Cheffin*, which perhaps is a term of endearment, but also could be interpreted as inappropriate when uttered in a diminutive manner.

Viewers soon comprehend that Anna Neubert is very proud to be part of one of Europe's largest and most expensive crisis response packages. As the story unfolds, the audience is led to notice the serious, diligent, and highly professional stance that Anna takes toward the execution of her work. Anna subsequently voices that her work revolves around cooperation, not confrontation. Viewers are left with an eerie feeling that this statement might be misconceived.

What becomes ever so clear as the story develops is that Anna's colleagues turn out to be anything but optimists, activists, and idealists. In reality, Anna Neubert's colleagues are better described as alcoholics, realists, and neurotics. Worst of all, they are indifferent. "*Willkommen im Irrhaus*" ("Welcome to the Madhouse"), is what Anna's boss tells her when he introduces her to her new

9 CIA World Fact Book Kosovo, https://www.cia.gov/the-world-factbook/countries/kosovo/ (retrieved 10 January 2024).

work. In the background, another of Anna's colleagues is loudly humming Beethoven's "Ode to Joy" (the official EU hymn…) in the face of a local victim of war. Things only go downhill from there.

3.3 *A Filmic Exaggeration with (More Than?) a Grain of Truth in It*

The film *Kill Me Today, Tomorrow I'm Sick* may be accepted as satire, but it is also a parody that unfailingly mocks one aspect of mission life that is a reality. What happens to Anna Neubert may be seen as an exaggeration – but there is some truth to it.

During my many years of deployment in various international, multilateral missions, I too encountered colleagues that resembled those in the film with Anna Neubert. I met neurotics who could not stop smoking, never slept, and only spoke about sex or themselves. In doing so, they would utterly discard the needs of the people they were supposed to protect. I also encountered realists, people who had lost their last spark of idealism in the execution of their highly demanding work. And I encountered many alcoholics, and people who were vain, people who lacked those empathic skills needed to understand the perspective of the other, people who were merely in it for the money, and people undergoing a so called *'white divorce'* (a status of semi-permanent separation from spouses, without taking the responsibility of filing for divorce, and thus withholding the stay-behind partner the opportunity to move on to a more loving, genuine, and generous life).

4 The 'Wounded Healer' Concept

> We don't really heal anything; we simply let it go.
>
> CARL GUSTAV JUNG (1875–1961). In: 'The Psychology of the Transference: The Practice of Psychotherapy' (CW 16, p. 422)

'Wounded Healer' is a concept first brought forth by Swiss psychologist Carl Gustav Jung. Jung based his notion on the idea that an analyst would feel compelled to treat patients because the analyst themselves is mentally or spiritually wounded. According to Jung, the best therapist is someone who has experienced trauma themselves, only to come out of it at the other side (Smith, 1997, p. 177; Thomson, 2024). Wounded healers are the spirit guides who have gone down to the underworld (when they got wounded) but have since found a way back to living and the light. The wounded healer can recognize the injuries in others, making them a better healer than those who do not carry (mental) scars themselves.

Jung, however, also recognized that wounded healers risk projecting, or transferring, their own wounds onto the individuals they work with. A deeply reflective and recovered wounded healer recognizes and understands this though, and is able to draw wisdom and insights from the injury and pain, emerging as an even stronger healer.

4.1 *The 'Wounded Healer' Concept and Moral Injury*

> They are each called to be the wounded healer, the ones who must not only look after their own wounds, but at the same time be prepared to heal the wounds of others.
>
> HENRI J.M. NOUWEN. In: 'The Wounded Healer' (1979, p. 90)

A relatively recent phenomenon in terms of thinking about the 'wounds of the wounded' is the concept of moral injury. As early as 1984, a forerunner of the term 'moral injury' was coined by Andrew Jameton.[10] Psychiatrist Jonathan Shay introduced the concept of moral injury for the first time (Shay, 1994; 2002). He defined the term as an injury to a person's moral conscience and values resulting from an act of perceived moral transgression inflicted on themselves or as suffered (and thus witnessed) by others. This type of injury, a mental injury, causes feelings of guilt and shame, of moral disorientation, and of societal alienation in the person who is suffering. In some cases, moral injury may even lead to feelings of betrayal by colleagues, commanders, organizations, politics, or society at large. This sense of betrayal can result in feelings of anger toward all aforementioned entities and structures.

4.2 *Frontline Personnel and First Responders*

Moral injury is most often studied in the context of military personnel. The term has also been applied to frontline humanitarian and first aid responders who have dealt with extremely stressful situations in which they were unable to provide care at a level that they were taught to, or the level they felt would be the required standard set by the organizations they represent, or – most

10 Jameton coined the term 'moral distress' to describe the psychological distress of being in a situation in which military is limited from acting on what they believe to be right. The concept quickly grew to encompass other professions and circumstances (Jameton, 1984; University of Nebraska Medical Centre (2022). *In Memoriam*, https://www.unmc.edu/newsroom/2022/12/14/dr-jameton-remembered-for-medical-ethics-expertise-curiosity/ (retrieved 14 February 2024).

prominently – the level they felt was demanded by their own internal standards set by their moral compass. The same could be said regarding those who are working for international, multilateral organizations that deploy in response to the worlds' most complicated security and humanitarian crises. Molendijk (2021) refers to the specific role of frontline personnel and first responders when she mentions:

> But what about other types of missions? Recent years have mostly seen peace missions for which the national and international leadership imposed tight restrictions on the use of force [...]. They show that while restrictions on the use of force may protect soldiers from doing things they might regret later, they may also render soldiers powerless when confronted by situations that do require force.
>
> MOLENDIJK, 2021, p. 40

Core to the concept of moral injury is the experience of a deployed staff member (military, police, civilian) in which someone who holds legitimate authority has betrayed what is morally right in a high-stakes situation. The trauma has the potential to affect the individual on various levels, including the psychological, social, cultural, and spiritual (Thomas, 2016, p. 77).

At the very core of the concept of moral injury is an individual's trust that has been broken. This can be the trust in an individual, leaders, governments, organizations, and institutions. It can also be trust in the people around the individual (family, friends, strangers) and even trust that the individual has in themselves. It is a trust that is broken in terms of no longer believing, or at least doubting, that others inherently act on the basis of what is (morally) just and good. What is eventually broken is the belief of the wounded individual that the world around them offers a safe and good place to live in, and that others mean well (Robben & Hinton, 2023).

Shay (2002) clearly differentiates moral injury from 'Posttraumatic Stress Disorder' (PTSD), explaining that, "for years, I have agitated against the diagnostic jargon 'Posttraumatic Stress Disorder' because transparently, we are dealing with an injury, not an illness, malady, disease, sickness, or disorder" (Shay, 2002, p. 42–43). As such, through his writings, Shay argues that PTSD is not an illness, but the persistence of adaptive behaviors needed to survive in a stressful environment. The wounds that the wounded healers are experiencing should not be seen as an illness, even though these wounds hurt. The wounds should be seen as proof of professional and personal development or growth, making the wounded healer an even more capable 'healer' (e.g.

security provider, protector of civilians, human rights activist, military, police, or psychotherapist).

5 Cultural Analogues between Jung's 'Wounded Healer' and Those Deployed in the Context of Crisis Response

> When we look around us, we see humans paralyzed by dislocation and fragmentation, caught in the prison of our own mortality. However, we also see exhilarating experiments of living by which people try to free themselves of the chain of our predicament, transcend our mortal condition, reach beyond ourselves, and experience the source of a new creativity.
>
> HENRI J.M. NOUWEN. In: 'The Wounded Healer' (1979, p. 21–22)

Everyone who is deployed in the context of international crisis response differs significantly from all the others who are also deployed in these contexts. People differ in personal features, personality traits, idiosyncratic (life) experiences, and (work) motivations.

Despite the obvious and many differences, there are also aspects between individuals in this line of work (e.g. military, police, civilians deployed in the context of international crisis response) that are similar. The work that is being performed in the mission often needs to be executed under (extreme) harsh conditions, unfamiliar circumstances, in unknown environments, and in a hostile climate with locals that are not always welcoming to the internationally deployed (to say the least). Therefore, the internationally deployed develop certain common characteristics.

5.1 *Higher Levels of Mental Strength*

Regarding common characteristics between professionals deployed in the context of crisis response, one could think of (higher levels of) resilience, agility, versatility, flexibility, stamina, and endurance. Also, internationally deployed personnel often have to perform tasks under extremely stressful conditions, in situations with high urgency. Facing the unknown can be a common task for the internationally deployed and it is at times completely overwhelming. Identifying these challenges can be a helpful first step in the process to overcome them as an individual, team, and wounded healers.

Professionals who are deployed in the context of international crisis response may struggle with having to be on duty – always. There might be some downtime or the occasional R&R (rest & recuperation), but schedules and expectations can change at any time due to developments on the ground. This leads to hyper vigilance (or hyper alertness) and a feeling of never being truly off-duty. This instability may require a higher level of mental fortitude and motivation by the internationally deployed. Professionals who are deployed in the context of international crisis response report that they always have to be ready to adapt. They may be faced with new job tasks, unfamiliar environments, new teams, new living quarters, new missions, and new supervisors.

Most of those who are deployed in the context of international crisis response must spend extended time apart from their family and friends. The individuals might be sent to remote duty stations or are even called on to go into a war zone with no definite return date. Those who are stationed on a ship will most likely deploy for many months at a time. Being away from loved ones for extended periods of time can influence (work) motivation, just as much as it can influence the vulnerability and susceptibility of becoming wounded mentally.

The mental challenges that these individuals face can be just as difficult to overcome as the physical ones – or even more so. It is argued that the physical challenges exacerbate or even create mental challenges of their own. Every practical or physical challenge an internationally deployed person faces comes with the mental challenge of maintaining sound reasoning, balance, homeostasis, and a personal sense of identity as they work through the mission experience.

No matter what position, function, or task the internationally deployed has in the mission, the main goal is always to maintain stability in their area of responsibility and to protect the lives of civilians. These mission goals are urgent under all circumstances and come with (great) dangers, critical timelines, and strict discipline and discretion. The urgency of one's mission can feel like a heavy weight that the internationally deployed cannot lift or release during the scope of their deployment, or even during post-mission years. Not being able to find release may further increase the risk of becoming overwhelmed or wounded.

And last – but definitely not least – missions require those who are deployed to traverse treacherous terrain, counteract chemical warfare, escape risky situations involving armed opponents, and manage with dwindling life-support resources or loss of communication with the base. It may be in these situations that the deployed personnel become aware of the increased possibility of personal injury or death. Especially in the case of younger personnel hitherto unbothered by feelings of their own 'transienceness' and mortality on this earth, the sudden onset of such emotions can feel like being hit by a brick.

5.2 *The Consequences*

It is argued that all the above puts the internationally deployed at risk of becoming mentally wounded or suffering from burnout, compassion fatigue, decreased empathy, and a sense of disillusionment or cynicism regarding the work. Left unaddressed, these effects can contribute to decreased job satisfaction and even lead some to leave their professions altogether. Worse, it can lead professionals to resort to the use of narcotic substances such as alcohol, turn from idealists into realists (or pessimists), or develop neurotic or obsessive behavior. Worse even, it can drive a person to abandon those behaviors that define us as good human beings such as the virtues of respect for others, patience, reliability, sincerity, courage, and compassion. and the will to do good upon others. These characteristics may be replaced by corruption, vanity, hypocriticism, or – worst of all – indifference.

6 The Motives of Those Opting for Deployment in the Context of Crisis Response

> Making one's own wounds a source of healing, therefore, does not call for a sharing of superficial personal pains, but for a constant willingness to see one's own pain and suffering as rising from the depth of the human condition that we all share."
>
> HENRI J.M. NOUWEN. In: 'The Wounded Healer' (1979, p. 96)

According to Sussman (1992), a commonly cited, rational, and conscious argument for wanting to become a therapist, helper, or healer is a desire to help others. This conscious argument is socially desirable and professionally accepted, but the choice of profession is most likely based on more unconscious and complex motives (Norcoss & Farber, 2005). What we consciously think we know about ourselves is only part of the story; to get the entire story of who we are and what our motives are, we need to explore our hidden intentions.

A large part of our mental life takes place at the unconscious level. These unconscious mental processes develop during our lives because of our interaction experiences with our environment. Firstly, (and primarily) our caregivers or parent(s), but also siblings, teachers, friends, colleagues, neighbors, and so on. These (past) experiences substantially influence our decision-making at any further stage in our lives, including the choice of a specific career.

6.1 *The (Unconscious) Way in Which We See Ourselves*

Malach-Pines and Yafe-Yenai (1999) write that the unconscious determinants of people's career choices can be traced back to the internalized image of the self, the other – usually the parent or caregiver – and the emotional relationship between the two. The authors further argue that the choice of a specific career allows the individual to repeat important childhood experiences, fulfill unsatisfied needs, or realize certain career goals, professional patterns, and expectations from their family of origin. In line with the literature on 'wounded healers', many therapists appear to have significant emotional challenges resulting from early childhood experiences (Sussman, 1992; Barnett, 2007; Steele, Boon & Van der Hart, 2017).

The desire to assist others may then be a disguised way to remedy something within themselves or to supplement previously incurred dissatisfaction or struggles. This is consistent with the fact that in addition to the altruistic intentions and desires to help others, there is usually a more unconscious desire to free the self from inner conflict and to satisfy unfulfilled needs. In this scenario, the healer indirectly acts more in self-interest than in the interest of the patient (Lindner cited in Sussman, 1992). This arguably goes against their professional responsibility. Moreover, there is a (presumed) lack of awareness that this entails risks for the healer themselves, including an increased risk of burnout (Sussman, 1992). Maroda (2022) claims that healers, based on their personal history, may be inclined to feel excessively responsible for the suffering of the individuals that they support. This is associated with feelings of guilt when the individual who is being supported is not doing well or worsening. Yet, at the same time, there is also a positive and encouraging message: insight into one's own difficulties could make a positive contribution to success in the support rendered to others (Sussman, 1992; Maroda, 2022).

6.2 *Deeper Layers of Understanding One's Own Weaknesses and Wounds*

To be able to perform the work of the internationally deployed effectively and sustainably, it is argued that it is important for professionals to gradually become aware of their unconscious motivations and how that shapes their work. Through this, a wounded healer is not merely someone who has endured painful experiences while being deployed, but is someone who has been able to process and integrate their experiences into the self in such a way that they become more able to offer help to another person. This allows the professional to place the other person first, instead of themselves (see also, Barnett, 2007). It may also lead to higher levels of awareness, knowledge, and understanding of their own weaknesses and wounds from 'regular' trauma that inherently comes with being alive.

7 Coping, Coping Strategies, and Coping Mechanisms

> It is an illusion to think that a person can be led out of the desert by someone who has never been there. Our lives are filled with examples telling us that leadership requires understanding, and understanding requires sharing.
>
> HENRI J.M. NOUWEN. In: 'The Wounded Healer' (1979, p. 79)

The term 'coping' refers to conscious and unconscious strategies that people use to lower the stress that comes from feeling unpleasant emotions. Strategies for coping can be in the form of thoughts (cognitions) or actions (behaviors) that an individual developed and these strategies could have originated from themselves, a social group, or their larger society (Abedi, 2022). One could claim that coping is a normal part of life, for dealing with the challenges and difficulties that life brings which are taxing for all of us. Coping, in its rudimentary form, is a way to deal with life's challenges and tragedies without becoming mentally or physically ill.

One model in the context of coping mechanisms that is useful for understanding 'wounded healer', is the BASIC Ph Model. I have been applying this model myself since I was first introduced to it in 1995 by Prof. Mooli Lahad from the Israel Trauma Coalition and Community Stress Prevention Centre (CSPC).[11] I apply the model in my international mission work, both in the context of the people I work with, as well as in the context of my own physical and mental well-being. I have found this model to offer a structure that aids me in my understanding of underlying traits and (work) motivations of those I work with, but also those of myself (including my own weaknesses and wounds).

> B – Belief
> Belief can be a powerful factor in resilience. This can be through faith or any other shared beliefs and relies on inner core values. Shared beliefs are particularly helpful as they also provide external support.

11 The Community Stress Prevention Centre (CSPC, est. 1981) provides worldwide disaster management consultation and psychosocial disaster intervention at the individual, family, group, community, organization and national levels. CSPC LinkedIn page, https://www.linkedin.com/company/community-stress-prevention-center/ (retrieved 11 August 2024).

A – Affect
Feelings or emotions. By expressing through emotions, we are able to share fears, anger, sorrow etc. and have these emotions validated externally to make us feel less alone.

S – Social
Via support-seeking through friendships or organizations we can gain a sense of responsibility within a group which can help us to stay grounded. A decrease in isolation alongside an increase in social responsibility can restore emotional security.

I – Imagination
Creativity is a method of coping with trauma which children are particularly adept at utilizing. Expression of thoughts and feelings in a creative manner can allow a safer feeling release of expression through art, writing, drama or music.

C – Cognitive
Cognitive coping skills utilize problem solving and a direct approach to the issue. Strategizing with others can make people feel less alone, and more in control of their situation.

Ph – Physical
Physical activity takes us back to our mammalian routes. It has the dual benefit of providing informal processing of a situation alongside a release of feelings in an indirect Brighton Therapy Partnership.[12]

In applying Lahad's BASIC Ph Model, I discovered that the model offers a robust framework for understanding my own challenges when it comes to the ways I think and act when confronted with stressful events in the mission environment. More importantly, I found that by applying Lahad's BASIC Ph Model, my understanding of the various coping strategies applied by others (e.g. the people I work with whilst deployed to a mission) has increased. Gaining insight into ways I can heal myself has improved my capacity to help and heal others.

12 See: Brighton Therapy Partnership, https://brightontherapypartnership.org.uk/resilience-trauma-basic-ph/ (retrieved 11 August 2024).

7.1 *Sri Lanka Post-Tsunami Crisis Response (January 2006)*

Lahad's ideas on working with affected individuals and communities includes dealing with individual cases and providing 'cascade' training to professionals ('train the trainers' or 'helping the helpers'). Once trained, these professionals can go on to train others. Lahad's cascading model helps to swiftly build a substantial force of counselors that are ready to venture out into communities and societies that are confronted with the negative effects of large-scale natural disasters, crimes against people, mass atrocities, and war. Lahad refers to this cascading model as 'building islands of resiliency.' I remember conducting post-Tsunami crisis response work in Sri Lanka in January 2006:

From the 14th to 28th of January, I joined Lahad's CSPC team in Colombo to contribute to a master trainers' course for Sri Lankan psychologists, pedagogues, social workers, health workers and security workers (military, police, airport and border security, members of the Sri Lankan coast guard) tasked with relief efforts for communities affected by the 2004 Indian Ocean earthquake and tsunami.[13] Our work was based on the BASIC Ph Model and our team consisted of Israel Defense Forces (IDF) (military) psychologists and psychiatrists (Israel Defense Forces), who were highly trained in dealing with victims of atrocities (and who were often 'wounded healers' themselves because all of them were on active duty during Israel's deadly Second Intifada between 2000 to 2005).

One of the first issues our team of trainers focused on was how to recognize a traumatized individual. As part of the training, a 24-year-old Sri Lankan man had been invited for a storytelling session. This man, a fisherman from a coastal village not far from Galle, was named Ranil (alias). On December 26, 2004, the humble homestead of Ranil had been washed away by the tsunami. With it, nearly all Ranil's family members had been swept away as well. Ranil's young wife, their two young children, Ranil's parents, his parents-in-law, Ranil's brother, and his wife's sister had all perished in the disaster, their bodies never to be found. The day the tsunami hit, Ranil had been in Galle city center to undergo a minor medical treatment. Consequently, Ranil had become his own families' sole survivor.

13 On December 26, 2004, a major earthquake struck with an epicenter off the west coast of northern Sumatra, Indonesia, causing a massive tsunami with waves up to 30 meters high, known as the Boxing Day Tsunami (after the Boxing Day holiday). The tsunami devastated communities along the surrounding coasts of the Indian Ocean, killing an estimated 227,898 people in 14 countries. The tsunami prompted a worldwide humanitarian response (U.S. Geological Survey, USGS). https://www.usgs.gov/centers/western-geographic-science-center/science/tsunamis (retrieved 11 August 2024).

During the session, Ranil was sharing with the audience how he had been feeling disconnected to his surroundings ever since that dreadful day of the tsunami hitting his coastal village. In the first days after the tsunami, he had been refusing food and drink. Ranil mentioned that he did so because he was not perceiving any feelings of hunger or thirst. Ranil had rushed back to his village when the tsunami hit. He had done so by foot because local transportation infrastructure had been washed away as well. When Ranil arrived in his village, he had not noticed that his feet were dripping from blood. His sandals had not been able to protect him well enough from walking over the debris left by the tsunami. Ranil had spent several days searching for his lost family members, but he was never able to locate them. Two years later, Ranil is still not able to utter much more during our training program than the sentences "I can't believe this happened," and "I don't believe it, I don't believe it."

Ranil had volunteered to meet with our training audience. He had mentioned that he wanted to do so as part of his own recovery and healing journey. Since the tsunami hit, Ranil had built himself a new dwelling at the same location where the little hut was that used to house his now deceased family. Meeting with Ranil offered the training audience a way to enhance their understanding of the individual coping skills of (one of the thousands of) tsunami victims. It did so also by having the trainees reflect on their own ways of coping with adverse events and trauma. Many of them had been affected by the tsunami themselves and had been working with tsunami survivors since the disaster. They mentioned how they had been experiencing difficulties with confronting and managing their own trauma while working with others who were traumatized. The healers were wounded themselves. By guiding the healers through the BASIC Ph Model, trainees were offered a pathway into understanding their own (unconscious) trauma responses and coping mechanisms better, making them more capable of supporting others.

8 Know Thyself: The End Is My Own Beginning

> There we come into contact with the center of our own creativity and find the strength to refuse to become passive victims of our own futurology. There we experience ourselves no longer as isolated individuals caught in the diabolic chain of cause and effect, but as beings able to transcend the fence of our own predicament and to reach out far beyond the concerns of self. There we touch the place where all people are revealed as equal and where compassion becomes a human possibility.
>
> HENRI J.M. NOUWEN. In: 'The Wounded Healer' 1979, p. 23

Those who are internationally deployed may experience emotional difficulties because of the hardships they witness and endure, similarly to the manner in which this may occur in therapists. It is argued that these experiences may be accompanied by internal difficulties and unfulfilled desires, which international responders may encounter through their work. When these inner difficulties and unfulfilled desires remain hidden from the conscious self, they may form an obstacle to the execution of the highly responsible and highly urgent work.

At the same time, there is a possibility that internal struggles can simultaneously contribute to work output in a positive and constructive manner, provided a person has sufficiently investigated it and dealt with them within themselves. This aligns with what Sussman (1992, p. 30) also argued is the case for psychotherapists. In other words, while our own unconscious vulnerabilities and motives can form a pitfall, examining and working through them in international work in the context of crisis response could actually improve our capability to help and become a stronger, more balanced, more reliable, more resilient and more effective (first) responder. This can be done by thoroughly inspecting the wounds that life has previously inflicted upon us (Barr, 2006) and especially those wounds that find their origin in our work within the worlds' bloodiest conflict zones.

To this end, it is necessary that we dare to enter the foggy and evasive regions of our own psyche, with the aim of gaining insight and a more stable basis on which to carry out our work. Receiving effective and adequate help from those around us (psychotherapists, psychiatrists, coaches, mentors, friends, family, supervisors, supportive community members and colleagues, including our peers and supervisors) matters and helps.

This position does not exempt professionals from inner conflict and certain unconscious desires in the work, but rather uses awareness of this as an opportunity to develop oneself further as a strong, robust professional in the field of peace and security. In addition, examining our own vulnerabilities, weaknesses, wounds, and desires allows us to better understand the people around us and to assist those in need as effectively as possible.

9 One Final Time: Closing Scene from *Kill Me Today, Tomorrow I'm Sick*

Going back to the satirical film *Kill Me Today, Tomorrow I'm Sick*, the ending leaves viewers with a heavy sensation in the pit of their stomach. Viewers who themselves are, or have been, part of such missions – may they be military, police, or civilian – are likely left with intense emotions, as the movie functions (to some extent) as a mirror to what they experienced or witnessed.

Upon my own viewing of the movie back in 2019, I noticed how I identified with Anna Neubert almost instinctively. Anna could have been my twin, my alter ego. She was the same age I was at the time of my first mission years in Kosovo, Montenegro, Serbia, Bosnia and Herzegovina, Belarus, and Ukraine. Anna Neubert and I were both well educated and well prepared (can one ever truly be well prepared before entering a conflict situation?). Both of us spoke (some of) the local languages, were single, and child-free. We were both confident, independent, and – significant in the light of 'wounded healer' – very proud to be part of Europe's most exorbitant aid mission. Lastly, we both wanted to contribute to the development of democratic, inclusive, and stable security infrastructure for countries following their years of oppression.

Thirty years along in my career as a professional in international peace and security – with further missions that brought me to Afghanistan, Georgia, Ukraine, again Afghanistan, Israel, and Palestine – I would have been very keen to meet-up with Anna Neubert if she had truly existed. Over coffee, I imagine how Anna and I would discuss our now three-decades long professional careers. I would inquire how Anna views her own career, and the ways in which her robust determination to assist those in need and to protect civilians evolved over the years. I would be curious to find out whether Anna's experiences would have – at least partially – moved away from idealism, toward realism, as I have found to be the case for myself.

At the same time, I would also expect for Anna to have engaged in personal introspection. She would have deeply examined the wounds that have been inflicted on her by war, wounds that have pained her, but have also helped her to understand herself and others better. And I would hope Anna would agree with me that, in the end, our wounds have made it possible for us to become better healers, better responders, better military, security workers, psychologists, civil-military experts, social workers, war crime investigators and, first of all, better protectors of civilians.

10 Conclusion

Those who are deployed in the context of international crisis response are at risk of becoming wounded, physically and mentally – or to suffer from burnout, compassion fatigue, decreased empathy, and a sense of disillusionment or cynicism regarding the work. If left unaddressed, these effects can contribute to decreased job satisfaction and may even lead some professionals to leave their professions altogether. Worse even, it can lead those professionals whose task it is to safeguard stability and security, and to protect the lives of civilians, to become corrupted, overly vain, hypocritical, and, worst of all, indifferent. Missionary, mercenary, madman.

In our times, rife with hatred, it is important for the wounded healer to not lose their belief in the power of ideals. The wounds that the wounded healers are experiencing should not be seen as an illness, even though these wounds do hurt. Such wounds may alternatively be seen as proof of growth, making the wounded healer an even more capable 'healer,' an even better security provider, protector of civilians, human rights activist, military, police, or relief worker. This requires having the power to manage (as a minimum requirement), surpass, and sometimes supersede individual responses to situations as abhorrent as conflict, war, mass atrocities, and crimes against people. This healing can be achieved through their own belief system, for instance, or through other methods incorporated in Mooli Lahad's BASIC Ph Model.

Let us not forget that trauma does not always make people stronger. Trauma can also damage the central nervous system, hijack the digestive system, and keep a person in a constant loop of hyper-alertness with anxious responses. To tell someone that they automatically become stronger because of trauma is to deny what it has cost them to survive (Houldley, 2022, p. 54).

When the end is the beginning, and the wounded healer is able to remain an idealist also toward the end of their career, remain an activist instead of turning into a realist (only), turns out to be able to nurture the optimist in themselves rather than the pessimist, and has not turned into an alcoholic or neurotic, perhaps then, at the very end of an individual's professional career, this is the highest moral achievement for professionals deployed in the context of international crisis response.

References

Abedi, S. (2022). Healing the Wounded Healers. *Psychology Today*, 5 August 2024, retrieved 1 July 2025 from https://www.psychologytoday.com/us/blog/healing-the-wounded-healers/202204/healing-the-wounded-healers.

Aeschylus (458 B.C.). *Oresteia*. Loeb Classical Library. Translation: A. Sommerstein (2008), 3 vols. London: Heinemann.

Barr, A. (2006). An Investigation into the extent to which Psychological Wounds inspire Counsellors and Psychotherapists to become Wounded Healers, the significance of these Wounds on their Career Choice, the causes of these Wounds and the overall significance of Demographic Factors. *The Green Rooms*, 15 January 2014, retrieved 26 September 2024 from https://issuu.com/imran_manzoor/docs/wounded_healer_research_alison_barr_part_1_of_2

Barnett, M. (2007). What brings you here? An exploration of the unconscious motivations of those who choose to train and work as psychotherapists and counsellors. *Psychodynamic Practice: Individuals, Groups and Organisations*, 13(3), p. 257–274.

Hooker, R. (1968). *MASH: A Novel about Three Army Doctors*. New York: William Murrow and Company.

Houldley, E. (2022). *The Vulnerable Humanitarian: Ending Burnout Culture in the Aid Sector*. London: Routledge.

Jameton, A. (1984). *Nursing Practice: The Ethical Issues*. New York: Prentice Hall.

Jung, C. G. (1969). The Psychology of the Transference. *The Practice of Psychotherapy*. London: Routledge.

Jung, C. G. (1916). *Psychology of the Unconscious: a Study of the Transformation and Symbolisms of the Libido, a Contribution to the History of the Evolution of Thought*. London: Kegan Paul Trench Trubner.

Jung, C. G. (1967). *Fundamental Questions of Psychotherapy*. London: Routledge.

Ledur, J. (2022). What Russia has gained and lost so far in Ukraine, visualized, *The Washington Post*, retrieved 11 January 2024 from https://www.washingtonpost.com/world/2022/11/21/russia-territory-gains-ukraine-war/

Malach-Pines, A., Yafe-Yenai, O. (1999). Unconscious influences on a choice of career: implications for organizational consultation. *Journal of Health and Human Services Administration*, 21(4), p. 502–5011.

Maroda, K. J. (2022). *The Analyst's Vulnerability: Impact on Theory and Practice*. New York: Routledge.

Molendijk, T. (2021). *Soldiers in Conflict: Moral Injury and Soldiers in Conflict, Political Practices and Public Perceptions*. London: Routledge.

Norcoss, J. C., Faber, B. A. (2005). Choosing Psychotherapy as a Career: Beyond "I Want to Help People". *Journal of Clinical Psychology*, 61(8), pp. 939–943.

Nouwen, H. J. M. (1979). *The Wounded Healer: Ministry in Contemporary Society*. London: Darton Longman & Todd.

Postlewait, H., Cain, K., Thomson, A. (2004). *Emergency Sex and other Desperate Measures: a Story from Hell on Earth*. New York: Hyperion.

Robben, A. C. G. M., Hinton, A. L. (2023). *Perpetrators: Encountering Humanity's Dark Side*. Redwood City: Stanford University Press.

Shay, J. (1994). *Achilles in Vietnam: Combat Trauma and the Undoing of Character*. New York: Simon & Shuster.

Shay, J. (2002). *Odysseus in America: Combat Trauma and the Trials of Homecoming*. New York: Simon & Shuster.

Steele, K., Boon, S., Van der Hart, O. (2017). *Treating trauma-related dissociation: A practical, integrative approach*. New York: w.w. Norton & Co.

Sussman, M. B. (1992). *A Curious Calling: Unconscious Motivations for Practicing Psychotherapy* (2nd edition). Lanham: Jason Aronson Inc.

Thomas, R. (2016). *Psychological Stress – Aid Workers in Complex Humanitarian Emergencies*. Saarbrücken: LAP Lambert Academic Publishing.

Thomson, J. (2024). The Chiron Effect: Are "Wounded Healers" Better Healers? In Big Think Neuropsychology, retrieved 21 April 2024 from https://bigthink.com/neuropsych/the-chiron-effect

Shay, J. (1994). *Achilles in Vietnam: Combat Trauma and the Undoing of Character*. New York: Simon & Schuster.

Shay, J. (2002). *Odysseus in America: Combat Trauma and the Trials of Homecoming*. New York: Simon & Schuster.

Smith, R. C. (1997) *The Wounded Jung: Effects of Jung's Relationships on his Life and Work*. Evanston: Northwestern University Press.

Zerubavel, N., O'Dougherty W. M. (2012). The Dilemma of the Wounded Healer. *Psychotherapy Theory Research Practice Training*, 94(4), pp. 482–491.

CHAPTER 11

How to Address Emotions from the Perspective of a Military Commander in UN Peace Operations

Patrick Cammaert

1 Introduction

The environment in which UN peacekeepers deploy is changing rapidly and has become very violent. UN personnel are confronted with atrocities against local populations, including conflict-related sexual violence. In the last few years, the UN was even targeted by armed groups in the Democratic Republic of the Congo (DRC), Central African Republic (CAR), and Mali.

These confrontations have an enormous impact on peacekeepers who are working and living in oftentimes austere conditions. This results in stressful, emotional, and sometimes traumatic experiences. Preparing during the pre-deployment training, keeping a sharp eye on the well-being during deployment, and providing good care after deployment must be jointly implemented to prevent post-traumatic stress disorder (PTSD) among UN personnel.

In this chapter I will describe this stress, the emotional impact of the work as well as how to address the impact it has on the performance and behavior of peacekeepers during peace operations. This will be done from a military commander's perspective using personal experiences. In doing so, several missions will be covered, namely those in Yemen, Cambodia, Ethiopia and Eritrea, Democratic Republic of the Congo, South Sudan, and Gaza (see also Bootsma, 2019).

2 Yemen

It is the year 2019. There is a small local hospital in a port called Hodeidah in West Yemen. As the Head of the UN Mission in Hodeidah, called the UN Mission to support the Hudaydah agreement (UNMHA), I went to visit a hospital to see the impact on the population after the warring parties denied the UN access to a food warehouse called the Red Sea Mills, located between the frontlines. There is enough food for millions of people, but the parties cannot agree to provide the population access through the World Food Program (WFP). I have seen pictures of the effect of malnutrition on small children, but I wanted to assess the situation with my own eyes. I am greeted in the hospital by doctors and administrators, all male, who start giving me a briefing. After ten minutes, I ask the lead doctor if there are female doctors in the hospital. He confirms this and states that I will see them when I am making the rounds. I insist that I would like to see them now and ask him to call them in. After five minutes, five female doctors arrive. Two speak English well, three not so much but we use our female interpreter to converse instead. The ladies are surprised when I call them in to attend the meeting and even more so when they are allowed to speak and answer my questions. For twenty minutes they tell me all the ins and outs of the hospital and about their patients: malnutrition, sexual violence, domestic violence, poverty, lack of medication, being shot at, non-stop bombardments during the night, etc. The men in the room continually try to get my attention back but I stay concentrated on the ladies' perspectives. I ask them to show me around in their respective departments. I have seen a lot of nasty scenes in my career, but I am not prepared for what the doctors show me. Mothers sitting on hospital beds with their babies or toddlers whose bodies appear as little skeletons. It hit me like a ton of bricks. They all look at me with big brown eyes and a somber expression: you are the one who will help us. I know I cannot help them, and I know for sure in a few days these children will die. It breaks my heart. I have difficulty controlling my emotions which is something that has increased over the last few years as I have gotten older. When we say goodbye to the female doctors, they want selfies and grab my hand, thanking me for empowering them. In the car ride back to my headquarters (HQ) tears begin to come. Also anger. Anger that the parties cannot agree to allow the UN access to the warehouse where so much food is being stored that will eventually rot. In the next meeting I angrily confront the parties about my experience and walk out of the meeting. This was the only moment I lost my temper. I said to both sides several times:

> If you don't leave your past in the past, it will destroy your future. Live for what today has to offer, not for what yesterday has taken away.

It is a saying from Buddha that I saw in an article on the plane to Aden when I deployed.

It took another three months before WFP got access to the warehouse. During long conversations with my wife back in New York, I shared my anger, my sadness and grief. She understood it and what I was going through. We served together in the DRC in United Nations Organization Mission in the Democratic Republic of the Congo (MONUC).

3 Cambodia

Let me go back in time now to 1992. My battalion is preparing for deployment to Cambodia to serve in the UN Transitional Authority in Cambodia (UNTAC). It is my first deployment for the UN. I am determined to prepare my unit for all worst-case scenarios present in our sector, such as the serious mine threats and hostile acts by the Khmer Rouge forces. I ask a friend who is a medical doctor in the Royal Navy and a former surgeon in the Falklands war to come over and brief the whole battalion on how to address gunshot wounds, mine victims, etc. He shows us the most gruesome pictures and films which became valuable later in the deployment. However, we first encounter how challenging it is to get in the right mindset. After arrival, when we crossed the border between Thailand and Cambodia by bus, there is a bathroom stop. Despite all the warnings about a mine threat, the first thing the boys do is pee in the grass alongside the road. But not long after settling in and starting their patrol schedule, they are confronted with mine victims, often children. This kicked in the lessons learned earlier, and these marines became more capable of saving lives. But they still need careful attention from each other and superiors because they have a lot of pressure on their shoulders and their minds are constantly occupied. Good counseling is necessary to deal with the difficult and stressful situations. Fortunately, they have a very good humanist counselor (*humanistische Raadsvrouw*) who frequently sees many of them.

Over the months tension rises. Not only outside the gates, on patrol, but also on occasion within the gates of various compounds. Internal interpersonal relations occasionally flare up and the resulting emotions are difficult to control, especially when compounds are shot at or under mortar attack. Sometimes one of the compound commanders becomes physically afraid and reacts unusually, not demonstrating leadership when it is needed. Most of those cases land on my desk and I must address them. I am often forced to make unpleasant, but unavoidable decisions, like sending people back home, removing them from their post or letting them hand in their weapon. In the evening when I sit on the balcony of my house in Sisophon, where our battalion HQ is based, I stare at the flame of an oil lamp and think about what will come next now that the tensions among the men and threats in the country are rising. Every evening, I write in my diary as a way for me to take the stress away.

Now the date for the elections is getting closer so the Khmer Rouge is becoming more and more hostile. This culminates with a patrol ambush by the Khmer Rouge and we sustain casualties. One Japanese UN police officer (who is part of the patrol) is killed, and all members of the patrol are wounded. I learn of the incident when I return from a subunit visit and as soon as I step out of the helicopter my operations officer tells me that we have a major problem but no details are known yet. When I enter the Battalion HQ the atmosphere is tense but also calm and controlled. Pre-deployment training pays off now. People know what to do and know to wait for the commanding officer to give further direction. A few hours later I visit the Field Dressing station to observe the work that is being done by the team of doctors, nurses and even by vehicle mechanics who assist in the operation theatre. It fills me with emotion and pride. I am glad that I had issued the order to wear flag jackets and helmets right on time, when the tension started to rise. During the ambush, many bullets hit the flag jackets which are bulletproof and meant to protect us. For mine threats in the meantime, we drive around with sandbags at the bottom of the vehicles and on our seats to protect us from a possible mine blast. After a patrol, good debriefs help to mitigate the stress and tensions among the patrol members.

Together we talk a lot about the security situation and the measures we must take to mitigate the risks. The unit regimental sergeant major advises me to have one of the more senior HQ personnel hand in his weapon because he is unstable and has difficulty dealing with the stressful situation. He leads a patrol and once encountered a very risky situation where he managed to avoid a major shoot out. It is now halfway the term and most people had their R&R (rest and recuperation) period back home or in the area, but I felt that the effort of patrolling and other activities demands more of the unit than the rest provided can compensate for. The company commanders are afraid the marines will be exhausted during the volatile period of the elections. So, I decide that a second period of R&R is needed to allow the men and women of the unit to let off steam. A deal with a UN helicopter unit to pick up 45 personnel along with a bed and breakfast facility in Phnom Pen (under supervision of the provost marshal) give the required period of rest and the result is fantastic. Without serious incidents everyone returns to their camps, ready to start the last period leading up to the elections.

Welfare is an important aspect to keep the unit's moral high. Loyalty can fluctuate and I often bring the importance to care for people under our wings to the attention of officers in the unit. Once when I was walking around in Battalion HQ, I saw a very competent corporal, whom I had known for a long time, looking sad and withdrawn. I asked him what is going on and offered a chat over coffee. He started to cry and told me he received a letter from his wife that she started an affair with their neighbor. What is one supposed to do under these circumstances? Sending the man on patrol is risky because he would be distracted by problems at home and not focused on the challenging patrol. But he could also not be sent home for welfare reasons as he did not fulfill the official criteria. So, we sent him to the marine barracks in Doorn, the Netherlands, with a special task to organize something for me. He also received the task to sort out the problem with his wife and come back afterward or, if that does not work out, to report to the welfare officer at home. Two weeks later he came back and said the situation was resolved. Years later, I see him at Schiphol airport. He is arriving, me departing. We spoke for a few minutes. How are you? I am good sir. I have two kids and we are very happy. Big smile. I feel great.

4 Ethiopia and Eritrea

My next mission is as Force Commander (FC) in United Nations Mission in Ethiopia and Eritrea (UNMEE) in 2000 (see also Cammaert & Sugar, 2015). Two countries who just signed a peace agreement. The UN troops must form a buffer zone between the parties who are still in their trenches, sometimes at shouting distance. However, there are some unresolved issues in the agreement. For starters, we do not know yet where the border is that the troops must withdraw to. It takes six months of almost non-stop negotiating for me, as FC to get the parties to agree to separate and form a Temporary Security Zone. What happens next felt unreal. I make a helicopter flight over the frontlines and the trenches. In an area in Assab, a port city in the South-East of Eritrea, the ground between the two trench lines is littered with mummified bodies of fallen soldiers. Both parties deny that they are theirs and point the finger at the other. After endless conversations, we persuaded the two parties to let us together take care of the bodies as a confidence building measure. Under the leadership of the UN and International Committee of the Red Cross (ICRC) the two parties and we took care of the bodies. We let the two sides pay their respects and brought them home to hand over to their families. It was a very emotional event for all involved. The sight of those fallen soldiers abandoned to rot under a blistering sun is unimaginable but it was very rewarding to allow a new chapter to begin by resolving this issue.

One of my battalions is Dutch. Before departing for Eritrea, the minister of defense wants to see me. He tells me that he has given the battalion strict instructions not to engage with the local population or do other humanitarian work. Too risky. I look at him in disbelief. So, our good practices learned in Cambodia, such as using our spare medical capacity to help the local population, are not allowed. That means that the doctors must sit idle when there are no Dutch military patients. It is not only very frustrating for me as Force Commander but also for the battalion who wants to do more. Other battalions do try their best to support the local population where they can. It is embarrassing.

Six months before the end of my term, I am in Addis Ababa with the Special Representative of the Secretary General (SRSG) for a meeting with the Prime Minister. We do this regularly but just before we drive to the PM's office, I get a message that I am not needed for this meeting. This is strange and unusual. When the SRSG comes back, he calls me in and he sits at his desk with his face buried in his hands. "Force Commander, Force Commander, what is wrong with those people." He is referencing the Ethiopian government. Apparently, there was an incident where a UN helicopter with the mission's chief public information had flown over a small village Badme, which is a sensitive area since the war started there. The Ethiopian authorities are not happy and are blaming me. I had nothing to do with it and did not know anything about it. The authorities had been very critical of the SRSG, but could not touch him. So, they lash out at me and tell the SRSG that I am not welcome in Ethiopia anymore. I am shocked. Fortunately, the SG and UN HQ in New York give me their full support. This allows me to stay in the mission, but henceforth, I operate only from Eritrea where we still have the majority of the 5000 troops. At the end of my tenure, the SG appoints me as the Military Advisor at the Department of Peacekeeping at HQ in New York.

5 Democratic Republic of the Congo

After two years in New York HQ as the Military Advisor of the Secretary General Kofi Annan and the Department of Peacekeeping, I am sent by him to the Democratic Republic of the Congo to be the General Officer commanding the Eastern Division of MONUC (The UN Organization Stabilization Mission in the DRC). I set up my Divisional HQ in Kisangani a city at the Stanly Falls in the Congo river. It is a commercial hub for river and land transportation and a major distribution center for the North Eastern Part of the country. It has a good airport and the E-Div has a strength of 15,000 troops from 38 countries. The UN Mission has lost its credibility due to inaction, so SG Annan has given a short order: please general, take action. Soon after arrival I sit with one of my brigade commanders in the district of Ituri where armed groups control the population through their use of violence and in particular sexual violence. Rape and gang rape are occurring at an epidemic scale. Torture and abduction of young girls and boys is staggering. Many troop-contributing countries are not prepared for what they encounter in the villages and hamlets. They do not have enough knowledge to know what they should do, what they can do, and what they are supposed to do. It is frustrating and sad. The expectations of the local population are high. They expect that the UN will solve their problems. So, with the words of the SG Annan in my head and heart, the Division begins to act and often with necessary force, using the Rules of Engagement (ROEs) to stop the violence and disarm the armed groups. We work together with our civilian UN colleagues from various parts of the UN mission such as political, human rights, conflict-related sexual violence, child protection, and others. Women and children suffer incredibly in the DRC. When a woman is raped, she is often abandoned by her husband and kicked out of the village with her children. They end up in the street in extreme poverty and are subsequently very vulnerable and exposed to even more violence. In Bukavu, in the South Kivu province, a local gynecologist named Denis Mukwege started Panzi hospital as a specialized clinic for treating rape and gang rape victims. The patients range in age between 3 and 83 years old. I visit Dr. Denis quite often and we have become good friends. Every time when I am frustrated with the UN, or with the risk-averse attitudes of some contingent commanders, or when I am impacted by the sadness and suffering of the locals that I witness, I take a helicopter and fly to Dr. Denis. Being there among the survivors of rape who are treated with compassion and love by the staff as well as talking to Denis all put into perspective that my problems are nothing in comparison to what those women and girls go through. It makes my problems and frustrations melt like snow in the sun. When I return to my HQ, I feel motivated again to continue pushing and inspiring the troops and my civilian colleagues to implement our mandate to protect civilians under threat of physical violence, including sexual violence. It is one way of addressing my emotions. Another is that I have a special advisor who I brought with me when I departed New York. He is a retired Lt Col from the French Army whom I knew from a previous deployment to the former Yugoslavia. He is very calm and while he is smoking his pipe, I can talk freely with him or yell at him to let off steam. It is important to have a sounding board to share your pain and stress with.

A very emotional moment is when a special forces unit is briefed by our Div HQ on a difficult mission. I say goodbye at the airstrip before they depart for their risky operation. A few days later, six of those soldiers are killed in a fire fight after a young lieutenant made some serious mistakes. It hits me hard. I start thinking, did I overlook something? Was the task too difficult for them?

Have I overestimated their capabilities? Command is lonely. Field Marshall Lord Slim said once:

> When times are bad … there will come a sudden pause when men stop and look at you. No one will speak; they will just look at you and expect leadership. Their courage is ebbing; you must force it to flow back, and it is not easy. You will never have felt more alone in your life.

Fortunately to control and share my emotions, I can talk to a friend, who is now my wife and also serves in the mission at Mission HQ in Kinshasa. She understands the challenges on the ground in the mission. For me, as the division commander, it is crucial now to talk to the unit who lost six soldiers and share their grief and sadness. They must continue with their operations and that is not easy. I decide to visit this unit more often and look out for them.

6 South Sudan

After my retirement, Secretary General Ban Ki Moon appointed me as head of an independent investigation in South Sudan after the hostilities in 2016 in Juba. As a follow-up of this report, the SRSG of the UN Mission in South Sudan (UNMISS) asked me to visit Juba again to assess their progress in implementing the recommendations of the investigation. One member of the previous investigation team accompanies me on this trip. Bertrand Bourgain is a retired but very experienced Colonel of the French Foreign Legion and a good friend. One day, we drive back from Juba to mission HQ which is outside the city. The dusted track runs alongside the fence of Mission HQ. Close to the fence, we see a small hamlet of huts where maybe 100 people live. We stop and talk to the village chief who invites us to the village center and wants to brief us on the situation. A group of women sit on a bench looking very distressed and sad. This is strange because most of the time we see them smile, even in their misery. We learn that there is no more clean drinking water. They fill their jerrycans with water from a pool and consequently many people in the village are sick. At the same time, a UN water bowser truck with *drinking water* on the side in big letters passes by. Seeing the misery of the local people who are supposed to be protected by the UN makes us both very emotional, sad and angry. Is nobody in this huge HQ aware of the situation? Has nobody stopped like us to inquire what is going on? When I have my wife on the phone, I have difficulty controlling my emotions. The same happened to Bertrand. We are both so upset. In the debrief that day we both ventilate our anger and frustration at the leadership of the mission. Please send one or two of the many water trailers that are parked in the compound to the little village every day with fresh water. Protection means to also protect people from diseases. The senior leaders look embarrassed. The next day we see a water trailer parked in the village. We are happy but still wondering why people don't observe or act on these things themselves.

7 Gaza

Finally, a few words on an experience that is still very often in my thoughts: another independent investigation that I headed for SG Ban Ki Moon, this time in Gaza after the 51-day war in 2014. The team holds meetings in Jerusalem, Ramallah, and Gaza. The situation on the West Bank, and particularly in Gaza, is alarming. The destruction in Gaza is shocking. We spoke with a lot of UN personnel who worked and lived in Gaza during the war. They had to enter UN schools after these schools were hit by Israeli artillery shells. Thousands of Palestinians shelter in these schools. After the bombardments, the UN colleagues must assist the people who are sheltering in these slaughterhouses. The chaos is difficult for them to describe to us. We walk around in silence, observing the destruction and thinking of what happened when the schools were hit. Their experiences during the 51 days created serious post-traumatic stress disorder among the staff. Some of my team members who have never been in a war situation like this look like they were shell-shocked. We spoke for a long time in the evenings with young Palestinian people who have just finished university. It is painful to hear the lack of perspective they have in their lives.

When back in New York, I brief SG Ban Ki Moon and among a lot of recommendations, one sticks out. I ask the SG to immediately send a team of PTSD specialists to Gaza to address the traumas of our UN colleagues. He takes note and promises to take action. He did.

8 To Conclude

Over the years I have learned that pre-deployment training, where the real circumstances are imitated closely, is vital. If possible, don't let people be surprised by events that can be avoided. Encourage others to seek out a buddy that they can talk to when experiences are stressful. Family and friends who understand what you are going through are important relationships to keep close to you. Communicate, don't push traumatic experiences away. If possible, inform people in stressful situations what you as the leader know. That avoids rumors spreading. Keep an eye on the symptoms of stress and trauma. Make sure that even if the circumstances are difficult, that troops can get rest, sleep, and mental health support when needed. Finally, the commander also needs somewhere where he/she can let off steam.

References

Bootsma, E. (2019). *Kijk niet weg: De Missie van Generaal Patrick Cammaert.* Atlas Contact.

Cammaert, P., Sugar, A. (2014) United Nations Mission in Ethiopia and Eritrea (UNMEE), In: Joachim A. Koops, T. Tardy, N. MacQueen, P. D. Williams (Eds), *The Oxford Handbook of United Nations Peacekeeping Operations* (2015; online edn, Oxford Academic.

Conclusion

Maartje Weerdesteijn

1 Introduction

The book allowed us to glance into the personal and professional lives of scholars, teachers, and practitioners who have dedicated their lives to understanding and countering mass atrocities. Our authors are diverse in terms of the jobs they occupy; they work or worked at (international) criminal courts and tribunals, non-profit organizations, the military, and at universities. They also differ in terms of their academic discipline, with contributors specialized in, among others, criminology, anthropology, history, and criminal law. Yet despite these differences, there are striking similarities between their experiences and observations.

2 Between Our Places of Origin, the Sites We Visited, and the People We Meet

In each of the chapters it becomes apparent that the personal backgrounds of those working in the field of mass atrocities matter. How anyone perceives and experiences the emotional and ethical dilemmas that are tied to the work is deeply impacted by who they are.

The perceived emotional and ethical dimensions of the work seem to be intertwined with the underlying reasons for working in this field. Smeulers' respondents, for instance, highlighted personal experiences as an important motivating force. Familial and personal ties to a conflict region, but also experiences with domestic criminality, may motivate scholars to strive for justice or to write in order to heal. Experiences in their personal lives oftentimes raised questions that their scholarly pursuit was meant to answer, marrying personal need with professional curiosity. Bouwknegt likewise reflects on his own reasons for working in this field, noting, "we all have our reasons, of which the personal … could be the trickiest driver." He highlights in his chapter how his family background was impactful on his decision to start working in the field. The experiences of his grandfather during his military service in the Dutch East Indies (now Indonesia), combined with several formative encounters during his teenage and early adult years, awakened his interest in the topic and he mentions the serendipity of doing so much of his research on the very grounds his grandfather used to visit because of the military barracks that once stood there.

For Sheremeti fleeing Kosovo as a child steered her professional path and significantly shaped her research. It motivated her, challenged her, and required resilience from her. Sheremeti rejects the idea that coming from a conflict region somehow imbues one with a natural resistance to emotional harm, although it could lead to a unique form of resilience. The chapters from Sheremeti and Smeulers both highlight that coming from the region and having affinity with its respective cultural sensitivities likely make scholars particularly suitable to conduct their research but can also make them particularly vulnerable to the emotional costs.

However, we are not only shaped by where we come from or who we are, we are also formed by the experiences we have as professionals and the people we meet, who shape our journeys, for better or worse. Traumatic experiences can accumulate and weigh heavily on scholars. Some of Smeulers' respondents indicate that the work gets easier over time, but as Smeulers emphasizes, this certainly is not the case for everyone. For many of the authors in the book, their experience in the field is not a cure to the emotional burden the work may impose. As Michels eloquently explained, she felt at times that "the contagious effect of trauma slowly crawled under [her] skin." Bouwknegt nuances the dichotomy between the work becoming easier or harder by arguing that although it became professionally easier through routinization, it continued to be difficult for him personally. Luckily, years of experience did provide him more insight into what he is willing and able to do.

3 Between Caring, Coping, and Containing Emotions

As Scherer (2005, pp. 700–701) argues, emotions are "relevance detectors" that signal what "must be relevant to the major concerns of the organism." Several scholars highlight the risk that compassion fades and one can become numb or even indifferent (see for example the chapters of Smeulers, Witteveen, and Van Peski). Indifference and numbing means losing sight of what is important. It is a real risk and a tremendous concern to those who work on sensitive topics such as mass atrocities (see also Hagan & Kay, 2011, p. 290). The indifference can relate to the mass atrocities or to everyday problems that seem to pale in comparison.

Witteveen even goes so far to call indifference "the biggest sin of all." He reflects on his struggle to prevent his own compassion from fading and making all harm, except for the most atrocious kind, seem trivial. Bouwknegt agrees that “an immense pitfall to the human as scholar or the scholar as human … is to either have too much empathy or to lose empathy entirely.” Luitjens found a balance that works for her by focusing on compassion rather than empathy. In doing so, she directs her attention to the motivation to relieve suffering for victims of mass atrocities instead of putting herself in the shoes of the other through an empathetic lens.

Although, to some extent, emotions are needed as a professional, the full weight of emotions may not be felt immediately while in the field. Smeulers found many of her respondents maintained a professional posture during interviews, while their emotions were felt afterwards. Luitjens observed a similar reaction in herself after attending the Srebrenica memorial; initially unable to grasp her feelings, they washed over her for days after.

Trying to ban emotions from either the personal or professional sphere thus seems both impossible and undesirable, leaving those who work in this field with the need to cope with them. The recommendations of how to cope with emotions vary as much as the personal experiences of those who felt them. Luitjens advises taking time to process emotions and to sit with them while Cammaert writes a diary and Witteveen finds a sense of purposefulness in his faith, seeking to “dig into my deepest emotions of faith to bring a spark of light.”

Coping and self-care is not only necessary for professionals but also for students as the chapters of McGonigle-Leyh and Christiaanse, and Aydin-Aitchison and Battista, emphasize. Students need resilience and coping skills to protect themselves from psychological harm. Course coordinators may facilitate this by providing them with “safety, trustworthiness, choice, collaboration, and empowerment” (see the chapter of McGonigle Leyh and Christiaans in this volume).

The importance of collaboration and fostering a caring community among colleagues, friends, and family is reiterated throughout the chapters. Sheremeti describes the importance of being able to share her stories and Bouwknegt similarly mentions the importance of colleagues who are also close friends. Michels even mentions the reverse, how detrimental a toxic work environment can be. Cammaert and Luitjens find support from their spouses.

4 Between Distance and Closeness

When does something get close, when does it touch our hearts? Smeulers and Sheremeti mention field work and interviews in person. Witteveen also stresses that the impact of being there to bear witness, the visual of harm, is particularly impactful. Luitjens, on the other hand, found that conducting interviews online essentially meant welcoming the legacies of atrocities into her home, thus collapsing the expected and much needed distance between the safety of one's private life and the horrors of what she investigated. Smeulers, recognizing this risk, echoes the advice of a respondent: "don't contaminate your home."

Beyond the physical distance to mass atrocities, emotional distance can be important. Luitjens mentions the emotional distance comes as soon as she steps into the role of an ethnographer and notes that this distance is also expected from her as an anthropologist during field-research. Like Luitjens, Sheremeti too seems to be constantly searching for the "right balance between professional detachment and human empathy."

Aydin-Aitchison and Battista translate this to a university teaching setting, discussing the tension of navigating how much distance to put between their students and the violence they teach. Graphic accounts or images of violence raise the need to avoid sensationalism while too much abstraction and emotional distance can obstruct learning.

5 Between Positive and Negative Emotions

Understandably given the gruesome nature of the topic, much of the emphasis of the authors is on the negative emotions that the work brings forth. Yet, in between the stories of emotional struggle are also many moments of joy, fulfillment, and a sense of community with colleagues.

Witteveen emphasizes that this line of work is not something anyone does for fun but also discusses moments of humor and laughter which facilitate coping. He and the respondents in Smeulers' chapter also highlight a profound sense of gratitude. Gratitude for matters that are otherwise taken for granted and for being able to do such work. For some of the students of mass atrocities, the negative emotions are counterbalanced by feelings of relief, thankfulness and hope as Aydin-Aitchison and Battista found.

It is, furthermore, worth acknowledging that the negative emotions are actually not entirely negative in its consequences. Some of the chapters suggest that the emotional traces that the work leaves can, and should, be embraced. They can motivate a person, contribute to devotion toward a cause or calling. As the respective chapters of Michels and Witteveen suggest, working on such a heart wrenching topic can provide a sense of meaning.

Van Peski, in addition, suggests that knowing who we are and why we do the work we do will make us better at what we do. She challenges us to rethink how we see the wounds that are inflicted to realize the potential they have to make us better at protecting others from harm. Luitjens emphasizes that traumatic encounters can lead to post-traumatic growth and De Brouwer highlights that while emotionally difficult, encounters with victims/survivors can also be beautiful, motivating, and profoundly inspiring. Importantly, for many the balance is ultimately positive.

6 Acknowledging Emotions as Good Ethical Practice

An important finding across the chapters is that acknowledging our emotions and the ways in which they, and who we are as individuals, impact our work is an important step to making us better scholars, teachers, and practitioners. We have to acknowledge that while sometimes our emotions may impact our work and pose challenges to staying objective, they are impossible to eliminate. What we can do is be honest about them, experience them consciously and conscientiously whilst deliberately counteracting any subsequent undesirable effects. Ultimately, the contributions show that having emotions should not be considered a failure, rather caring and coping should be considered an important part of being successful. Luitjens even argues that learning about secondary and vicarious traumatization allowed her to become a better researcher. Sheremeti seems to agree and emphasizes that acknowledging the emotional challenges, reading the literature and familiarizing yourself with the experiences of others, allows scholars to prepare better for the work. Van Peski, furthermore, highlights that having gone through traumatic events, and acknowledging the existence of the wounds these experiences left, can make for better practitioners. Cammaert stresses the importance of recognizing emotions, but also of acting upon them, for oneself and to help others. In doing so, he emphasizes the importance of caring for those who work for you by, for instance, ensuring that soldiers have sufficient time to rest and recuperate.

We can get ahead of the game by incorporating this insight into our teaching since today's students are the professionals of the future as McGonigle Leyh and Christiaanse point out. They found students felt calmer after having their feelings acknowledged. In addition, as Aydin-Aitchison and Battista stress, it can help them be deliberate about when and how they want to be exposed to mass atrocities and open up conversations about how these emotions may be coped with. In doing so, Aydin-Aitchison and Battista argue, "instructors can act as models of compassion and integrity in how they handle material and interact with others."

7 A Final Reflection on This Book and Future Research

This book is hopefully a first step in breaking the taboos that so often cling to the emotional dimensions, and ethical considerations they bring forth, of working in the field of mass atrocities. As such we believe it is an important endeavor which captured unique, highly personal reflections. While – as was stated in the introduction – this book makes no claim to universality, its obvious limitations in that respect warrant further acknowledgment. As Mesquita et al. (2017) argue, emotions are not only human traits but also very cultural phenomenon. In that respect it is important to address the Euro- and Western-centric contributions in this book. While not an excuse, the focus can be explained by limitations in our own network and the sensitivity of the topic. Given the fact that we asked the authors to put rather personal and sensitive reflections on paper, we asked people whom we thought would be able to do so. This ultimately led to the undesirable situation that less diverse voices were heard. We hope and encourage other scholars to rectify this in future research.

References

Mesquita, B. Boiger, M. De Leersnyder, J. (2017). Doing emotions: The role of culture in everyday emotions. *European Review of Social Psychology*, 28(1), pp. 95–133.

Scherer, K. R. (2005). What are emotions? And how can they be measured? *Social Science Information*, 44(4), pp. 698–729.

Hagan, J., Kay, F. M. (2011). The Emotional Toll and Exhilaration of Human Rights Activism: Gender and Legal Work at the Hague International Criminal Tribunal. *Queens Law Journal*, 37(1), pp. 257–301.

Index